The United Nations
and
Dependent Peoples

By
EMIL J. SADY

THE BROOKINGS INSTITUTION
WASHINGTON, D.C.

Printed in the United States of America

The George Banta Company, Inc.

Menasha, Wisconsin

Preface

IN THE SUMMER OF 1951, the Brookings Institution began a series of studies on the United Nations. The series was initiated by the late Dr. Leo Pasvolsky who, until his death on May 5, 1953, was Director of the International Studies Group at the Institution. The general plan for the research was formulated in the winter of 1949-50 when many proposals for changes in the United Nations system were being widely discussed in the United States. Much of the public discussion indicated the need for a systematic analysis of the issues arising from the experience with the United Nations system and for a careful evaluation of the immediate and ultimate implications of the various courses of action being proposed. To assist in meeting this need became, therefore, the central purpose of the Brookings studies.

While this research has been under way, new developments have further affected the attitude of many Americans toward the United Nations. Paramount among these have been the difficulties encountered in dealing with aggression in Korea and in trying to achieve a settlement of the situation there, within the broader context of the whole Far Eastern situation. Some American pressures for changes in the United Nations system have been increasing, and now that the General Assembly and the Security Council have agreed in principle that a General Conference should be called for the purpose of reviewing the Charter, it is hoped that the Brookings studies will be of special value in contributing to better public understanding of the problems that will be involved.

The studies are being published in seven volumes, of which some have already appeared. Although these volumes form a related series, each of them constitutes a separate study of a major feature of the United Nations system. The order given below is not the actual order of publication, but it represents the logical arrangement of the series.

One volume is entitled *A History of the United Nations Charter*. It will present, from the American point of view, the evolution and negotiation of the Charter as part of the developing United Nations system during the period from 1940 to 1945. A major purpose of the volume will be to show the principal ideas and proposals con-

iii

sidered by the United States Government in reaching its final position on the specific provisions of the Charter.

Three volumes will analyze and appraise the principal activities and organizational problems of the United Nations and its related agencies since January 1946 when the Organization came into being.

One of these, entitled *The Organization and Procedures of the United Nations,* will cover the general organizational development of the United Nations. It will be concerned both with particular organizational problems in each of the principal organs—the General Assembly, the Security Council, the Economic and Social Council, the Trusteeship Council, the International Court of Justice, and the Secretariat—and with some of the general problems encountered, such as the interpretation of the Charter, the definition of domestic jurisdiction, and the admission of new Members.

The second of these, which has already been published, is entitled *The United Nations and the Maintenance of International Peace and Security.* It deals with methods and processes for maintaining peace and security through the United Nations. It covers the procedures that have been developed under the Charter for the peaceful settlement or adjustment of disputes and situations, the use of collective measures in threats to or breaches of the peace, and the regulation of armaments, and seeks to evaluate these methods and processes in light of the conditions in which the United Nations has had to function.

The third, entitled *The United Nations and Promotion of the General Welfare,* will cover the major activities undertaken by the United Nations in response to the insistent pressures that, during the postwar period, have brought to the fore issues in the field of general welfare. The work of the Organization and its related agencies in dealing with problems of international co-operation in economic and social affairs, in the promotion of human rights, and in the advancement of dependent peoples will be analyzed and the efforts made to harmonize conflicting national views in solving these problems will be appraised. The chapters dealing with human rights that will comprise Part Three of this volume have already been published separately under the title of *The United Nations and Human Rights.*

Another volume in the series will deal with *Regional Security and the United Nations.* It will analyze and appraise the history and activities of the principal regional security, collective defense, and similar arrangements that have developed within the framework of the United Nations Charter. The volume will describe how and why the arrangements came into existence and the manner in which they have functioned, and will analyze some of the problems raised by their establishment and operation, both within the scope of the individual groupings and in relation to the broader United Nations system.

A sixth volume, which has already been published, is entitled *Proposals for Changes in the United Nations*. It presents a description and analysis of the principal proposals advanced by governments and by private groups and individuals for changes in the United Nations system. The analysis includes a review of the major arguments advanced both for and against particular proposals, the impact of the proposals on the United Nations, and their implications for United States policy.

The final volume, entitled *The United States and the Future of the United Nations,* will attempt an over-all appraisal of the United Nations system from the American point of view. This volume, which will be based primarily on the studies in the other six volumes, will present general conclusions and recommendations regarding such changes as may appear to be desirable in the United Nations Charter or in the organization and functioning of the system.

The present publication consists of the chapters, dealing with dependent peoples, that will comprise Part Four of the volume on *The United Nations and Promotion of the General Welfare.* Because of the current public interest in the subject of these chapters, they are being published in advance of the rest of the volume, which will include them when it appears early next year.

A special word should be said regarding the scope of this study. It covers events through the tenth session of the General Assembly, which adjourned in late December 1955. In some instances, however, references have been made to important subsequent developments that occurred during the spring and summer of 1956. It should also be noted that the conclusions in the present study are those of the author, based on his analysis and appraisal of the facts he has examined. The general conclusions and recommendations that will be made in the final volume on *The United States and the Future of the United Nations* will take into account the conclusions reached in this and the other studies in the series, but they will be formulated from the point of view of the United Nations system as a whole and of United States policy with respect to it.

This study has been written by Emil J. Sady. Much of the factual material in Chapters III and IV relating to events prior to January 1953 was drawn from a special study made by Elizabeth H. Armstrong while she was temporarily on the Brookings staff four years ago. A. Evelyn Breck, with the aid of Medora Richardson, edited the final manuscript.

The author and the Institution acknowledge with gratitude the many thoughtful comments and constructive suggestions made by a number of present and former officials in both government and international organizations who responded to inquiries or read drafts of the manuscript. Their courtesy and willingness in making their expert knowledge and experience available have aided in clarifying many difficult points and issues. Although custom precludes the citing of these persons by name, the Institution greatly appreciates the individual assistance of each of them.

After Dr. Pasvolsky's death, Robert W. Hartley was given the responsibility for bringing to completion the Brookings studies on the United Nations, and the manuscript for the present publication has been prepared under his direction. We have had the benefit of continuing consultation with Ernest A. Gross, James N. Hyde, Joseph E. Johnson, C. Easton Rothwell, and Willard L. Thorp, who comprise an informal group, organized during the summer of 1953, to advise on the direction of the project, and to whom the Institution is heavily indebted for many helpful suggestions.

Finally, on behalf of the Institution, I wish to express grateful appreciation to the A. W. Mellon Educational and Charitable Trust of Pittsburgh for the generous grants that have made possible this series of studies on the United Nations system. The conclusions and recommendations of these studies have been reached, however, wholly independently of the Mellon Trust, which is not to be understood as approving or disapproving the views expressed in this and the other volumes in the series.

ROBERT D. CALKINS
President

October 29, 1956

Contents

THE UNITED NATIONS AND DEPENDENT PEOPLES

CHAPTER I

The Colonial Setting of the United Nations Charter

The "COLONIAL PROBLEM" has been a major concern of the United Nations from the very beginning. It was the cause of much debate at the United Nations Conference on International Organization, held at San Francisco in 1945. The dimensions of the problem, which caused the Conference to give special attention to it, were largely determined by the scope and nature of colonial rule prior to the war; by the impact of the war on colonial peoples and authority, particularly its stimulation of nationalism and of economic and social change; and by the national interests of the Members of the United Nations in colonial issues. In drafting the Charter, the Conference had the precedents from the League of Nations and other international experience to draw on, and the provisions finally written into the Charter relating to dependent territories reflected both these precedents and the new international concern with the colonial problem.

Colonial Rule Prior to the Second World War

About one third of the population and land area of the world was under some form of colonial rule prior to the Second World War. There were over eighty separate colonial jurisdictions (*i.e.*, colonies, protectorates, mandates, territories) located in Asia, the Middle East, Africa, Oceania, and the Western Hemisphere. Great Britain, the Netherlands, France, Belgium, Portugal, Italy, and Spain, having a combined population of about two hundred millions, had control over most of the seven hundred million people in dependent territories. The United States had jurisdiction over about fifteen millions and Japan over about sixty millions.

The territories differed in size from the subcontinent of India, with a population of three hundred fifty million, to the tiny mandated territory of Nauru, with a population of three thousand.

They ranged in culture from highly complex and advanced civilizations to those of the typically stone-age type. Some, especially the large territories in Asia, were in the throes of powerful nationalist movements; in others the largest political unit was the tribe or clan. Some territories were rich in resources, which benefited the colonial powers; others were poor and dependent financially on their metropole. One thing they had in common, which distinguished them from neighboring independent nations, was that they were governed by a people of another race or culture whose homeland in almost every case was thousands of miles away.

Modern colonial systems had their origins in the period of European "discovery" of the rest of the world more than four hundred years ago. European history of the colonies is not one of their peoples but of their discovery and subjugation by others, their inevitable role in international conflicts, and their value to other nations as sources of raw materials, man power, markets, and strategic bases. Colonial government was not, however, the unmitigated evil that it is often pictured. The United Kingdom, for example, asserted its political authority in West Africa partly out of the humanitarian impulse to abolish slavery and the slave trade. Colonial authority frequently served to hold intertribal rivalry in check and provided the basis for unifying small tribes and princely states into larger and more viable units, more capable of becoming independent nations. Western democratic institutions, which were introduced into many territories during the colonial period, served as the foundation for their government when they became independent states. Although new diseases brought in by Europeans decimated the population in many areas, scientific medicine was also introduced, making the colonies in due course more healthful places for the indigenous people as well as for European settlers. Capital investment, while benefiting interests within the administering nations, also contributed to the economic and social progress of the colonial peoples and indirectly to the growth of nationalism among them.

Colonial policies were generally the product of the world of their time, and more enlightened policies followed—although belatedly— the development of more liberal ideas in the world at large. The early influence of humanitarian thought led to a policy of protection, as contrasted with the present emphasis on advancement of dependent peoples. The modern principle that the interests of indigenous peoples is paramount was formally recognized but, unfortunately, its implications were rarely accepted when these interests conflicted with those of the administering nation or of European settlers.

In only a very few of the territories did the inhabitants have any certainty of achieving independence or an equality of status with citizens in the metropolitan area of the colonial power. The idea that the British Commonwealth could include member states in which nonwestern peoples were dominant, although perhaps implied in British policy, had not been established. And the Netherlands, as late as 1938, had rejected a request of Indonesian nationalists for dominion status. The idea of associated states in a French Union had also not been conceived; the transformation of French territories into overseas departments had occurred only in the coastal area of Algeria, which was regarded legally as part of metropolitan France; but the three French departments in northern Algeria were governed more like colonies than metropolitan departments. In fact, the Philippines was the first territory for which the granting of independence was planned on a long-range basis, with dates set for phasing an orderly transition (e.g., removal of tariff preferences) and for the final event. It was true, of course, that the *principle* of self-determination for all peoples had been proclaimed, but except for the Philippines, it had not yet been applied by the metropoles on their own initiative in any of the classical colonial situations.

The reins of government in *all* colonies were held, in the final analysis, by the colonial power even though some of the colonies enjoyed a degree of self-government. Where indigenous systems of government were recognized, they became instruments of colonial administration, and tribal chiefs were vested with powers far beyond those assigned to them under the traditional systems. With rare exceptions, the best government jobs were filled by specially trained civil servants from the metropole; local personnel, who were almost always in subordinate positions, were not given the same training opportunities, and the only official language was that of the metropole. Leaders who spoke out against government policies and actions or tried to organize the people for political action were kept under police surveillance and often exiled or imprisoned. There was little identity between the people and their government.

The territories were dominated economically as well as politically by the colonial powers. They served as sources of raw materials, outlets for investments, and markets for the manufactured products of their metropoles. They were heavily in debt to their metropoles, which kept a tight rein on their fiscal policies. Nationals of the mother country occupied all significant positions of ownership, management, and control. Tariff arrangements were designed with the view to serving the interests of people elsewhere, and although the local inhabitants benefited directly and indirectly from economic development, this development was geared primarily to interests extraneous to those of the inhabitants.

Social services, such as education, were grossly inadequate in many colonies. The revenue-producing capacity of most colonial territories was greater than was drawn upon to provide such services and developmental subsidies were rare. Heavy reliance was placed on religious missions to supply social services, and with few exceptions, the restriction on educational opportunities in the territories coincided with the political policy of the colonial power. Higher education of the people would, it was felt, eventually threaten the colonial structure and, except in a few territories, was not encouraged.

The color or culture line existed to some extent in almost every territory.[1] It was manifest in the complexion of electorates and legislative bodies, in the establishment of segregated schools and hospitals, in the granting of special economic privileges, in officially supported private clubs, and in other ways. Regardless of the official position or intellectual attainments of a local person, he could not participate on equal terms in the social life of the white community. More than any other element of colonial administration, the color or culture line seared the sensibilities of local people and separated them from their rulers.

The double standard in political philosophy, in public services, and in human relations provided the stimulus for the growth of nationalism. The riots and bloodshed in India and the imprisonment of its renowned leaders in the cause of Indian independence had aroused feelings throughout the world. Furthermore, political

[1] The Japanese, for all their use of slogans such as "Asia for the Asiatics" and their propaganda efforts to establish a common racial front among Asians against the white peoples, drew a color line that set themselves above and apart from the people they ruled. For a fuller discussion of the nature of colonialism, see Raymond Kennedy, "The Colonial Crisis in the Future," *The Science of Man in the World Crisis*, Ralph Linton, Ed. (1945) pp. 306-46.

grievances in many territories were aggravated by the world depression of the 1930's from which some of them had not yet recovered at the outbreak of the Second World War. Asian nationalists had, of course, won certain concessions from their rulers and had gained confidence in themselves as Asians by noting the ability of Japan to industrialize and to achieve recognition as a major power. But European authority—both official and personal —however much hated and resisted, seemed invincible in the colonies as the Second World War began.

The Impact of the Second World War on the Colonial Problem

During the first year of the Second World War, three colonial powers—Belgium, the Netherlands, and France—were overrun by the Nazi war machine. The status of the dependent areas of these colonial powers quickly became precarious. German and Italian forces occupied North Africa; Vichy France acquiesced, under German pressure, in Japanese occupation of northern Indo-China; and other territories of the occupied nations were effectively cut off from political and economic relations with their metropoles. Except in some French territories, colonial authorities courageously refused to recognize the puppet regimes that had been established in their homelands by the Axis powers. Because of Vichy leadership in French Caribbean territories and the power vacuum elsewhere in the Caribbean, the American republics agreed at Havana in July 1940 on a temporary system of "collective trusteeship" for any European possession in the Western Hemisphere whose status was threatened.

Hitler's attack on the Soviet Union in June 1941 relieved the Japanese warlords of their preoccupation with a Soviet attack, and they moved their forces, again with Vichy acquiescence, into the southern half of Indo-China. With the attack on Pearl Harbor, Japan began its conquest of the rest of Southeast Asia. Malaya, Singapore, the Netherlands Indies, Burma, Guam, the Philippines, the Gilbert and Ellice Islands, the Solomon Islands, and parts of New Guinea were soon occupied by Japanese forces.

The ease with which Japan overran Southeast Asia and conquered many of the prized colonial possessions of major world powers shocked the world. It also obliterated the fiction of white supremacy in the eyes of the colonial peoples. The lack of support given by the colonial peoples to their rulers in opposing the Japanese conquest revealed the inherent weakness and shallowness of the relationship between the colonial powers and their dependent peoples. Only in the Philippines did large segments of the population demonstrate their allegiance to the mother country by resisting the invader, by participating in underground movements during the occupation, and by co-operating subsequently in their liberation.

Military conquest was only one of many effects of the war on colonial peoples. The war increased greatly the contacts of many of the colonies with the outside world. Substantial numbers of soldiers from India and Africa, for example, fought in places distant from their homes. And the establishment of American military bases in colonial areas had a profound psychological, as well as an economic, impact on the peoples of the territories. In the Caribbean, strategic considerations, the shipping and food crisis brought on by the war and the accumulation of need resulting from past neglect, led to the creation of the Anglo-American Caribbean Commission—after the war enlarged to include France and the Netherlands and renamed the Caribbean Commission—to promote the economic and social advancement of the region.

The ideas that united the nations arrayed against the Axis powers and that gave moral strength to their cause struck a responsive chord among colonial peoples, especially those in the more advanced territories. The promise in the Atlantic Charter, later reaffirmed in the Declaration by United Nations, to "respect the right of all peoples to choose the form of government under which they will live," appealed to nationalist sentiment as a universal principle applicable to the peoples of colonies as well as to those in independent nations. The wartime attack on Nazi racist doctrines also dealt a blow to the theory and practice of racial superiority and discrimination in colonies.

As allied forces began their liberation in Europe and the Pacific, two problems arose that indicated the need for broad postwar action in the colonial field. One of these involved the disposition of territories formerly held by the Axis powers. The fate of the Italian colonies in Africa, which were occupied by the armed forces of the United Nations coalition in the process of defeating Italy, had to be decided. Similarly, decisions had to be made, in anticipation of the defeat of Japan and the occupation of the territories that it held, regarding the disposition of those islands and territories that would be taken from Japan pursuant to the terms of the Cairo Declaration. The other problem was the future of the territories administered under the mandates system of the League of Nations, which came to the fore once agreement was reached at the Moscow Conference, in late 1943, to proceed with the establishment of a new international organization to replace the League.

In the spring of 1945, as the war in Europe ended, and the outcome—although not the duration—of the war with Japan became certain, a wave of idealism seemed to sweep the world. There was a sense of opportunity for fulfilling ideals, and an urgency to do something about international problems like colonialism, which conflicted with them. There was little public sympathy generally for the restoration of the *status quo ante bellum* in the colonies either of the Axis powers or of the Members of the United Nations. Furthermore, it seemed possible that some form of international accountability for the administration of colonies of all types, and not of the mandated territories alone, would be included in any plan for the postwar organization and maintenance of international peace and security. It was in this atmosphere of high ideals and of restrained self-interest in connection with the colonial problem that the San Francisco Conference opened.

National Interests of Member States in the Postwar Colonial Problem

There was common recognition among the nations represented at the San Francisco Conference in 1945 that the international community had a stake in the destinies of colonies. Humanitarian regard for the welfare of dependent peoples seemed to be the dominant motive, tempered in the case of the colonial powers by a regard for their own essential interests. In order, however, to appreciate the political dimensions of the colonial problem within the United Nations since it first appeared during the San Francisco Conference, it is important to understand the variety of other factors that have influenced the attitude of Member states on this issue.

First, and perhaps most important of all, is the fact that more than half of the Member states of the United Nations trace their independence to some form of liberation from colonial rule and for that reason are strongly inclined toward an anti-colonial position.[2] A strong anti-colonial position by representatives of these states in the United Nations is not only popular in their countries, but also in some cases politically essential to them at home. Some of these representatives often express more moderate views in private, but in the open meetings—with world-wide publicity being given to their remarks—they speak for home consumption.

Another important factor is that those Member states that are linked by cultural or regional ties with one another can be expected to form a solid bloc if the interests of one of them clash with those of a colonial power. Thus, for example, the Arab states tend to vote together on colonial issues arising in the non-self-governing territories in the Mediterranean area. The same is true of Latin American and Asian states with regard to issues arising in their areas. Furthermore, the three groups will normally support one another on colonial issues if they have nothing to lose in so doing.[3]

There is also the fact that the racial and cultural aspect of colonialism is offensive to the many Member states with predominantly non-European populations, and the knowledge that their own people are not free of race or caste problems does not soften their feeling about racism in the colonies. Moreover, anti-colonialism forms a partial vent for their antagonism toward the present or traditional position of authority, economic domination, or social prestige of Europeans. In the world forum, colonialism is almost a synonym for racism.

Indeed, colonialism is an important issue in international politics largely because it affords nations with predominantly non-Caucasian populations an opportunity to express resentment against the dominant position in world power that has been held by Western Europeans for many centuries. In addition, the issue gives smaller states an opportunity to assert their independence of the major

[2] Of the 51 original Member States, the following 27 are in this category: Argentina, Bolivia, Brazil, Chile, Colombia, Costa Rica, Cuba, Dominican Republic, Ecuador, Egypt, El Salvador, Guatemala, Haiti, Honduras, India, Iraq, Lebanon, Mexico, Nicaragua, Panama, Paraguay, Peru, Philippines, Syria, United States, Uruguay, and Venezuela. Of the 25 states that have subsequently been admitted to membership, the following 11 are in this category: Burma, Cambodia, Ceylon, Indonesia, Israel, Jordan, Laos, Libya, Nepal, Pakistan, and Yemen. Association with the United Kingdom in the British Commonwealth of Nations has in varying degrees mellowed anti-colonial sentiment in Australia, Canada, and New Zealand. The Union of South Africa is a special case, more the prototype of a colonial power.

[3] For a detailed analysis of bloc voting, see the volume in this Brooking series, *The Organization and Procedures of the United Nations.*

powers. In almost all matters involving international security, and in many relating to economic and social development, the small nations are of necessity dependent on, or are dominated by, the major powers, and colonial issues are among the few in which the smaller nations can put the major Western powers on the defensive. Other Member states are anti-colonial in the extreme because they want to incorporate into their metropolitan area neighboring territories of colonial powers. For example, Argentina claims title to the Falkland Islands, which the United Kingdom administers; Greece wants to annex Cyprus; Guatemala and Mexico have long standing claims on British Honduras; India wants to take over the possessions of Portugal that are contiguous to its boundaries as it has those of France; Indonesia calls Western (Netherlands) New Guinea "West Irian" and asserts the right to sovereignty over it; Yemen claims title to Aden, which is a British protectorate. The interest in colonial issues is enlivened because some territories have substantial numbers of settlers, other than those from the metropole, who are citizens or former citizens of Member states such as India and China. These settlers retain cultural, religious, and even political ties with their homeland and are often discriminated against in the territories. Furthermore, the interests of some Members are affected by economic considerations relating to colonies, because they compete with colonies in seeking markets for their primary products. Or they covet the raw materials or the markets for manufactured products that colonies afford.

Still another important factor is the ignorance in many countries, and among many of their representatives in the United Nations, of the problems and programs of government in the different territories. Few nonadministering Member states maintain consulates in dependent territories or employ specialists in colonial matters, and consequently, they are unable properly to inform or instruct their representatives. In the circumstances, these representatives tend to be uninhibited and undiscriminating in their criticism of colonial administration and to be guided more often than not by considerations other than an understanding of the needs of dependent peoples.

Probably the most disturbing national interests in colonial issues are those of the Soviet Union. Although it would be ridiculous to regard the attack on colonialism as being wholly or even primarily Communist-inspired, it is exacerbated by the Soviet Union and, among other purposes, serves those of the Soviet Union. It is one of the most divisive elements among non-Communist nations. It creates pressure to force the premature withdrawal of the authority of the metropole before democratic institutions are strong enough to avoid the chaos in which communism thrives. It undermines relations between the colonial powers and the dependent peoples, thus lessening the possibilities of their developing some 'form of permanent association and tending to create a vacuum that the Communists hope to fill.

Despite the espousal by the Soviet Union of anti-colonialism and of proposals whereby the trusteeship system or its equivalent would be applied to all non-self-governing territories, the Soviet Union has maintained a colonial-type relationship with the "nationalities" within its borders, has deprived millions in Eastern Europe of self-governing powers that they previously enjoyed, and has not offered either to return to Japan or to place under trusteeship the former Japanese territories that it took over militarily at the end of the war with the sanction only of the Yalta agreement. However, these have not been dealt with as colonial problems in the United Nations, and the Soviet Union has largely escaped the reaction that its hypocrisy on this issue has deserved.

All of these factors, taken together, have meant that since the earliest days of the San Francisco Conference, the principal colonial powers have been on the defensive in the Organization. Their attitude, in general, was that they had nothing to gain and much to lose from the activities of the United Nations in the field of trusteeship and non-self-governing territories. Their opposition at the San Francisco Conference was formidable and their posture was weak. However, they defended resolutely and with pride their colonial record and have continued to do so despite uprisings within their territories and attacks on colonialism from without. Their reaction to criticism in the United Nations has often been conditioned by public opinion at home and in the territories. As new trusteeship or colonial issues have arisen in the United Nations and the colonial powers have been increasingly confronted by implacable majorities against them, they have closed ranks. Despite the fact that their colonial policies and programs have undergone substantial transformation along the lines envisaged in the Charter, they regard with suspicion all moves in this field in the United Nations.

The Union of South Africa, which played a constructive role at

San Francisco, must be placed in a category by itself for its subsequent defiance of the United Nations in refusing to place the former mandated territory of South-West Africa under trusteeship, for its extreme racist doctrines, and generally for provoking some of the most virulent, broadside attacks that have been made on colonialism. The Union has weakened the position of the colonial powers generally because they have often felt it necessary, although distasteful, to support the Union in order to avoid setting legal precedents that seemed even more distasteful.

The rest of the administering nations—Australia, Denmark until 1954, New Zealand, and the United States—have been caught in the cross-fire of the two extreme groups. At the San Francisco Conference, they had what might be called a mild anti-colonial bias; but to a varying extent, they have since modified their position— Australia more than the rest. They have not wanted to identify themselves with the extreme position of the principal colonial powers, but they could not, because of their own territorial and other interests, join in the attack against those powers. As a result, the attack on colonialism, although not focused on them, has often encompassed them in its broad sweep. The uncomfortable position of this middle group has been eased only by the self-discipline and the sense of fairness displayed by many of the Member states that are nonadministering nations.

Especially has the official attitude of the United States toward colonial issues changed since the final months of the war. Having achieved nationhood as a result of revolt against colonial rule, the United States developed early in its relations with other nations a position in support of the aspirations of dependent peoples for self-government or independence. That position, which became firmly established in the American value system, happily coincided with the interests of national security of the United States, of American missionaries in the welfare of people concerned, and of private corporations in the raw materials, trade, and investment opportunities in the colonies. Furthermore, the United States, although having dependent territories, did not regard itself as a colonial power. Until recent decades its treatment of American Indians was inept and at times cruel, but it did not associate its policies toward Indians with those of European settlers toward the inhabitants of some African colonies.

The first adjustment in the traditional position of the United

States took place during the Second World War in the process of deciding whether the former Japanese Mandated Islands in the Pacific should be placed under a form of trusteeship that protected the strategic interests of the United States, or directly under United States sovereignty. Its difficulties in reaching a decision in favor of strategic trusteeship and the consequences of the decision itself tempered the general approach of the United States to trusteeship matters in the United Nations. Another sobering influence, although not of great weight at the time, was the realization that whatever international responsibility was established over colonies generally would also apply to Guam, Puerto Rico, perhaps Hawaii and Alaska, and other territories under the sovereignty of the United States.[4]

The threat of Communist domination in Western Europe during the immediate postwar years provoked another adjustment in the American position. The United States was trying to build a defensive alliance. This involved strengthening the colonial powers economically and militarily and maintaining mutual confidence among the peoples concerned. A strong anti-colonial position by the United States would, it was felt, have impaired these basic objectives. The United States had to be mindful of the political effects, within the metropoles, not only of its own policies on colonial issues but also of changes in the colonial policies of the metropoles themselves. Moreover, the cold war brought a realization that the continued orientation of dependent peoples toward Western democracy is essential to the free world and that this required not only fulfilling the aspirations of such peoples for self-government or independence, but also creating conditions to ensure that their new governments would remain democratic after this goal was achieved. Finally, American officials and scholars are far better informed about problems and programs in dependent territories than in the past, and this, coupled with the position of the United States as a leader in world affairs, has had a moderating effect on the reaction of the nation to specific colonial issues. Thus, although the United States continues to be motivated by faith in government by consent of the governed and by a genuine regard for the welfare of dependent peoples, its approach has been tempered by changes in the circumstances, in the interpretation of its national interests, and in its understanding of colonial problems.

[4] For a detailed account of this developing American attitude, see the volume in this Brookings series, *A History of the United Nations Charter.*

Precedents in International Organizations and Treaties

The conflict in the colonial field between national self-interest and moral principles has existed from the earliest days of European colonialism. During the eighteenth and nineteenth centuries, the ethical approach to colonial administration gained strength from the humanitarian movement, and more specifically from the opposition to slavery and the slave trade, in the parliaments of Western Europe. But it was not until the end of the nineteenth century—at the height of European rivalry over colonies in Africa—that action was taken on a multilateral basis to safeguard the welfare of inhabitants of colonies. Beginning in 1885, a series of international agreements, known as the Congo Basin Acts, was concluded with the primary objective of avoiding international disputes over colonies in the Congo Basin and of ensuring equal access by all nations to trade and navigation in the region. They also provided for (1) the abolition of slavery and the slave trade, (2) the protection of the local inhabitants and the improvement of their moral and material well-being, (3) the suppression of traffic in arms, ammunition, and spiritous liquors, (4) the control of diseases, and (5) the preservation of wild life. The experience gained under the Congo Basin Acts in minimizing conflict over territories and in formulating principles for the guidance of administering nations had a significant influence on the later development of the mandates system under the League and of regional co-operation among nations in matters affecting dependent areas.

League of Nations Mandates System

Under the terms of the Treaty of Versailles, the former overseas possessions of Germany and Turkey were ceded to the Principal Allied and Associated Powers, and the Supreme Allied Council decided which territories were to become mandates, the mandatory power for each, and the terms of the mandates.[5] The mandatory

[5] The mandatory powers and the territories under their administration were: United Kingdom—Iraq, Palestine, British Togoland, British Cameroons, and Tanganyika; France—Syria, Lebanon, French Togoland, and French Cameroons; Belgium: Ruanda-Urundi; Union of South Africa: South-West Africa; Japan—Marshall, Caroline, and Northern Mariana Islands; New Zealand—Western Samoa; Australia—New Guinea; Great Britain, New Zealand, and Australia (administered by Australia)—Nauru.

The Council of the League indirectly suggested that the United States serve as trustee for Armenia, and the Supreme Allied Council submitted the suggestion to the United States Government. Although "Wilson did not shrink

power was required to submit annual reports, on the basis of a comprehensive questionnaire, to the Council of the League. The Permanent Mandates Commission, a body comprising ten to eleven experts appointed by the Council, examined the reports and advised the Council not only whether the mandatory power remained within the limits of its powers but also whether it made good use of them. These experts were not officials or otherwise representatives of their governments. In practice, however, four were usually colonial experts, one each from the United Kingdom, Belgium, France, and Japan, and three were nationals of those Members of the League that possessed dependencies other than mandates (the Netherlands, Portugal, and Spain). Only three or four posts were held by nationals of noncolonial powers, but these were among the most influential and useful members of the commission.[6] The hearings of the commission, which were not open to the public, were attended by representatives of the territorial governments, who were closely questioned by members of the commission.

In addition to the annual reports submitted by the mandatory powers, the commission also had access to other documents and reports, both official and unofficial. It was empowered to examine written petitions, which it received from the mandated territories through the mandatory powers. The mandatory powers often withheld transmittal of petitions until they took corrective action. The commission felt that hearing oral petitions would weaken the authority of the mandatory powers and individual members of the commission were allowed to hear them only in an unofficial capacity.[7] The petitions system strengthened the principle of international accountability for the administration of mandated territories and provided a useful source of information to the commission, but the right to petition was known to only a few people in the mandated territories and still fewer were willing to assume the risks involved in exercising the right.

from the burden," Congress rejected the proposal. Francis Paul Walters, *A History of the League of Nations*, Vol. I (1952), p. 109.

[6] Arthur N. Holcombe, *Dependent Areas in the Post-War World* (1941), p. 62.

[7] The International Court of Justice, in an advisory opinion of June 1, 1956 on the question whether the Committee on South-West Africa could grant oral hearings, held that the Council of the League having established the right of petition and originated the manner of its exercise was competent to authorize the Permanent Mandates Commission to grant oral hearings had it seen fit to do so. See International Court of Justice, "Admissibility of Hearings of Petitioners by the Committee on South West Africa," Advisory Opinion, June 1, 1956, *I.C.J. Reports, 1956*, p. 23.

Despite its limited powers, the commission helped to develop improved standards in the administration not only of mandated territories but also of other territories. The members of the commission supplemented their formal reports to the Council of the League with informal advice to officials of the mandatory powers on problems relating to the mandates and to neighboring territories. The commission gained respect within the international community for its impartiality and competence, and in view of the publicity given to its reports to the Council, no mandatory power could disregard the advice of the commission without exposing itself to the sanctions of public and parliamentary opinion.[8]

Whereas conflicts were to arise in the United Nations in the relationships between the General Assembly and the Trusteeship Council, the relationships of the various organs of the League of Nations to one another and to the mandatory powers did not cause difficulties. The Covenant assigned to the Council of the League the task of supervising the administration of mandated territories, with the advice and assistance of the Permanent Mandates Commission. The right to make decisions on mandate questions belonged to the Council, and although the commission had direct contact with representatives of the mandatory powers, its observations were addressed to the Council. The Secretary-General of the League included in his reports to the Assembly of the League a summary of the work of the commission.

The annual discussion in the Assembly was usually based on the section dealing with mandates in the Secretary-General's report, which was regularly referred to a committee of the Assembly for consideration. The discussions and resolutions of the Assembly focused world attention on matters of major importance relating to mandates, but its specific recommendations were addressed to the Council because its principal function was to maintain contact between public opinion and the Council.[9] The Assembly had confidence in the ability and integrity of the commission and also undertook to ensure that its members were free of pressure from the Council.[10] The commission was aided not only by the mandates section of the Secretariat, which made substantive proposals to it, but also by the various other functional units of the Secretariat.

[8] William E. Rappard, "The Mandates and the International Trusteeship Systems," *Political Science Quarterly*, Vol. 61 (1946), p. 412.

[9] League of Nations, *The Mandates System: Origin, Principles, Application* (1945), p. 35.

[10] Quincy Wright, *Mandates Under the League of Nations* (1930), pp. 88-89.

Under the League system, the mandatory powers were secure in their authority within their territories. They were free to accept or reject observations or suggestions made by organs of the League, but they were answerable to world opinion. Except for several on-the-spot inquiries by special missions sent by the Council and for occasional hearings by members of the commission of oral petitioners, there were no direct official contacts between the organs of the League and the people in the mandated territories. The mandatory powers sent their top territorial officials to appear at the hearings of the commission on their annual reports, and these officials also sat as voting members of the Council when actions were taken relating to their mandated territories. It is to their credit that none of them invoked a veto on any of the proposed actions of the Council, even though all such actions required a unanimous vote. The unanimity rule with its threat of a veto did, however, enable the mandatory powers to bring about changes in resolutions that might otherwise not have been made.

The principal weakness of the mandates system was that it depended on facts supplied by the mandatory powers and on the sensitivity of those powers to world opinion. The system could work satisfactorily only to the extent that the mandatory powers were honest in their reporting, faithful to their "sacred trust," and responsive to world opinion in assessing their responsibility, policies, and programs. The full measure of the weakness of the system was exemplified in the case of the Japanese Mandated Islands in the Pacific. The Permanent Mandates Commission was unable to determine whether Japan, in violation of the terms of its mandate, was establishing fortifications in the islands as the commission suspected it was. An appeal to world opinion was useless because Japan was insensitive to it. Moreover, the Council of the League lacked the power and inclination to compel Japan to abide by the terms of its mandate. In the absence of any deterrent, Japan was able to violate with impunity its mandate and the Covenant of the League and also its treaty with the United States, by which the latter obtained certain rights in the islands.

Other Experience with
International Co-operation

The mandates system, although the most notable, was only one part of the experience between the two world wars with international co-operation in the problems of dependent areas. Article 23(b) of the Covenant of the League reflected the international concern for the welfare of people in *all* dependencies and not of the mandates alone. In this respect, it provides the precedent for the "Declaration Regarding Non-Self-Governing Territories" that forms Chapter XI of the United Nations Charter.

Under Article 23 of the Covenant of the League of Nations, the members of the organization agreed, "subject to and in accordance with the provisions of international conventions existing or hereafter to be agreed upon," to undertake a wide range of activities in promoting the general welfare. More specifically, they agreed, in Article 23(b), to "undertake to secure just treatment of the native inhabitants of territories under their control." Although the other activities envisaged by this article—*e.g.,* improvement of labor conditions, control of the traffic in dangerous drugs, control of the white slave traffic, prevention and control of disease—were carried out under the auspices of the League, nothing specifically was done nor was a special organ created by the League to satisfy itself that these obligations of its members were being carried out.

The League, of course, in carrying out many of its activities in promoting the general welfare, also was helping to improve conditions or to correct situations that existed in the dependent areas. For example, the Assembly of the League created committees on the problem of slavery, which existed in many dependent territories, and sponsored regional conferences on health and other matters in Africa and Southeast Asia. The approach of the League to the problems of dependent areas was, however, essentially a functional one, and it did not attempt to deal with them separately as "colonial" problems.

The International Labour Organisation did more work relating specifically to dependent areas than any other technical organization in the League system. It had a representative serving in an advisory capacity to the Permanent Mandates Commission, and its members were obligated to apply conventions "to their colonies, protectorates and possessions which are not fully self-governing . . . [with] such modifications as may be necessary to adapt the convention to local conditions."[11] It developed conventions on forced labor, recruitment of workers, penal sanctions, and contracts of employment that were especially aimed at conditions in dependent

[11] Constitution of the International Labour Organization, Art. 35(1).

areas. Perhaps the most far-reaching attempt made by the Organisation to deal with dependent areas was at its conference in the spring of 1944. There, recommendations were developed containing some fifty detailed provisions on the "Minimum Standards of Social Policy in Dependent Territories."

Provisions of the United Nations Charter

The legacy of the experience of the League in dealing with the problems of dependent peoples was a rich one for those who formulated the provisions of the United Nations Charter covering non-self-governing territories and the international trusteeship system. A detailed account of the planning and development of those provisions is presented elsewhere.[12] Therefore, it will be necessary here only to sketch briefly the background of these provisions and their essential features.

Negotiations Prior to and at the San Francisco Conference

The Dumbarton Oaks Proposals, which were developed during the late summer of 1944, did not contain specific provisions relating to dependent peoples. But at the Crimea Conference, held in Yalta during early February 1945, the United States, Great Britain, and the Soviet Union agreed, on the basis of a proposal made by the United States, that they and France and China, as sponsors of the forthcoming San Francisco Conference, would consult together prior to the Conference regarding the details of an international trusteeship system for dependent areas. They agreed that such a system would apply only to (1) existing mandates of the League of Nations, (2) territories to be detached from enemy states as a result of the Second World War, and (3) any other territory that might be voluntarily placed under trusteeship. The Yalta agreement also provided that no discussion of actual territories was contemplated in the preliminary discussions or at the San Francisco Conference, and that it would be a matter for subsequent agreement which territories in the three categories would be placed under trusteeship.[13]

[12] See the volume in this Brookings series, *A History of the United Nations Charter.*

[13] U.S. Department of State, *Postwar Foreign Policy Preparation, 1939-1945,* Publication 3580 (1949), pp. 392, 397, 662-63.

Failure to include provisions for dependent territories in the Dumbarton Oaks Proposals did not indicate a lack of interest in the subject at the time. The United States Government, which had taken the lead during the war in formulating plans for a postwar international organization to replace the League of Nations, had reached the tentative conclusion that an international trusteeship system should be an integral part of the postwar organization. Disagreement arose, however, within the government, during the early summer of 1944, regarding the scope of such a system, with the result that the matter was not the subject of formal discussion during the Dumbarton Oaks Conversations. At the root of the disagreement was the question whether the Japanese Mandated Islands in the Pacific, which Japan had used as bases for its operations in the Second World War, should be placed under international trusteeship with the United States responsible for administration or should be placed under the sovereignty of the United States.[14]

During the months following the Dumbarton Oaks Conversations, the disagreement was resolved to the extent that the United States was able to make a formal proposal for an international trusteeship system, which was the basis of the agreement reached at the Crimea Conference. The five-power consultations envisaged in the agreement made during the meeting at Yalta, however, were delayed by further disagreement within the United States Government over the details of the proposed trusteeship system. The result was that when the San Francisco Conference opened in April 1945, the consultations had not been held, and the sponsoring powers had not yet agreed on proposals for a trusteeship system. Finally, however, firm agreement was reached within the United States Government on the essential details of such a system. The United States proposal embodied special arrangements for "strategic area or areas," such as the Pacific Islands, and this was submitted to the Conference along with separate proposals made by Great Britain and France.[15]

The proposals submitted to the Conference by the major powers and by other participating nations were primarily concerned with the establishment of a trusteeship system, although the United Kingdom and Australia envisaged a general declaration of principles that would be applicable to all dependent territories.[16] After

[14] *Ibid.*, pp. 276, 295-96.
[15] *Ibid.*, pp. 412-13, 428-34, 445-46.
[16] The United States proposal was concerned solely with an international trus-

the Conference began, consultations were held among the five major powers on all of the proposals that had been submitted, and they presented a "Working Paper" to the Conference as a basis for discussion.[17] This paper was divided into two principal sections: the first comprised a proposed general statement of policy that would be applicable to all dependent territories, and the second outlined a proposed international trusteeship system.

During the subsequent debates in the committees, commissions, and plenary sessions of the Conference, the two sections of the Working Paper were gradually developed into what are now Chapter XI of the Charter, entitled "Declaration Regarding Non-Self-Governing Territories," and Chapters XII and XIII, entitled "International Trusteeship System," and "The Trusteeship Council," respectively. It became clear during the proceedings of the Conference that, regardless of what some Member states may have hoped, only a few, if any, of the non-self-governing territories of the major colonial powers would be voluntarily placed under the international trusteeship system that was being created. Attention of the anti-colonial nations was, accordingly, concentrated on trying to strengthen the provisions of what became Chapter XI of the Charter in the hope that some form of limited international supervision might be achieved for all dependent territories.

Declaration Regarding
Non-Self-Governing Territories

From the outset of the San Francisco Conference, it seemed to be generally assumed by the colonial powers that the inclusion in the Charter of some provisions along the lines of Chapter XI was not only inevitable but also desirable in order to forestall provisions of a more drastic nature. Thus, Section A of the Working Paper relating to non-self-governing territories in general, and on which Chapter XI was founded, was based on a proposal made by the United Kingdom.[18]

---

teeship system and did not include a general declaration of principles along the lines that had been earlier considered within the government. For the latter, see *ibid.*, pp. 110, 189, 254, 470-72.

[17] For text, see U.N. Information Organization and U.S. Library of Congress, *Documents of the United Nations Conference on International Organization,* Vol. 10 (1945), pp. 677-80. (Hereinafter referred to as *UNCIO Documents.*)

[18] For the text of the entire British proposal, which also included provisions for a trusteeship system, see *UNCIO Documents,* Vol. 3, pp. 609-14.

The first paragraph of Section A, as put forward by the sponsoring powers, contemplated that Member states administering dependent territories would accept, as a primary obligation, "the general principle that it is a sacred trust of civilization to promote to the utmost the well-being of the inhabitants of these territories within the world community." To this end, they would (1) "insure the economic and social advancement of the peoples concerned," (2) "develop self-government in forms appropriate to the varying circumstances of each territory," and (3) "further international peace and security."[19] As finally expanded and modified by the Conference into Article 73 of the Charter, these general and implementing obligations became as follows:

1. Under the opening paragraph of Article 73, the general obligation of the Member states administering non-self-governing territories is to "recognize the principle that the interests of the inhabitants of these territories are paramount, and accept as a sacred trust the obligation to promote to the utmost, within the system of international peace and security established by the present Charter, the well-being of the inhabitants of these territories."

2. The first of the implementing obligations in the Working Paper, which became Article 73(a) of the Charter, was expanded to include "political" and "educational" advancement as well as "economic" and "social" advancement of the peoples concerned, and the administering states also undertook to ensure "their just treatment, and their protection against abuses." These obligations are to be carried out, however, "with due respect for the culture of the peoples concerned," a phrase that could serve either to guide, or to excuse negation of, the undertakings.

3. The second of the implementing obligations in the Working Paper, which became Article 73(b) of the Charter, also was expanded so that the administering states are obligated to develop not only "self-government," but also "to take due account of the political aspirations of the peoples, and to assist them in the progressive development of their free political institutions," with the explicit understanding that this obligation will be carried out "according to the particular circumstances of each territory and its peoples and their varying stages of advancement." The extent of this obligation was a central issue at the Conference, with some anti-colonial nations strongly advocating the inclusion of the

---

[19] *UNCIO Documents,* Vol. 10, pp. 677-78.

specific word "independence," and the colonial powers strongly resisting its inclusion.[20] The issue was resolved by agreement that in the context of this obligation, "self-government" comprehended the possibility of independence, and that "independence" would be included among the objectives of trusteeship.[21]

4. The third of the implementing obligations in the Working Paper became Article 73(c) without change, but two other such obligations were added by the Conference. One of these, which became Article 73(d), obligates the administering states to "promote constructive measures of development, to encourage research, and to co-operate with one another and . . . with specialized international bodies" in the achievement of these purposes, and thus comprehends the idea of establishing in other areas regional commissions along the lines of the Caribbean Commission. Under the other added obligation, which became Article 73(e), the administering states agreed to "transmit regularly to the Secretary-General for information purposes, subject to such limitations as security and constitutional considerations may require, statistical and other information of a technical nature relating to economic, social, and educational conditions" in their non-self-governing territories, with the exception of those under trusteeship.

There was no misunderstanding at the San Francisco Conference on the nature of the obligations undertaken by administering states under Article 73, or of the fact that the Charter contained no provision for machinery to supervise the administration of any non-self-governing territories that were not placed under trusteeship. There was apparently agreement at the time that the purpose of Article 73 was to lay down a set of principles that the nations concerned would undertake to follow in the administration of such territories; and also that the sole reason for requiring the transmission of information under Article 73(e) was to inform the world of the extent to which the Members that were administering powers were fulfilling their obligations. The type of information to be reported was specified, and no requirement was imposed for reporting "political" information. Finally, the Conference neither defined precisely the term "non-self-governing territories" nor specified criteria

---

[20] Eugene P. Chase, who served as secretary of Committee II/4 (on the trusteeship system) at the San Francisco Conference, states that "the colonial powers led by the United Kingdom refused to approve the Declaration if it mentioned 'independence' as a possible objective." *The United Nations in Action* (1950), p. 318.

[21] *UNCIO Documents*, Vol. 10, pp. 562.

for determining when a territory is, or ceases to be, "non-self-govern-ing." Many of these points were later to pose great problems with respect to the interpretation of and compliance with Article 73.[22]

Article 74 was based on the second paragraph of Section A of the Working Paper. The draft proposed by the sponsoring powers was accepted by the Conference with practically no change. It has been the source of little difficulty and little interest. Under Article 74, the Member states administering non-self-governing territories recognize that other countries have social, economic, and commer-cial interests in dependent territories and promise that their policy with respect to the territories will be based on the principle of "good neighborliness." The article seems to afford moral, although not legal, protection against discriminatory policies, such as the closed-door in relation to trade, that an administering Member might be tempted to establish and to justify as being necessary under the guise of the paramountcy clause in Article 73.

International Trusteeship System and the Trusteeship Council

The provisions of the Charter creating the international trus-teeship system and prescribing the powers and functions of the Trusteeship Council were based on Section B of the Working Paper, and this section was in turn based on the proposal made by the United States.[23] Chapter XII of the Charter, which com-prises Articles 75 to 85, inclusive, deals with the trusteeship sys-tem, and Chapter XIII, comprising Articles 86 to 91, inclusive, with the Trusteeship Council.

The objectives of trusteeship, as outlined in Article 76, can be viewed as supplementing the principles set forth in Article 73, which, except for paragraph (e), seems to apply to trust as well as to other dependent territories. These objectives include "progressive development towards self-government or independence" in accord-ance with the "freely expressed wishes of the peoples concerned," and the encouragement of "respect for human rights and for funda-mental freedoms for all without distinction as to race, sex, language, or religion." The provision in Article 76 for equal treatment for all Members and their nationals in trust territories is more explicit

---

[22] See below, Chap. III.
[23] For text of the United States proposal, see *UNCIO Documents*, Vol. 3, pp. 607-08.

than the provisions in Article 74, although the qualifications in Article 76 negates its legal effect. Taken together, Articles 73 and 76 represent a tremendous advance over Articles 22 and 23(b) of the Covenant of the League of Nations, in the development of international principles and obligations relating to the administration of dependent territories.

Whereas Chapter XI of the Charter applies to all non-self-governing territories administered by Member states, the trusteeship system, by reason of Article 77, applies only to such territories in the following categories as are placed under it by means of trusteeship agreements: (1) territories held under mandate; (2) territories that may be detached from the enemy states as a result of the Second World War; and (3) territories voluntarily placed under the system by states responsible for their administration. In this respect, of course, the Charter only reaffirms the agreement on this matter reached at the Crimea Conference, but in addition, Article 78 provides that the trusteeship system cannot be applied to territories that have become Members of the United Nations.

The administering authority of a trust territory may be one or more states or the United Nations itself (Article 81). The terms of trusteeship for each territory and any amendment thereof must, according to Article 79, be agreed upon by the "states directly concerned, including the mandatory power in the case of territories held under mandate," and must be approved, under Article 18(2). The question what states other than the mandatory powers are "directly concerned" was later to pose a difficult problem.

All or part of a trust territory may be designated as a strategic area or areas (Article 82). The basic objectives of the trusteeship system continue to apply to the people of a strategic area, but under the terms of Article 83(1), all functions of the United Nations in such areas are performed by the Security Council, instead of the General Assembly. The Security Council is to avail itself of the assistance of the Trusteeship Council on functions relating to political, economic, social, and educational matters in strategic areas. This formula for strategic trusteeship, which, as has been noted, was proposed by the United States, was the best means conceived at the time for adhering to the principle of territorial non-aggrandizement and at the same time protecting United States security interests in the former Japanese Mandated Islands. A strong case can be made that a regular trusteeship provides greater protection to the national interest of an administering authority than a strategic trusteeship, one reason being that any permanent member of the Security Council can veto amendments to a strategic trusteeship agreement whereas only the administering authority can veto a proposal to amend a regular agreement. The additional veto that a permanent member of the Security Council acquires on becoming an administering authority of a strategic area is without value.

The administering authority has the duty of ensuring that each trust territory, whether or not strategic, "shall play its part in the maintenance of international peace and security" (Article 84). To that end, it may make use of voluntary forces and facilities from the trust territory "in carrying out the obligations toward the Security Council undertaken in that regard by the administering authority." As will be noted later, controversy developed over the significance of the latter provision of Article 84 when the trusteeship agreements were being considered in the General Assembly.[24] In contrast, under the mandates system of the League of Nations, there were specific prohibitions applicable to "B" and "C" mandates against the establishment of fortifications and against the military training of the local inhabitants for other than police purposes and the defense of the territories.

The functions of the United Nations with regard to trust territories not designated as strategic are exercised by the General Assembly, but the Trusteeship Council, "operating under the authority of the General Assembly, shall assist the General Assembly in carrying out these functions" (Article 85). These functions include, according to Article 87: (1) consideration of annual reports submitted by the administering authority on the basis of a questionnaire formulated by the Council; (2) receipt and examination of petitions; and (3) periodic visits to the territories. The functions with respect to petitions have been deemed to include the hearing of oral petitions. When it is recalled that the League of Nations had the authority only to review annual reports, to examine written petitions forwarded by the mandatory power, and to make "observations" on the administration of the mandated territories, it can be seen that the powers of the United Nations under the trusteeship system are substantially greater.

The Trusteeship Council is designated by Article 7(1) as one of the principal organs of the United Nations and, under Article 86(1),

----

[24] See below, Chap. IV.

it consists of the following Member governments: (1) those Members administering trust territories; (2) the permanent members of the Security Council; and (3) as many other Members elected for three-year terms by the General Assembly as are necessary to ensure that the Council has an equal number of governments that administer trust territories and those that do not. As a result of a compromise between those who wanted an expert body such as the Permanent Mandates Commission and those who preferred a body consisting of government representatives, Article 86(2) provided that each of these governments shall select "one specially qualified person to represent it" in the Trusteeship Council.

The broad powers of the General Assembly in trusteeship matters, its relationship to the Trusteeship Council, and the governmental character of the membership of the Council contrast sharply with the limited powers of the Assembly under the League of Nations mandates system, the subordination of the Permanent Mandates Commission to the Council of the League, and the independent status and technical competence of the members of the Mandates Commission. These contrasts may have a bearing on the fact that conflict has developed between the General Assembly and the Trusteeship Council, whereas the Assembly of the League respected the Permanent Mandates Commission and sought to insulate it from pressure by the governments represented on the Council of the League.

Although the Charter contains special provisions relating to trust territories and other non-self-governing territories, the general provisions of the Charter and the general powers and functions of the organs of the United Nations and of the specialized agencies also apply in such territories in the same manner as in the metropolitan areas of the Member states. The General Assembly has the power to consider problems in dependent areas on the same basis as problems elsewhere. A situation in a non-self-governing territory threatening international peace and security could be—and has been —brought before the Security Council. The full scope of the powers and activities of the United Nations must be kept in mind in considering the past and future role of the United Nations in dependent territories.

CHAPTER II

Postwar Developments and the United Nations

THE NATURE and dimensions of the colonial problem have substantially changed since the end of the Second World War. Basic changes in the political status of many territories, in the policies of the colonial powers, and in the pace of advancement make this postwar period one of epochal significance in the history of colonies. The principal developments in dependent territories administered by Members of the United Nations and the direct role therein of the Organization and the specialized agencies need to be examined in order to assess what the future relationship of the United Nations should be to the problem of dependent territories.[1]

Political Advancement of Dependent Peoples

The phenomenal changes that have occurred in the political status of dependent territories during and since the Second World War have radically reduced the size of the problem from what it was at the outbreak of the war. In the brief span of fifteen years, over half a billion people who were previously living under some form of colonial rule have become citizens of independent nations, incorporated into the metropolitan area of an existing state, or associated on the basis of mutual consent with the metropole

[1] Portugal and Spain became Members of the United Nations toward the end of the tenth session of the General Assembly. Both are usually considered as colonial powers. Their overseas territories appear to be "territories whose peoples have not yet attained a full measure of self-government." However, as neither has been an administering Member during the period under review and neither has made known whether it intends to regard its overseas territories as non-self-governing within the meaning of Article 73(e) of the Charter, reference is made to them in this study only to the extent that they have been or may become involved in colonial issues in the United Nations. It may be noted, however, that political and economic progress in their territories has in general lagged behind that in the territories of other colonial powers.

that formerly exercised colonial authority. The political developments during this brief period in territories that are still non-self-governing have been equally important, with many of the peoples advancing rapidly toward self-government or independence.

General Changes in Status

A variety of causes underlie the recent changes in non-self-governing territories, some, as has been noted earlier, traceable directly to the war.[2] The sudden collapse of Japan and the resulting chaos in Southeast Asia enabled nationalist groups to obtain arms from Japanese troops and other sources and, except in Malaya, to consolidate their positions before the authority of the colonial powers could be effectively restored. Also as a result of the war, nationalist sentiment was stimulated in all of those territories that were in advanced stages of political development, thus contributing to the achievement of independence by Syria, Lebanon, Burma, Ceylon, India, Pakistan, Laos, Cambodia, and Viet Nam. Other territories—such as Korea and Libya—underwent a political transformation as a result of wartime agreements among the major powers or of the terms of the peace treaties, which stripped Japan and Italy of sovereignty over their prewar colonial empires. Only the people of the Philippines had a prewar promise of independence, and they asked that it be granted without delay despite the severe war damages they had suffered.

The table on pages 32-33 shows the striking changes that have taken place since 1939 in the status of non-self-governing territories.[3] None of the prewar territories listed in this table are now

[2] See above, Chap. I.

[3] Basic to any discussion of the change in the status of "non-self-governing territories" is a definition of the term itself. Article 73 of the United Nations Charter refers to them as "territories whose peoples have not yet attained a full measure of self-government," but, as will be noted later, the General Assembly has been unable to elaborate on this definition. (See below, Chap. III.) For purposes of the discussion here, the definition suggested by the United States delegation in 1946 will be used; namely, that the term "non-self-governing territories" as used in the Charter "would appear to apply to any territories administered by a Member of the United Nations which do not enjoy the same measure of self-government as the metropolitan area of that Member," qualified, however, by actual experience in the United Nations in the application of the term. (See U.N. General Assembly, First Session, *Report of the Secretary General, Non-Self-Governing Territories: Problems of Transmission and Organization*, Doc. A/74 (Oct. 21, 1946), pp. 5-6.)

Under such a definition, it is clear that the term "non-self-governing terri-

regarded as non-self-governing, and the twenty-eight territories involved, with a prewar population of about 570 millions, comprised about four-fifths of the 700 million people who were living under some form of colonial rule prior to the war. From these twenty-eight territories, nineteen independent nations have emerged and thirteen areas have been either incorporated into the metropolitan area of an existing state or associated, on the basis of mutual consent, with the metropole that formerly exercised colonial authority.

In most cases, these changes in status have greatly increased the participation of the people in their government. In some cases, however, the change may lessen rather than increase local powers of self-government—as, for example, the elevation of a French territory to the status of a department under the highly centralized system of French local government. Moreover, the substitution in North Korea and Manchuria of a government dominated by the Soviet Union for one dominated by Japan can hardly be regarded as an achievement in self-determination, and the government of northern Viet Nam is now dominated by an avowedly Communist party that hailed the revolt against France as an integral part of the world revolution led by the Soviet Union. Postwar events in North Korea and Viet Nam accentuate the danger of a new form of imperialism replacing the old and reveal a new dimension of the colonial problem.

Although the changes of recent years have reduced the magnitude of the colonial problem, there has been no decrease in the intensity and importance of the problem in international affairs. Mounting world sympathy generally for the plight of dependent peoples was reflected, as has been noted, in the provisions of the Charter of the United Nations, and the Organization has manifested a continuing interest in the advancement of such peoples since it

---

tories" would not apply to areas recognized by most Member states as independent nations. Furthermore, the United Nations has not regarded as non-self-governing territories such places as the Northern Territory of Australia, the Northwest Territory of Canada, the territories of Quintana Roo and Baja California in Mexico, which fit the definition given but which—unlike the classical type of colony—are within, contiguous to, or near the metropolitan boundaries of the administering nation. There remain, in effect, only those areas that the administering nations themselves regard as "non-self-governing territories," and it is in this sense that the term is used here to identify both prewar and postwar areas and to assess the political changes that have taken place in all such territories.

Changes in Areas No Longer Dependencies[a]

Dependency in 1939	1939 Population (In thousands)	Status September 1956
ASIA		
Burma (United Kingdom).....	16,000	Independent Republic
Ceylon (United Kingdom).....	5,900	Independent member of the British Commonwealth
Formosa (Japan)............	5,800	Seat of the National Government of China
French Settlements in India...	323	Part of India
India (United Kingdom)......	350,000	Independent states of India and Pakistan, both members of the British Commonwealth
Indo-China (France)..........	23,600	Independent states of Cambodia, Laos, and (Southern) Viet Nam recognized by the West, each linked differently with the French Union; and the Democratic Republic of (Northern) Viet Nam, recognized by the Soviet bloc
Korea (Japan)..............	22,000	Independent Republic of Korea, with status of North Korea in question
Manchuria (Japan)..........	37,000	Part of China
Netherlands Indies..........	69,400	Independent Republic of Indonesia, excluding Western New Guinea
Philippines (United States)....	16,200	Independent Republic
WESTERN HEMISPHERE		
French Guiana..............	40	Department of France
Greenland (Denmark)........	19	Part of Denmark
Guadeloupe (France)........	300	Department of France
Martinique (France).........	247	Department of France
Netherlands Antilles.........	100	Self-Governing Territory
Netherlands Guiana.........	330	Self-Governing Territory of Surinam
Puerto Rico (United States)...	1,800	Self-Governing Commonwealth, associated by compact with United States
MIDDLE EAST		
Lebanon (French Mandate)....	1,100	Independent Republic
Libya (Italy)...............	900	Independent Kingdom
Morocco (French Protectorate).	6,650	Independent, with agreement pending to define future relationship with France

[a] List of dependencies in 1939 from Arthur N. Holcombe, *Dependent Areas in the Post-War World* (1941), pp. 95–97. Population figures from United Nations *Demographic Yearbook, 1953* and *1955.* Population shown is for 1939 or closest year thereafter for which data are available. Status and population from *Statesman's Yearbook, 1940* and *1953* and other sources.

Dependency in 1939	1939 Population (In thousands)	Status September 1956
Palestine (United Kingdom Mandate)................	1,500	Independent Republic of Israel constitutes main portion of previous mandate
Anglo-Egyptian Sudan........	3,553	Independent
Transjordan (United Kingdom Mandate)................	300	Independent Kingdom of Jordan
Syria (French Mandate).......	2,500	Independent Republic
Tunisia (French Protectorate)..	3,231	Independent, with agreement pending to define future relationship with France
OTHER		
Malta (United Kingdom)......	240	Constitutional dyarchy, self-governing in local matters
Newfoundland and Labrador (United Kingdom)........	290	Confederated with Canada
Réunion (France)............	200	Department of France
Total population..........	569,523	

came into being in 1946. In fact, colonial issues are among the most important in international relations, and are a cause of tension between nations both inside and outside the United Nations.

The debates in the United Nations with respect to the territories that are still non-self-governing have, with rare exceptions, emphasized the faults of colonial administration and have therefore tended to obscure the many advances that have taken place. The war weakened the major colonial powers—particularly the United Kingdom—and awakened the conscience of their domestic public opinion, making them less able and generally less inclined to resist the insistent demands of dependent peoples for more self-government. These conditions, together with the pressure of world opinion to which the United Nations has contributed, have encouraged the colonial powers to adopt more enlightened policies toward almost all of their territories and have facilitated the making of long-overdue changes.

British Territories

Recent political progress in the non-self-governing territories administered by the United Kingdom has been the most outstanding. In almost all of the forty-four British territories,[4] constitutional re-

[4] Considering the five territories of the Windward Islands and the island

forms have been instituted that have increased popular representation in either legislative or executive bodies or in both. Furthermore, these reforms have benefited primarily the non-Caucasian inhabitants, except in several of the white-settler-dominated territories in Africa.

In the Gold Coast, for example, the Prime Minister and all cabinet ministers are now elected members of the legislative Assembly, and all members of the Assembly are elected by secret ballot. Final steps are being taken to elevate the Gold Coast to the status of an independent member of the British Commonwealth of Nations in 1957. It is expected that among these steps will be the termination of the international trusteeship status of British Togoland—heretofore administered as an integral part of the Gold Coast—and its unification with the Gold Coast in accordance with the wishes of the inhabitants as expressed in a recent plebiscite.

A federal government has been established in Nigeria, with the central House of Representatives and the assemblies in the three regions composed almost entirely of elected members. The executive councils of the central and regional governments also have a majority of elected members. Only a beginning, however, has been made in organizing political parties on a national basis. The lack of nationwide political parties and the cultural differences between the regions have complicated the functioning of a parliamentary system. Nigerian leaders have been assured their independence within the framework of the Commonwealth and are working toward achieving it within the next few years.[5] Prior to that time, the people of the Trust Territory of the British Cameroons, which forms an integral part of the political and administrative structure of the Nigerian government, will probably be asked to decide whether they wish to have their territory united with an independent Nigeria.

In the British West Indies, the peoples of Barbados, Jamaica, and Trinidad have elected majorities in their legislatures, and a majority of their cabinet ministers are elected by universal adult suffrage in their respective constituencies. Almost all of the territories in the

---

groups in the Western Pacific as separate units and those territories such as the Leeward Islands having a common legislature as an individual unit.

[5] The target date for full self-government is 1959. Leaders in Northern Nigeria are especially conscious of the need for time to train personnel and to develop the institutional foundation for self-government. See *New York Times* (Sept. 9, 1956), p. 7.

Leeward and Windward Islands have acquired elective majorities in their legislatures. As a result of several postwar conferences of representatives of the British Caribbean territories and other measures, final steps are being taken to establish a Federation of the British West Indies as a fully self-governing member of the British Commonwealth. A constitution for the federation is being drawn up. The Bahamas, the British Virgin Islands, British Guiana, and British Honduras are not expected to join at the outset, but one or more may subsequently join. The new federation will start out with a population of about three millions. Elections to the federal government are scheduled to take place in 1958.

In Southeast Asia, the Federation of Malaya, created in 1948, has developed rapidly toward full self-government. British and Malayan representatives recently signed an agreement to make every effort toward Malayan independence within the British Commonwealth by August 1957.[6] Singapore, which is not in the Federation, poses a special problem for the British because of its strategic importance. Although the self-governing powers of the people of Singapore were increased under a constitution adopted in 1955, they were confined to domestic matters and were subject to a degree of control by the colonial governor that is resented by the local political leaders. Further changes are in sight, but it remains to be seen whether they will satisfy the political aspirations of the people.

There are British territories at every stage of self-government, and the recent effort toward making government more representative is evident even in the least advanced. Constitutions that had not been revised for as long as a half century have been modified since the Second World War.

The pattern of political progress in British territories is clear, although there are individual variations. Authority is highly decentralized. Except for certain reserved powers, such as over defense, foreign affairs, and the negation of local acts, that are exercised by the United Kingdom Government, the authority and machinery of government are established in each territory regardless of its stage of development. In the earliest stages, the government of a territory is vested in a governor, who is responsible to the Secretary of State for Colonies. The governor is aided by an executive council that serves as the embryo of the cabinet and legislature. Its members, most or all of whom might in the beginning be officers in

[6] *New York Times* (Feb. 9, 1956).

the British colonial service, provide the basis for the official majority in the legislature. The legislature may consist of one or two houses. If there are two houses, the official majority will usually be found in the upper house, with the lower elected by universal, or by restricted, franchise. Political progress tends to be conceived in terms of increasing the representative character of the executive and legislative councils through the addition of elective members, reducing the qualifications for voting, diminishing the powers of the governor as ministerial responsibility develops, and finally removing the reserved powers. Although the Secretary of State for Colonies is responsible, together with his cabinet colleagues, to the Parliament in London for the government of the colonies, territorial law emanates not from London, but at the outset from the governor, next from the governor with the advice of his council, and then from the legislature with the assent of the governor. Unlike other colonial powers, the home ministries responsible for civil functions in the United Kingdom do not exercise authority in the colonies. Conceptually, the British system, more than any other, permits self-government to develop according to the circumstances of each territory.[7]

There have been setbacks, however, and weaknesses have appeared in certain territories. In British Guiana, the constitution had to be suspended to safeguard the territory from communist domination. In Cyprus, a combination of Greek-inspired nationalism, the belief of the United Kingdom that it could not make effective military use of the island if it granted Cypriots the right to decide their own national status, and the concern of Turkey for its national minority in Cyprus, led to guerrilla warfare and bitterness, weakened the Western defensive alliance, and dramatized the illusion of security obtained at the price of the freedom of another people. In Kenya, the Mau Mau uprisings, detested by many Africans as well as others, focused world attention on the explosive race relations in that territory and helped to bring about political and economic reforms benefiting the African inhabitants.

Leading Africans view the creation of the Federation of Rhodesia and Nyasaland, and to a lesser extent the East African High Commission (Kenya, Tanganyika, and Uganda) as a means for extending the area of political domination by white settlers—wholly apart from

[7] For details, see The Hansard Society, *Problems of Parliamentary Government in Colonies* (1953).

their merits from the standpoint of public administration. In fact, the system of restricted voting rights, of fixed racial quotas for membership in legislatures, and of constituencies formed on the basis of race still exists in a number of British territories with white and alien Asian settlers, and although this system may be an expedient for introducing the principle of representative government among people at varying stages of political development, it becomes an instrument for political domination of one racial group over another and aggravates racial conflicts in all fields. It is encouraging to note, however, that in the reform of municipal and other forms of local government instituted in 1947 throughout the British colonial world, a trend away from racial constituencies in local government elections is discernible in white settler areas.

If the greatest source of weakness in British colonial administration now lies in the entrenched political position of white-settler minorities in some territories, its greatest strength since the war lies in its clear definition of political goals, including the path to their attainment, and in the compatibility of these goals with nationalist sentiment. Independence within the British Commonwealth seems to provide a workable and a psychologically satisfactory basis for self-determination in almost all territories, assuming it is not attained on the terms of the white settler minorities. There remains, however, the development of suitable formulas for strategic areas, such as Cyprus, Hong Kong, and Singapore, that will enable Britain to meet its security requirements while satisfying the political aspirations of the people, and for small territories in the Western Pacific, which may be unable to stand on their own feet as independent nations. In the latter connection, the relationship that has been worked out between the United Kingdom and the independent Kingdom of Tonga is suggestive of the kind of arrangements that might be developed. For example, by mutual consent, the United Kingdom could conduct foreign relations on behalf of a small territory while, except on request, scrupulously avoiding interference in domestic matters. There is also the possibility of small island territories attaining full self-government through federation.

French Territories

Political developments since the war in non-self-governing territories under the administration of France have also surpasssed those of any previous period. They are traceable in part to the creation of the French Union under the Constitution adopted in 1946, which consists of: the French Republic, which comprises Metropolitan France, the Government General of Algeria (including three departments), four overseas departments, and nine overseas territories;[8] and the associated territories (the trust territories of French Togoland and Cameroons) and associated states (Viet Nam, Laos, and Cambodia until they became independent). France also has a condominium with Great Britain over the New Hebrides. By definition, only the overseas territories, the associated territories, and New Hebrides are considered in this study as non-self-governing territories.[9]

The effect of the French Union on the overseas and associated territories has been to increase their participation in government, but to do so in such a way that their status has become somewhat ambiguous. They are partly integrated with, and partly independent of, the central government in France, with the way not clear for them to move more completely in either direction. They have been assigned forty-three of the six hundred twenty-seven seats in the French National Assembly, which has much the same power to legislate for the territories as it does for the departments of France. But this representation is not proportionate to population and could not be substantially increased without jeopardizing further the power of the French people over their home government. On the other hand, the territorial legislatures have power over budgetary and revenue matters, which the French departments do not have. The territories are autonomous financially, except for deficiency and developmental grants from France, and their executive departments, except for defense and foreign affairs, function independently of the normal operations of French ministries in the rest of the Republic. Moreover, an act passed by the French Parliament on June 23, 1956, paves the way for further decentralization

---

[8] The eight territories of French West Africa are considered as a single unit as are also the four territories of French Equatorial Africa.

[9] It can be argued, particularly in view of the Arab revolt against French authority in Algeria, that the Algerian departments have a colonial type of government both in terms of its structure and of the political control exercised by French settlers over it; and that the four overseas departments have lost powers of self-government in the process of gaining political equality with the metropolitan French departments. This illustrates the difficulty of defining and applying the term "non-self-governing territories." However, peculiarities in jurisdictional relationships exist elsewhere in the world, and it seems proper here to regard the constitutional changes in these areas as having removed them from consideration as non-self-governing territories.

of legislative and executive authority to the overseas territories. In French West Africa, the Africans have large majorities in legislatures at every level of government, and the use of separate voting rolls for Europeans, including assimilated Africans, is disappearing.

Political developments in the other French territories have been along similar lines, but serious political tensions exist in several of them. Although France can perhaps be credited with good intentions to effect political reform, it has not been quick enough or generous enough in its grant of political authority to avoid the tragedies that have occurred in Viet Nam and North Africa. Disaffection also is becoming increasingly evident in the Trust Territory of the Cameroons under French administration.

France at times seems as willing as Britain to increase the participation of its dependent people in their government, but unlike Britain, it is bound by traditional concepts of centralized control—of viewing metropolitan France and the overseas areas as a unit, with control centered in Paris. Territorial participation in government has meant taking a share, necessarily limited, in the legislative organs of the French Republic and Union and not merely that of achieving complete autonomy in local affairs. The French system is defective in that it stops short of goals that are politically practicable for the metropole to concede, and that would, at the same time, be capable of satisfying the political aspirations of the territorial peoples concerned. Moreover, racial discrimination by the French in their territories is another obstacle to closer association. A fundamental change for the territories appears inevitable, and it seems likely to be in the direction of greater local autonomy instead of more complete integration in the central government of France. African deputies in the French Parliament who oppose both departmentalization and the concept of the "associated state" express their aim in the phrase "an autonomous state within the French Republic."[10] Recent use of the term "independence within interdependence" in referring to Morocco and Tunisia and their respective relationships with France is also suggestive of the trend. The concept has yet to be elaborated, but it seems to involve, first, that France recognize the independence of a territory and subsequently negotiate with its government on the basis of equality the special relationship that shall exist between them.

[10] Kenneth Robinson, "French Africa and the French Union," *Africa Today,* C. Groves Haines, ed. (1955), pp. 311-36.

Belgian Territories

Postwar political development in the Belgian Congo and the Trust Territory of Ruanda Urundi, the only territories under the administration of Belgium, have been negligible. Belgian territorial administration is highly centralized and authoritarian. All laws, including the annual budget, for Belgian territories are enacted by the Belgian legislature or by royal decree. Control is exercised by the central government over almost all aspects of life in the territories. Although there is one Governor-General for both territories, the Governor of Ruanda Urundi has virtually a complete and separate administrative staff. Consultative councils were appointed in 1947 to advise the chief executives of these territories, but there are no elective offices at territorial levels or in the sections of urban areas inhabited by Europeans and Asians.

Urban areas in Belgian territories are administered directly by the central territorial governments, with Africans participating under the direction of European officers in the executive activities of the African sections of the cities. Elections to local African councils were recently instituted in African communities in Ruanda Urundi. Draft legislation has also been under consideration for several years to establish an elective city council in Leopoldville, capital of the Congo. The decision whether separate voting rolls should be established for the various racial communities, with reserved seats in the city council for each, or whether constituencies should be formed without regard to race, could have a profound influence on the future political and social life of the Congo.

The Belgian theory of colonial administration has been that political advancement should follow economic and educational progress, and consequently, territorial authorities have taken measures to discourage the development of nationalist sentiment. The fact that European and Asian settlers do not have the same kind of privileged political position as those in British East and Central Africa also has undoubtedly helped to minimize political discontent among Africans and to retard the growth of nationalist sentiment. This does not mean that racial segregation and discrimination do not exist in the Congo. They do, and there is bitterness and a sense of deception among educated Africans who feel that their progress has provoked manifestations of the "color bar."[11] But the

[11] Guy Malengreau, "Recent Developments in Belgian Africa," *Africa Today,* Haines, ed., pp. 337-57.

Belgian Government may succeed in its desire to avoid the explosive tensions that exist in certain other multiracial societies in Africa if it continues to accelerate the rate of economic and educational advancement of the Africans, and to postpone the creation of legislative bodies at the territorial level and in urban areas inhabited by various races until all elements of the population concerned can vote and be represented on these bodies without regard to race. Belgium has not proclaimed this to be its policy with respect to voting but the course it has been following enables it to institute such a policy. This policy could be highly successful if it is clearly not used as a device for delaying unnecessarily the establishment of representative government.

Territories Administered by Other Member States

Of the other administering Members of the United Nations—the Netherlands, the United States, Australia, and New Zealand and, until 1954, Denmark—only the Netherlands has been regarded traditionally as a colonial power.

The responsibilities of the Netherlands for the administration of non-self-governing territories have been considerably decreased by reason of postwar developments. Indonesia became an independent republic after prolonged armed conflict, which the United Nations helped to end. Two other prewar colonies, Surinam and the Netherlands Antilles, have recently achieved the status of self-governing territories. The only remaining dependent territory administered by the Netherlands is Western New Guinea, in which the people are in the earliest stages of political development and in which advancement is likely to be slow even under the most ideal circumstances.

Postwar political progress in dependent territories under the administration of the United States has exceeded that of any previous decade since the turn of the century. The outstanding developments have been the achievement by the Philippines of its independence and the achievement by Puerto Rico of its unique status as a self-governing commonwealth, associated freely by compact with the United States. Some progress has been made toward the achievement by Alaska and Hawaii of statehood. Although the necessary enabling legislation has not yet been adopted by the United States Congress, both national political parties and their leaders have supported the enactment of such legislation. Meanwhile, constitutional conventions have been held in both territories, and the constitutions there drawn up have been approved by overwhelming majorities of the respective electorates. In Guam, citizenship and civilian government under an organic act, including legislative power on all local matters, have been granted to the people. And civilian government has replaced naval administration in American Samoa and in most of the Trust Territory of the Pacific Islands.[12]

A great weakness in the territorial policy of the United States has been that full statehood or complete independence was the only objective conceivable for territories under the federal system. However, the concept of commonwealth status for Puerto Rico, if it is perfected, could provide a formula for the future political evolution of unincorporated territories such as Guam and the Virgin Islands which have no prospect of statehood. No such policy has been adopted, however, and the future political status of the unincorporated territories is uncertain. Moreover, there remains unresolved, or at least not clearly stated, the political future of the inhabitants of the Bonin-Volcano Islands and of Okinawa and other southern Ryukyu Islands, in which the United States exercises full jurisdiction although the islands are still under Japanese sovereignty. Growing sentiment within Japan and on Okinawa for restoration of Japanese jurisdiction in the southern Ryukyus makes it highly desirable for the United States to make known at an early date what its plans are with respect to the government of these islands.

Australia has the extremely complicated task of developing self-government in Papua and the Trust Territory of New Guinea where, outside the urban areas, the people have little feeling of common identity or interest. In some parts of the territory, the language of one village may differ from that of a neighboring one. The government is still in the process of establishing friendly contact with groups in the interior that have had little or no contact with the outside world. A legislative council was established, however, for Papua and New Guinea, and includes several indigenous persons among its members. Also, new systems of local government have been introduced in Papua, New Guinea, and the Trust Ter-

[12] In approving their future state constitution in April 1956, the Alaskan electorate also adopted an ordinance calling for the election of two United States senators and a representative at the next general election. The persons so elected, however, will be unable to take their seats in Congress until the Congress enacts legislation admitting Alaska into the Union.

ritory of Nauru. The main problems in the foreseeable future are likely to be race relations and the relationship of the western part administered by the Netherlands to the rest of New Guinea.

The Government of the Trust Territory of Western Samoa, with New Zealand as administering authority, has been transformed in the last decade from one that was typically colonial to one that is largely representative, founded on the broadly based Samoan chieftain system. A proposed timetable for the remaining stages of constitutional advance short of final achievement of self-government has been developed through consultations between representatives of the Samoan people and New Zealand officials. The most important event in this regard was the holding of a constitutional convention in 1954. The timetable calls for the establishment of the essential elements of a parliamentary and cabinet system in the territory by 1960, leaving only the change in the status of the representative of New Zealand in the territory and the assumption by the premier of the proper powers and functions of that office to be worked out. Samoan leaders have insisted that eligibility for voting and for holding office should continue to be limited to the *matais* or heads of extended families, consistent with Samoan tradition, and notwithstanding recommendations of the Trusteeship Council that more modern democratic methods be instituted.

Denmark, having granted the people of Greenland full self-government, is no longer an administering member. In response to a request from representatives of the Greenland legislature, an amendment to the Danish constitution, adopted in June 1953, has made Greenland an integral part of the Kingdom of Denmark. Greenland has proportionate representation in the Danish Parliament.

To summarize briefly, the Members of the United Nations that administer non-self-governing territories now generally seem disposed, with the exception of Belgium, to grant political authority to the people of dependent territories, and they have devised systems of varying effectiveness for doing so. With relatively few exceptions, the peoples in these territories either are moving forward with the co-operation of their respective metropole toward known and desired goals or are indifferent or reconciled for the time being to uncertainties in their political future. The fact that evidences of racism, defiant colonialism, and neglect still exist in some territories makes it necessary in any constructive criticism of colonial administration to distinguish between the policies of the various colonial powers and also between the policies in the various territories they administer.

Role of the United Nations

There is no way of assessing with any degree of precision the extent to which the United Nations has helped to bring about the vast political changes that have occurred in non-self-governing territories since the Second World War. The lofty principles contained in Chapter XI of the Charter, the sections on self-determination and racial equality in the Universal Declaration of Human Rights and in the draft covenants, and the debates in the United Nations on colonial issues have probably contributed indirectly to the rise of nationalism, to policy changes, and to constitutional advances in dependent territories. The activities of the Trusteeship Council have influenced constitutional changes in some trust territories and have probably stimulated political developments in neighboring territories. The possibility that debates might take place in the United Nations or that the Organization might take action when a crisis occurs in a colony has added a weapon to the nationalist arsenal. This possibility may, in some instances, have induced the administering nations to take a more conciliatory approach to nationalist demands, but in other instances, it may have hardened their attitude. The desire generally to remove the subject of colonies from the arena of the United Nations also may have accelerated constitutional changes in some territories, but there is no clear evidence to substantiate this conclusion. To credit the Organization with a predominant role would belittle the efforts of nationalist leaders in most territories and the progressive policies initiated by some of the administering nations.

Nevertheless, it is clear that the United Nations, in intangible as well as in tangible ways, has significantly influenced the postwar efforts that have been made to deal with the colonial problem. It undoubtedly has contributed greatly to the formation of the world opinion that has spurred constitutional advances in most of the eighty-odd prewar territories. The only territories, apart from the trust territories and South-West Africa,[13] in which the United Nations played a direct role in influencing constitutional change, however, were the Netherlands East Indies, Palestine, Korea, and the former Italian colonies. Although organs of the United Nations

[13] See below, Chap. IV.

discussed proposals that might have injected the Organization into constitutional issues in other territories, such as Tunisia, Morocco, and Cyprus, they did not approve them. Also the United Nations was not directly involved in the agreements reached at Geneva in July 1954 that ended the fighting in Viet Nam.

Palestine, Former Italian Colonies, and Korea

Of the four colonial areas outside the trusteeship system in which the United Nations became directly involved, three of them—Palestine, the former Italian colonies, and Korea—presented situations of the kind that are not likely to arise in other territories.

The Palestine case sheds useful light on the national interests of Member nations in a territorial problem, on the manner in which the machinery and powers of the United Nations can be brought to bear on a complex and explosive situation such as might develop in any territory, and particularly on the value of nongovernmental experts in contrast with government representatives as mediators.[14] The special Arab-Jewish problem in Palestine and the fact that the mandatory power—the United Kingdom—was desirous of terminating the mandate and, therefore, requested the General Assembly to devise a solution to the problem, made the situation unique. With that request, an essential ingredient of a colonial problem—namely, a colonial power that is interested in maintaining its position in the territory—was no longer an important element in the situation. It is noteworthy, however, in view of the later emphasis placed by the United Nations on satisfying the "freely expressed wishes of the peoples concerned" in the Togolands and on self-determination for all peoples, that no plebiscites were held in Palestine, and the Arabs, who constituted two thirds of the population in 1947, bitterly opposed the partitioning of Palestine, which the General Assembly recommended.

Similarly, in the case of the former Italian colonies, Italy—as the former administering power—was an interested party, but it was not in a position to assert any demands.[15] The Italian peace treaty provided that if France, the Soviet Union, the United Kingdom,

---

[14] For an analysis of the action by the United Nations in the Palestine situation, see the volume in this Brookings series, *The United Nations and the Maintenance of International Peace and Security.*

[15] For a more detailed account of the postwar negotiations on the former Italian colonies, see Redvers Opie and Associates, *The Search for Peace Settlements* (1951), pp. 130-43.

and the United States were unable to agree on the disposition of the former Italian colonies within one year from the effective date of the treaty, the question would be referred to the General Assembly for recommendation, which the four powers agreed to accept. When the four powers failed to reach agreement within the prescribed time, they referred the problem to the General Assembly. It recommended in 1949 that: (1) Libya be granted its independence effective in 1952 after a transitional administration under United Nations supervision; (2) Italian Somaliland be placed under the international trusteeship system with Italy as the administering authority for ten years, after which Somaliland would become an independent state; and (3) Eritrea be federated as an autonomous unit with Ethiopia, under the sovereignty of the Ethiopian Crown, with a United Nations commissioner to assist in the preparation of a democratic constitution for Eritrea.[16]

The handling of the former Italian colonies illustrates the value of the United Nations in resolving differences between the major powers over the disposition of territories and in providing machinery for supervising the administration of such territories. It also demonstrates the faith of the major powers in the United Nations in 1946, when the treaty was agreed upon. The action of the General Assembly in determining the disposition of these colonies—being in the nature of a purely legislative act—was unprecedented in international affairs. The decisions made, however, were the result of political compromises, and it remains to be seen whether they will prove sound.[17]

Except for the light it sheds on Soviet imperialism, the Korean case is atypical and has little bearing on the handling of the colonial problem as such in the United Nations.[18] It is worth recalling, however, that the United States, the United Kingdom, and the Soviet Union agreed at the Moscow Conference in December 1945, with China later concurring, that a provisional government for Korea and a four-power trusteeship to last for five years should be established to prepare the Koreans for complete independence.

[16] Res. 289(IV), Nov. 21, 1949.

[17] A more extended analysis of the features of United Nations action in dealing with the question of the former Italian colonies is given in the volume in this Brookings series, *The United Nations and the Maintenance of International Peace and Security*.

[18] For a more detailed account of the Korean case, see Opie and Associates, *op. cit.*, pp. 302-17, and the volume in this Brookings series, *The United Nations and the Maintenance of International Peace and Security*.

Negotiations to implement this agreement became deadlocked, and the Koreans themselves opposed trusteeship on the grounds that it would continue outside control and postpone independence.[19] In view of the intransigence of the Soviet Union during the negotiations and its subsequent support of the North Koreans in their attack on the Republic of Korea in June 1950, it is apparent that the Soviet Union had no intention of abiding by the Moscow agreement. It is, therefore, idle to speculate whether the Korean war might have been averted and the goal of a free and united Korea achieved if Korea had been placed under the United Nations trusteeship system. Nevertheless, the availability of the trusteeship alternative served a useful purpose by providing a plausible solution, which merited widespread support, and by revealing more clearly than otherwise the hypocrisy in the approach of the Soviet Union to the problem.

Indonesian Case

In contrast to the situations in Palestine, the former Italian colonies, and Korea, the involvement of the United Nations in the Indonesian situation is more typical of the kind that might occur with respect to other territories. The Indonesian situation presented the classic problem of a colonial power attempting to maintain its privileged position in one of its non-self-governing territories, when confronted by the demands of a rebellious, indigenous people for self-government and independence. A brief analysis of the steps taken by the United Nations to deal with the situation is, therefore, helpful in appraising the possible future role of the Organization in similar situations.[20]

Although special circumstances of the Second World War created the immediate situation in Indonesia with which the United Nations had to deal, Indonesian nationalism had its origins in conditions that existed long before the war. Despite stern measures taken by the Netherlands to quell the nationalist movement, it continued to grow. Its leaders were encouraged by advances of nationalism

[19] Cf. James F. Byrnes, *Speaking Frankly* (1947), p. 222.

[20] For further information on the events in Indonesia during this period and the relationship of the United Nations therewith, see G. Kahin, *Nationalism and Revolution in Indonesia* (1952); J. Foster Collins, "The United Nations and Indonesia," *International Conciliation* (March 1950), and the volume in this Brookings series, *The United Nations and the Maintenance of International Peace and Security*.

elsewhere in Asia, particularly in India and the Philippines. During the war, the Japanese success in arms and propaganda against the Netherlands and their promises of Indonesian independence, heightened nationalist sentiment.

The power vacuum that appeared in Southeast Asia when Japan surrendered in August 1945, provided the opportunity for Indonesian nationalists to declare their independence of the Netherlands. By the time British forces, which were responsible for receiving the Japanese surrender in Indonesia, arrived, the Indonesians had obtained arms and ammunition from the Japanese troops. The subsequent arrival of a small contingent of Netherlands forces precipitated hostilities between them and the Indonesian Republican forces. Except for a few centers controlled by British troops, Java and Sumatra remained under control of the Indonesians, but the Netherlands re-established its control over the rest of the islands.

The tense situation began to ease as the Indonesian leaders were persuaded to negotiate with the Netherlands. While these negotiations were proceeding, however, the Ukranian representative to the United Nations brought the situation in Indonesia to the attention of the Security Council in January 1946. The Ukrainian complaint alleged that British and even Japanese troops had been used against the Indonesians and requested that the Council carry out an on-the-spot investigation. The Ukrainian proposal was rejected after the United States expressed the view that such an investigation would serve no useful purpose and, in fact, might prejudice the negotiations then taking place.

The Netherlands-Indonesian negotiations culminated in the Linggadjati Agreement of November 1946, which provided for: de facto recognition of the Republic of Indonesia, to include Java, Madura, and Sumatra; the formation by January 1949 of a sovereign democratic state on a federal basis embracing all of the Netherlands Indies; and a Netherlands-Indonesian Union to be established under the Dutch Crown. Although the agreement encountered opposition in both the Netherlands and Indonesia, it was finally signed in March 1947; but differences among the Indonesians over the agreement soon widened. New problems and misunderstandings also arose between the Indonesians and the Dutch, which resulted in new fighting between them, and in July 1947, the Netherlands took military measures, described as a temporary and limited "police action," to restore order.

India and Australia thereupon brought the matter before the

Security Council, which in August 1947, called on both parties to cease hostilities and to settle their dispute by peaceful means. Some fighting continued, and the Council later established both a commission to report on compliance with its cease-fire orders and a Good Offices Committee to assist the parties in reaching a settlement. The Good Offices Committee consisted of three members of the Council, one selected by each party (Australia by the Indonesians and Belgium by the Netherlands) and the third (the United States) designated by the two thus selected. An Australian proposal for arbitration of the dispute was rejected as was also a Soviet proposal to establish a commission, composed of representatives of all members of the Council, to supervise a "cease-fire" order.

From the outset in early 1946, of the consideration of the case by the Security Council, the Netherlands had insisted that the situation in Indonesia was within the domestic jurisdiction of the Netherlands and thus, by reason of Article 2(7) of the Charter, was outside the competence of the United Nations. Consequently, when the Council, during the summer of 1947, was contemplating what action to take, Belgium proposed that the International Court of Justice be asked for an advisory opinion on the competence of the Council to deal with the question. This proposal was rejected, although the United States supported it in order to determine the right of the Council to impose a specific solution.

The Member states on the Council not only differed in their interpretation of the Charter and in their respect for its provisions, but also had conflicting interests in the outcome of the Indonesian situation. France, Belgium, and the United Kingdom, with investment and trade interests in Indonesia and mindful of the danger of precedents in any action by the United Nations on colonial issues, supported the Netherlands. The British position was tempered somewhat by the involvement of British forces in Indonesia, by the pro-Indonesian sentiment in Asian areas associated with the British Commonwealth, and by a frank recognition of the need to satisfy the legitimate aspirations of Asian peoples. Syria and the Philippines, which had only recently become independent states—the former linked by Islam with the Indonesians—strongly sided with them. India, although not then a member of the Security Council, was itself taking the final steps toward independence and sought to enlist the support of the United Nations in the Indonesian cause.

The Soviet Union, Poland, and the Ukraine supported the Indonesians and made the most of the opportunity to attack the "imperialism" of the Netherlands and the other western democracies.[21] Australia was moved to support the Indonesians because of propinquity, domestic political considerations, and a desire to enhance its position among the peoples of Southeast Asia. China was torn between its natural sympathy with the striving of fellow Asians for independence and its regard for the suffering of Chinese living in the Republican areas. The United States, which was confronted by a clash between its interests in Europe and those in Asia, took a position more nearly between the two extremes than any other member of the Council, but it inclined toward the Indonesian side, reflecting the traditional sympathy of Americans for the aspirations of dependent peoples for independence.

The Good Offices Committee aided the parties in working out plans for a truce and a set of principles for a political settlement, which were embodied in the Renville Agreement signed in January 1948. Disagreement arose, however, over the practical application of these principles, and with the object of narrowing the differences between the two parties, the Australian and the United States members of the Good Offices Committee made a proposal, which the Indonesians at first were willing to accept, but which the Netherlands refused to discuss. Mutual distrust between the parties, and to some extent distrust by the Netherlands of the Australian and United States members of the Good Offices Committee, resulted in another breakdown of negotiations.

The actions of both the Indonesians and the Netherlands seemed so hostile to each other that they dissolved such understanding as had been reached in the Renville Agreement on ultimate goals. The Indonesian Republicans viewed Netherlands actions to create separate states in the portions of Java, Madura, and Sumatra that were occupied by the Netherlands forces in July 1947 and to control the trade of the Republican area with the outside world as efforts to "divide and rule" and to strangle the new Republic of Indonesia. The Netherlands, on the other hand, contended that the Indonesian leaders were holding Dutch nationals as hostages, that they did not have the support of the people throughout Indonesia, and that control of trade with Indonesia was necessary to prevent shipment of arms, which could only aggravate the security problem.

Without warning, in December 1948, the Netherlands resorted to a second "police action," which it declared was necessary to

[21] Later when the Indonesians suppressed a Communist revolt, the official line in the Communist press was that the president and vice-president of the Republic were traitors to their country.

establish peace and security. Dutch troops occupied the principal Indonesian Republican centers and imprisoned the Indonesian leaders. The Security Council called for a cessation of hostilities and the release of the prisoners, but full compliance was not obtained until after the Council had reiterated its call several times. The Council then adopted a resolution in late January 1949, one part of which reconstituted the Good Offices Committee with wider powers as the United Nations Commission for Indonesia.[22] A principal task of the commission was to submit recommendations to the Council on the nature and powers of a United Nations agency, which would be established after an agreement between the parties had been reached, to remain in Indonesia until sovereignty was transferred to a United States of Indonesia.

After further negotiations, during which two proposals made by the Netherlands for reaching agreement and establishing a United States of Indonesia were rejected, the plan of the Security Council for reopening discussions in Batavia, in April 1949, was agreed upon by both parties. The desire of the Netherlands to achieve a quick settlement was probably heightened by a pending action in the General Assembly to take up the Indonesian question and by the threat of the withdrawal of United States economic assistance to the Netherlands. As a result of the agreements reached at Batavia and of the subsequent agreements concluded at a conference at the Hague, sovereignty was transferred to the Republic of Indonesia at the end of 1949.

Although the Indonesian case does not provide an adequate basis for generalizations, it suggests certain conclusions and questions. The intervention by the Security Council probably made more certain the achievement of full independence by the Republic of Indonesia. On the other hand, the intervention also may have deepened and permanently injured the kind of Netherlands-Indonesian relations that held mutual advantages to both—although Netherlands intransigence alone might have foreclosed the development of such relations and brought more extremist Indonesian elements into power. The United Nations intervention certainly wounded the national pride of the Netherlands and made it bitter toward nations that it had formerly esteemed.

The experience of the United Nations in this case raises a serious question whether the criteria for, and the scope of, intervention by the Organization in this type of situation are adequately defined. Rejection of the Belgian proposal to seek an opinion from the Inter-

[22] U.N. Doc. S/1234 (Jan. 28, 1949).

national Court of Justice on the question of the competence of the Security Council to intervene left the resolution of this question to political instead of legal determination. Furthermore, intervention by the United Nations was not restricted to cessation of hostilities. It extended to participation by the Council in the final constitutional arrangements between the Netherlands and Indonesia. As many Members of the United Nations have vital national interests in colonial issues, it is questionable whether the Organization should, in future situations, become involved to the extent that it did in the Indonesian situation. If such involvement by the United Nations is necessary, it is worth considering whether other means for mediation—such as through nongovernmental experts—might be more suitable than the use of official representatives of governments.

Economic, Social, and Educational Advancement

It is more difficult to evaluate the improvements that have taken place since the Second World War in economic, social, and educational conditions in non-self-governing territories than it is to evaluate their advances in political development. The latter are often concise, dramatic, and readily effected by legislation or executive decree of the administering nation. The former are subject to many variables outside the control of the administering nations, are more difficult to measure, and take more time to make themselves evident. Wholly apart from philosophical considerations of what constitutes a good life, improvements in economic, social, and educational conditions must be reflected in better use of human and natural resources, better health and living conditions, improved relations between people of different races and cultures, and a citizenry better adapted to the world in which it lives. They are meaningful only to the extent that they touch and enrich the life of the individual and his community and contribute at the same time to the well-being of the rest of the world.

The measure used above for postwar political progress, however, is the extent to which the administering nations granted powers of self-government to the people of their dependencies, without inquiring whether the people exercised these powers effectively. Similarly, the emphasis below is on the effort of the administering nations to improve economic, social, and educational conditions, the extent to which they have co-operated with one another in this task, the contribution of the United Nations and the specialized agencies in this field, and the special problems meriting attention by the United Nations.

Reference will frequently be made in the following analysis to the expansion of public services, the increases in outlays for development purposes, and other phenomena implying an accelerated rate of growth over past periods. The conclusions are made on the basis of official reports from the administering Member states and from the United Nations, but no inference should be drawn that the improvements noted have altered in any fundamental way the conditions in which most inhabitants of many dependent territories still live. Illiteracy, poverty, malnutrition, disease, and poor housing are still widespread, and the population in most territories is growing at an ever-increasing rate, thus requiring an ever-expanding program of public services in order merely to keep pace with the level of services provided in the past. Furthermore, with the increasing awareness among dependent peoples of a better life, through their more intimate contact with the outside world and through their leaders, the felt need—indeed, the demand—is far greater than in prewar years and calls for greater effort than ever before.

Expansion of Public Services

There has been an extraordinary expansion in education, health, public utilities, and other services in most dependent territories since the war. This is partly due to the wartime accumulation of deferred needs and, in some areas, of substantial reserves with which to fill them. More, however, than just replacement and normal expansion has taken place since the war. The postwar expansion has been unusually great, and the trend in most territories toward higher levels of public service appears constant. For example, of the twenty-five institutions of higher education in dependent territories, fifteen have been founded in the past decade. Also, the percentage of children of school age enrolled in school has increased in almost every territory.[23] Similar increases have occurred in hospital and clinical facilities and in other public services. In addition to improvements in territorial government services, attention has been given, especially in the British territories, to strengthening various programs, such as those relating to local government,

[23] U. N. Secretariat, *Special Study on Educational Conditions in Non-Self-Governing Territories*, Doc. ST/TRI/SER.A/8/Add. 1 (December 1953), pp. 12 and 111.

community self-help, co-operatives, and labor unions, which add substantially to the means for improving living conditions.

In general, the indigenous people have probably gained to a greater extent than other elements of the population from this expansion in public services. The United Nations and political leaders in administering states have exerted pressure to end racial discrimination and segregation in the territories.[24] Segregation in public facilities, however, on both racial and religious bases, which is costly financially and divisive socially, still exists in many territories.[25] Such segregation usually breaks down, and race relations generally improve when the majority of legislators are elected on the basis of universal suffrage. This has been the experience in West Africa and the Caribbean.

Most of the expansion in public services has been met through increases in territorial revenues, but administering nations have also greatly increased their grants to make up deficiencies in the operating budgets of some territories. Such deficiency grants are in some cases a mixed blessing. Unless a territory is to be (1) incorporated into the metropolitan area of the administering nation, (2) freely associated with its metropole or some other state or states on terms of political equality without regard to the subsidies it derives therefrom, or (3) joined politically with a more wealthy neighboring territory, the expansion of services beyond the foreseeable capacity of a territory to pay for them might permanently render the peoples concerned dependent politically as well as financially. Such a situation appears to be developing in French West Africa and in two or three insular areas under the jurisdiction of the United States. The problem everywhere, however, is one of increasing productivity, attracting capital investments, realizing present revenue potential, training local personnel, and stimulating community self-help activities.

Development Programs

Since the end of the war, almost all of the administering powers that are Members of the United Nations have launched ambitious

---

[24] See, for example, *Labour's Colonial Policy—The Plural Society* (London, 1956), p. 42. "The next Labour Government . . . will direct all colonial governments to remove all administrative and statutory discriminations, except those expressly designed to protect under-privileged racial groups. Ultimately, all racial discrimination must be abolished."

[25] U.N. Secretariat, *Race Relations in Non-Self-Governing Territories*, Doc. A/AC.35/L.193 (Mar. 10, 1955).

development programs. These include such major projects as: construction of multipurpose dams and harbor improvements; industrial development through government corporations and inducements to private investment; and substantial development grants, supplementing territorial funds, for improving public and community services through research, training, community self-help, and other means.

The United Kingdom voted to spend from its own revenues a maximum of £1 million annually beginning in 1929 for development purposes in the colonies. By 1940, this had increased to £5 million annually for development and £500,000 annually for research. Under the Colonial Development and Welfare Act of 1945 as amended, the amount was again increased to a maximum of £25 million annually and a total of £120 million for the subsequent ten-year period. All of the latter has been committed, and about £70 million has already been spent. Projects financed with these funds are drawn up by the territorial governments and approved by the Secretary of State for Colonies. Over half of the funds have been devoted to economic development, including communications; the balance has been devoted to education, health, housing, and other social services.[26]

In 1948, the British Colonial Development Corporation and the Overseas Food Corporation, with a borrowing power of £165 million, were established to foster economic growth and stability through means not comprehended within the development plans. By March 1956, the Development Corporation had invested £65 million in hydroelectric power, drainage, cement production, and other capital schemes in the territories.[27] There has also been a great increase in the last decade in the amount of territorial government loans raised on the London market with the backing of the United Kingdom Government.

France also has various schemes for fostering development, the principal one being the Plan for the Modernization and Equipment of French Overseas Territories, which was established in 1946. Under it, 65 billion francs ($185 million) was allocated for expenditure during 1949-52 for improvements in communications, public

[26] See British Information Services, *British Colonial Development and Welfare Acts, A Brief Review to March 1951.* I.D. 892 (Revised, March 1952), and *The United Kingdom Dependencies, 1952-53: A Summary of Developments,* I.D. 1177, (June 1953), pp. 7-9.
[27] Great Britain, *The Colonial Territories, 1955-56,* Cmd. 9769 (May 1956), p. 77.

works, agriculture, industry, health, education, and other activities in the overseas territories. The French Ministry for Overseas France has established a number of public corporations and promoted the formation of semipublic corporations to stimulate production in specific fields, such as electric power, agriculture, and mines.[28]

The Belgian Government approved, in 1951, the expenditure of 20 billion francs ($400 million) on a Ten Year Plan for the Economic and Social Development of the Belgian Congo, of which 7 billion francs ($120 million) had been obligated by mid-1954. The Belgian Government created an Indigenous Welfare Fund in 1947, to which it deposited 2 billion francs ($40 million) in repayment to the Congo and Ruanda Urundi for funds advanced to Belgium during the war. This fund, which has been augmented from other sources, has stimulated improvements in various fields.[29]

The United States has fostered postwar development in its territories through separate programs in the territories. For the Virgin Islands, the Congress has appropriated, since 1944, over $11 million for public works, and in 1949, it created the Virgin Islands Corporation (successor to the Virgin Islands Company), capitalized at $9 million. In Alaska, the Federal Government has spent, since the war, $75 million in rehabilitation of the Alaska Railroad and $125 million for road construction. In 1949, the Congress authorized the expenditure of $70 million for the construction of community facilities in Alaska, of which $41 million had been spent by mid-1954. The economic development program in Puerto Rico, while it was still a territory, was launched with federal funds made available mainly through the Puerto Rican Reconstruction Administration and through the wartime accumulation in the local treasury of federal taxes on rum shipments to the United States. A large public works program in Guam has been financed out of direct federal appropriations and by the deposit to the Guam treasury of all federal taxes collected locally. Both American Samoa and the Trust Territory of the Pacific Islands receive operating subsidies

[28] For general background data see France, *The French Union: Political and Administrative Structure* (undated); *France Moves Forward: The Story of Economic and Technical Progress* (1954).

[29] For an account of developments in the Belgian Congo, see "Belgian Congo: A New Frontier in World's Industrial Development," *New York Herald-Tribune* (Nov. 25, 1951). See also U. N. Secretariat, *Information from Non-Self-Governing Territories Transmitted During 1952*, Vol. 2, Doc. ST/TRI/SER.A/ 7/Add. 1 (1953), pp. 3-28. Belgium, *La Situation Economique de la Belgique et du Congo Belge* (January 1954).

annually to supplement local revenues as well as subsidies for the construction of public facilities.[30]

The United States has also provided substantial technical and financial aid to the dependent territories administered by the United Kingdom, France, and Belgium. Under the agreements between the United States and these three governments covering United States assistance for European recovery, assistance was also made available to their territories in several ways: (1) the administering nation could either divert part of its own aid allocations or grant counterpart funds to its territories; (2) the territories could draw on an Overseas Territorial Development Fund, which totaled nearly $65 million by 1951; (3) funds were made available for scholarships and special training in the United States, for United States technicians to visit territories, and for research to be carried out in American institutions; and (4) loans were made available on condition that repayment would be made in strategic materials.

India and several other countries also provide a relatively small amount of assistance, primarily through fellowships, to non-self-governing territories.[31]

Multilateral Co-operation

The South Pacific Commission was formed in 1947, along lines similar to the Caribbean Commission, to foster the economic, social, and educational advancement of dependent peoples in the region. The members of both commissions are the governments that administer non-self-governing territories in the respective regions.[32] Each member government appoints commissioners to serve on the commissions. Each commission has a secretariat and is assisted in

---

[30] Unpublished data obtained from the Office of Territories, U. S. Department of the Interior.

[31] The Soviet Union has not extended technical assistance in the usual sense to dependent territories. Senate Committee on Foreign Relations, *Soviet Technical Assistance,* Committee Print Staff Study No. 7, 84 Cong. 2 sess. (July 12, 1956). There are, of course, occasional reports that terrorist leaders in the territories have received their schooling in the Soviet Union. Moreover, Soviet offers of aid to Egypt and other independent countries in Africa may be made with a view to penetrating into North Africa and ultimately to political and commercial predominance in all of Africa by nonmilitary means. Kenneth Love, "Moscow Spurs Africa Drive with Diplomacy and Trade," *New York Times* (May 26, 1956), p. 1.

[32] France, the Netherlands, the United Kingdom, and the United States are members of both commissions; Australia and New Zealand are members of the South Pacific Commission.

its work by a research council made up of specialists and by a conference held periodically, which is attended by representatives of the peoples of the territories. The existence of the conference shows how aware the member governments concerned are of the necessity and, in varying degree, of the desirability of associating the peoples concerned in regional efforts on their behalf.

Both commissions serve in an advisory, consultative capacity, undertake research on practical problems of general interest in the region, hold technical conferences, provide technical advice and assistance, act as a clearing house for information, and otherwise assist the governments in the respective areas.[33] Although the transformation of French Caribbean territories to the status of departments had no discernible effect on the participation by France and the areas concerned in the Caribbean Commission, recent changes in the political status of Puerto Rico, Surinam, and the Netherlands Antilles will necessitate basic changes in the composition and functioning of the commission and its auxiliary bodies. Consultations have been held on proposed changes, but it is too early to predict what the outcome will be. The same problem could arise in connection with the South Pacific Commission when the Trust Territory of Western Samoa achieves full self-government.

There is no organic relationship between the Caribbean Commission and the South Pacific Commission on the one hand, and the United Nations on the other, although there are informal working arrangements, and the commissions constitute the kind of intergovernmental co-operation provided for in Article 73(d) of the Charter. The specialized agencies and the United Nations Secretariat occasionally send representatives or observers to the conferences of the commissions, and a few specialized agencies have provided funds to the commissions for projects of mutual interest. Secretariats of the commissions maintain informal contact with the secretariats of other international agencies, principally for the purpose of exchanging information and avoiding duplication of effort.

A Commission on Cooperation in Technical Matters in Africa

---

[33] For background material see Great Britain, *British Dependencies in the Caribbean and North Atlantic, 1939-1952*, Cmd. 8575 (June 1952), pp. 73-74; Caribbean Commission, *West Indian Conference* (Fifth Session, 1952). Emil J. Sady, *Report on the South Seas Conference: With An Analysis of the Agreement Establishing the South Pacific Commission*, U. S. Department of State Publication 2796 (March 1947); "New Agreement Extends Territorial Scope of South Pacific Commission," Statement by Felix M. Keesing, U. S. Department of State *Bulletin,* Vol. 25 (Dec. 24, 1951), pp. 1038-39.

South of the Sahara was established in 1950. It consists of representatives of the governments of Belgium, France, Portugal, Southern Rhodesia, the Union of South Africa, and the United Kingdom. Provision has been made for other countries south of the Sahara to be admitted to membership and also for attendance by representatives of other countries and of international organizations at meetings of the commission and at technical conferences sponsored by the commission.[34]

Also in 1950, seven members of the British Commonwealth, acting through a Consultative Committee, created the Colombo Plan for Cooperative Economic Development in South and Southeast Asia. Subsequently, nine Asian countries and the United States became members of the consultative committee. The plan contains six-year development programs for the Commonwealth members and British territories within the region. The estimated cost of those parts of the plan relating to the dependent territories is £107 million, which will be paid by the Commonwealth members of the plan other than the United Kingdom.[35] The plan, which was to end in 1957, has been extended at least until 1961.

The United Nations and Specialized Agencies

The United Nations has fostered economic, social, and educational advancement in the territories in various ways. First, on the level of policy and principle, all recommendations in this field of the General Assembly and the Economic and Social Council, including its subsidiary organs, are equally applicable to both non-self-governing territories and independent nations.[36] Of the various

[34] See address by George C. McGhee, "Africa's Role in the Free World Today," U. S. Department of State *Bulletin*, Vol. 25 (July 16, 1951), pp. 97-101. See also Great Britain, *The Colonial Territories, 1952-53*, Cmd. 8856 (May 1953), pp. 115-16 on international co-operation other than through the United Nations in Africa.

[35] See Commonwealth Consultative Committee on South and South-East Asia, *New Horizons in the East: The Colombo Plan for Co-Operative Economic Development in South and South-East Asia (1950)*; Great Britain, *The Colombo Plan: The First Annual Report of the Consultative Committee on Economic Development in South and South-East Asia* (Karachi, March 1952), Cmd. 8529 (May 1952), and subsequent reports; D. G. Bridson, *Progress in Asia: The Colombo Plan in Action* (1953).

[36] The recommendations of the General Assembly that relate specifically to non-self-governing territories and to trust territories are discussed below in Chapters III and IV.

subsidiary organs of the Economic and Social Council, the Commission on Human Rights, the Subcommission for the Prevention of Discrimination and Protection of Minorities, and the regional economic commissions of the United Nations in the Far East and Latin America deal with matters most directly involving non-self-governing territories. Some of the principles contained in the Declaration of Human Rights and in the draft covenants were drawn up especially with the territories in mind. The Economic Commission for Asia and the Far East includes representatives from the dependent territories of the region who participate as associate members, without the right to vote. Dependent territories in the Caribbean could, through sponsorship of their application by the respective governments responsible for their international relations, become associate members of the Economic Commission for Latin America, but none of them has yet taken advantage of this opportunity.

Dependent territories may participate in some specialized agencies but not in others. The qualifications and rights of membership differ as between agencies. In some cases, these differences appear reasonable, in others they seem wholly unreasonable.

The Universal Postal Union allows certain dependent territories, which were members before 1947, to retain their full membership, but only sovereign states can now become members, and there is no provision for associate membership. The International Telecommunications Union grants full membership to certain groups of territories, which were full members of its predecessor organization, and for those territories that do not so qualify, an associate membership status is provided. Membership in the World Meteorological Organization is open to dependent territories as well as to independent nations, but there are constitutional and other matters on which the territories cannot vote.

The World Health Organization, the United Nations Educational, Scientific and Cultural Organization, and the Food and Agriculture Organization permit dependent territories to become associate members, with the rights of ordinary members except the right to vote. The Pan American Sanitary Bureau, now a regional agency of the World Health Organization, also provides for participation of non-self-governing territories without voting rights. The International Labour Organisation has no provision for associate membership, but, as in the case of other international organizations, the member governments sometimes include on their conference delegations advisers from their dependent territories. Underlying the provisions for associate membership for dependent territories in specialized agencies is the principle of allowing those territories that are fully self-governing in the particular field being dealt with by an agency to have at least a voice in the proceedings, so that the international agency will, to the fullest extent consistent with the rights of independent nations in the organization, avoid detracting from the self-governing powers that the territories have. Relatively few territories, however, have taken advantage of the special membership provisions that have been made for them, and it is unlikely that many more of them will do so.

Associate membership in specialized agencies, as the principle has developed to date, appears suitable only for politically advanced territories that are moving toward full independence. It is unlikely to be sought by or for a territory that will probably be integrated completely into the political life of the metropole. Moreover, since associate membership has been designed for "non-self-governing territories," it is unlikely to attract self-governing communities such as Puerto Rico, Surinam, and the Netherlands Antilles, which are neither independent states nor dependent territories but are associated freely with an independent state. Although consideration should be given to amending the provisions for associate membership to remove any connotation that such membership is designed solely for dependent territories, it is doubtful that this would make associate membership politically acceptable to the self-governing communities. The latter will probably be satisfied with nothing less than full membership or a new type of membership, *e.g.,* associated state membership.[37]

The United Nations and the specialized agencies have directly contributed to the advancement of non-self-governing territories through their programs of conferences, research, scholarships, and above all, technical assistance. There is increasing participation of dependent territories in these programs. In addition, research publications of the United Nations Educational, Scientific and Cultural Organization, the World Health Organization, the International Labour Organisation, and the Food and Agriculture Organization

[37] For a related discussion of the need for bringing self-governing communities in the Western Hemisphere into inter-American technical organizations, see Emil J. Sady, "European Territories in the Caribbean and the Inter-American System," *Estudios Antropologicos,* published in honor of Dr. Manuel Gamio (University of Mexico, 1956).

have direct relevance to problems of dependent territories, although it is difficult to assess the extent to which their findings have been applied in the territories.

The most direct benefit that non-self-governing territories have received from international agencies has been through scholarship, fellowship, and technical assistance programs. When these programs were first initiated, the administering nations were, on the whole, skeptical about them because of the elaborate procedures involved in obtaining the assistance, doubts about the personnel and motives of international agencies, and the feeling that their own development programs were of sufficient magnitude to fill urgent needs and that assistance from other sources could not readily be absorbed or fitted into these programs. This feeling still exists to some extent, but there are clear signs that it is disappearing.

Requests for all types of assistance have increased. The United Nations, the specialized agencies concerned, and the United Kingdom concluded, in June 1951, a basic agreement that laid down the general principles on which technical assistance would be granted by the United Nations and the specialized agencies to British territories, thus simplifying subsequent arrangements for such assistance.[38] Similar agreements were subsequently concluded by the United States, France, and the Netherlands governing the provision of international technical assistance in their respective territories. Although the administering nations must approve of the assistance to be granted, the initiative often comes from the territories, and the details are worked out directly by the territorial governments and the agencies concerned. Experience has proved that international technical assistance can effectively supplement other available means for territorial development. In 1954, about $400,000, constituting about 2 per cent of the total amount spent by the United Nations and the specialized agencies for technical assistance projects, was devoted to work in eighteen dependent territories. For 1956, over $1,000,000, more than 3 per cent of the total, has been approved by these agencies for expenditures in twenty-seven territories. These are exclusive of regional projects, many of which benefit non-self-governing territories.

[38] For text of the "Basic Agreement between the United Nations, ILO, FAO, UNESCO, ICAO and WHO and the Government of the United Kingdom of Great Britain and Northern Ireland for the Provision of Technical Assistance to the Trust, Non-Self-Governing and other Territories for whose International Relations that Government is Responsible," see U. N. Secretariat, *Information from Non-Self-Governing Territories Transmitted During 1951*, Vol. 1, Doc. ST/TRI/SER.A/6 (1952), pp. 145-48.

In addition to providing scholarships and fellowships, these funds are used on the request of the administering Member states to carry out various kinds of projects in dependent territories. For example, the World Health Organization has provided assistance in malaria control in North Borneo and the Trust Territory of Somaliland.[39] The International Labour Organisation has helped Jamaica to set up a system for collecting labor statistics and to establish a pension fund for sugar workers. The International Bank for Reconstruction and Development has made valuable economic surveys in a number of non-self-governing territories and has granted loans to the Belgian Congo and Northern Rhodesia for development purposes.

These international programs, although insignificant in comparison with those carried out by the administering nations themselves, are of great importance. The international assistance is felt and appreciated in the territories. Despite the large amount of aid granted by the metropole, territorial and development budgets are often tight. A small contribution can often be meaningful. Furthermore, the territorial personnel are stimulated by association with experts of other nationalities having wide experience in other underdeveloped areas. But perhaps most significant of all is the psychological effect of the aid program, enabling other governments to share in the responsibility for the development of dependent areas, familiarizing their nationals with the technical problems posed, allowing in some cases experts from the territories to serve on projects in independent nations, and giving the territories generally a sense of belonging to a friendly world community.

Two conclusions regarding the role of the United Nations in the postwar political development of non-self-governing territories can be drawn from the experience during the past decade. The first is that in most cases, the administering nations are capable, without direct intervention by the United Nations, of working out with representatives of their territorial populations mutually satisfactory arrangements that will ensure progress in self-government. The second is that, in view of the numerous guerrilla wars, disturbances, and other disorders that have provoked constitutional changes in

---

[39] U.N. Secretariat, *International Technical Assistance to Non-Self-Governing Territories,* Doc. A/AC.35/L.227 (Apr. 3, 1956). See also, U.N. Economic and Social Council, *Eighth Report of the Technical Assistance Board to the Technical Assistance Committee,* Doc. E/TAC/REP/66 (1955), and U. N. Economic and Social Council, *Second Part of the Eighth Report of the Technical Assistance Board to the Technical Assistance Committee, Doc.* E/TAC/REP/68 (Apr. 30, 1956).

a number of territories and the anti-colonial sentiment of a majority of the Member states, the United Nations has exercised admirable restraint in not intervening directly more often in the problems of dependent areas.

The United Nations helped create the atmosphere that produced these developments, but it participated directly in relatively few of the constitutional changes that occurred. The action by the United Nations in the Indonesian situation suggests the need for defining more precisely the criteria for and the scope and form of future intervention by the Organization in similar situations. Furthermore, as many Members of the United Nations have vital national interests in colonial issues, the United Nations should consider using nongovernmental experts rather than representatives of governments if and when its mediation efforts in colonial disputes extend to constitutional arrangements.

The postwar effort to foster economic, social, and educational advancement in dependent territories emphasizes that a new epoch of colonial history is in the making, which contrasts sharply with that of the prewar period. The administering nations have created special funds and corporations and have spent substantial sums, unparalleled in colonial history, for development purposes. Regular public services in the dependent territories have also been expanded.

The United States and to a lesser extent other nations have, through bilateral arrangements, contributed financial and technical assistance to dependent territories of other nations. The administering nations are co-operating with one another through regional commissions and other means to improve the welfare of dependent peoples. The United Nations and the specialized agencies are providing increasing technical assistance to the dependent territories, which is of far greater significance than the financial cost would indicate, and advancement in the territories is being stimulated also by other activities of the United Nations, including those of the Economic and Social Council and its subsidiary organs.

The new spirit of colonial administration is not universal, nor has it penetrated every aspect of life in dependent territories. The living conditions of the people in most territories are still deplorable, but the efforts now being made by territorial leaders, by administering nations individually and collectively, and by international organizations to improve conditions provide the basis for hope that the fundamental political and social changes that are still in the offing in many territories can take place without causing a world upheaval.

CHAPTER III

The General Assembly and Non-Self-Governing Territories

Some of the most contentious issues in the United Nations have developed out of the consideration by the General Assembly of matters relating to Chapter XI of the Charter. Underlying most of these issues is the conflict over the respective rights and obligations of the administering states and of the United Nations in relation to non-self-governing territories. In general, Member states have approached these problems from one of two diametrically opposed positions. On the one hand, the Members with an anti-colonial bias see little good in colonial relationships and have seized on Chapter XI as a weapon by which they might expand the international accountability of the colonial powers for their stewardship of dependent peoples and thereby hasten the dissolution of the relationships. On the other hand, Members administering non-self-governing territories have generally sought to guard their prerogatives with respect to their territories and to minimize the role of the United Nations in colonial affairs. There are, of course, degrees of moderation between these two extreme positions.

Chapter XI of the Charter, as entitled, is a "Declaration Regarding Non-Self-Governing Territories," by "Members of the United Nations which have or assume responsibilities for the administration of territories whose peoples have not yet attained a full measure of self-government." The Charter did not otherwise identify the nations that made this declaration, or the territories involved, and by design did not create special machinery to ensure fulfillment of it. In this declaration, the administering nations accepted as a sacred trust the obligation to promote the political, economic, social, and educational advancement of the inhabitants of territories under their administration, but their only specific undertaking toward any organ of the United Nations is contained in Article 73(e): "to transmit regularly to the Secretary-General for information purposes, subject to such limitation as security and constitutional considerations may require, statistical and other information of a technical nature relating to economic, social, and educational conditions in the territories for which they are respectively responsible" other than trust territories. The word "political" was omitted from the categories of information to be transmitted, and the Charter is silent on what the United Nations should do with the information it receives.

Committee on Information from Non-Self-Governing Territories

The debates on whether there should be any machinery for implementing Chapter XI of the Charter, and if so, what its attributes should be, reveal the differences in attitudes among Members regarding the nature of Chapter XI and the role of the United Nations in relation to the obligations assumed by the administering Members thereunder. The focal point for these debates has been the question initially of the creation of, and later of continuing the existence of, the Committee on Information from Non-Self-Governing Territories, and its predecessor committees.

Establishment of the Committee

At the first part of the first session of the General Assembly in 1946, the Fourth (Trusteeship) Committee undertook to discuss Chapter XI and to make recommendations on its implementation as well as on matters relating to trusteeship. In the general discussion, the Australian delegate said that machinery should be set up for safeguarding the fulfillment of the explicit obligations to promote the welfare of inhabitants of non-self-governing territories. He raised these questions: What was to happen to the information transmitted under Article 73(e) of the Charter? How was this information to be made available to the Members of the United Nations? What advice did the General Assembly need to arrange for receiving, circulating, and classifying the information?[1]

[1] U.N. General Assembly, First Session, First Part, Fourth Committee, *Official Records*, 4th Meeting (Jan. 23, 1946), pp. 13-14. It has been pointed out that until 1950, Australia often took a "broad construction" of the Charter on issues relating to human rights and to trust and non-self-governing territories, whereas after the change from Labour to Conservative leadership, the Australian Government has consistently taken a "strict construction" of the Charter in these matters. See the monograph in this Brookings series, *The United Nations and Human Rights*, p. 149n.

Australia submitted a proposal that contained a provision directing the Secretary-General to present to the Assembly during the second part of the first session a report indicating how the United Nations should exercise the functions pertaining to it under Chapter XI, including the manner in which information transmitted under Article 73 should be communicated to other Members as well as to the Assembly. This proposal was rejected, and in its place the Fourth Committee adopted without objection a proposal made by China that the Secretary-General should include in his annual report "a statement summarizing such information as may have been transmitted under Article 73(e) of the Charter." A resolution with this included was adopted unanimously by the General Assembly on a roll call vote.[2] The unanimity achieved on this resolution, and the fact that a relatively moderate proposal was offered by a nonadministering state and was accepted in preference to a more far-reaching one suggested by an administering state, are noteworthy in view of the controversies that later developed.

At the second part of the first session of the Assembly, the Secretary-General submitted a special report of the type envisaged in the Australian proposal that had been rejected. The report stated that "Members responsible for . . . transmission will no doubt wish . . . to secure an adequate examination of the summaries to be made by the Secretary General." It pointed out the absence of a provision for channeling the information through the Trusteeship Council or the Economic and Social Council and went on to suggest the need for an expert body to assist the Secretary-General in preparing the summaries and the General Assembly in giving the summary "the attention which it may merit."[3]

Thus, the first concrete suggestion for a special committee to examine either the information transmitted by the Member states or the summaries prepared by the Secretary-General emanated from the Secretariat. In a working paper to the Fourth Committee, the Secretariat suggested that the committee might wish to consider appointing a committee that would meet before the opening of the second session to examine the Secretary-General's summary and the information on which it was based. In addition, the paper suggested, the Fourth

[2] Res. 9 (I), Feb. 9, 1946.
[3] U.N. General Assembly, *Non-Self-Governing Territories: Transmission of Information by Members Under Article 73(e)*, Doc. A/74 (Oct. 21, 1946), pp. 12, 13. See also U.N. General Assembly, First Session, Second Part, Fourth Committee, *Official Records*, Annex 14, p. 245.

Committee might consider recommending the temporary appointment of an *ad hoc* committee comprised of certain named governments, and that this committee might be given instructions to suggest procedures for the future.[4] The reaction in the Fourth Committee to these suggestions was varied, and the whole question of procedure was referred to a subcommittee of the Fourth Committee.

Opinion differed in the subcommittee on the question of what use should be made of the information transmitted. Belgium, Denmark, France, the United Kingdom, and the United States expressed the view that the Secretariat was the best agency to deal with the information transmitted, primarily because it had the necessary technical competence. The United States and Denmark also mentioned the possibility of creating an *ad hoc* committee or a subcommittee during the second session of the Assembly. The United Kingdom stressed that according to the Charter, the only purpose of transmitting information is "for information purposes," and France held that if no executive or supervisory body had been provided it was because it had not been intended to create one.[5] The non-administering states held that an expert body was needed to co-ordinate and correlate the information and that the Trusteeship Council, which they termed "an impartial and expert body," was the best qualified to perform this function. For legal and practical reasons, however, some of these states suggested that at that particular time an *ad hoc* committee should be established to examine the information. They believed that the information should be examined and judged, perhaps in the form of resolutions and not just filed away, and that because the examination of the information was a function of a political character, it would be inappropriate for the Secretary-General to perform it.

Two proposals were submitted and were rejected by a narrow margin. China suggested that the Trusteeship Council should receive and examine the information from non-self-governing territories and the Secretary-General's summary thereof, and Cuba, on the basis of a suggestion by the Secretariat, proposed an *ad hoc* committee composed of an equal number of administering and non-administering states.[6]

---

[4] U.N. General Assembly, *Non-Self-Governing Territories: Working Paper to the Fourth Committee,* Doc. A/C.4/29 (Nov. 1, 1946), p. 3.

[5] U.N. General Assembly, Fourth Committee: Sub-Committee 2, *Summary Record of Fifth Meeting,* Doc. A/C.4/Sub. 2/19 (Nov. 22, 1946), p. 8.

[6] The Secretariat played an unusually active role throughout the deliberations

As a compromise, a draft resolution was submitted by Denmark, the Netherlands, the United Kingdom, and the United States. It requested the Secretary-General to summarize, analyze, and classify the information transmitted during the course of 1947 and to include this information in his report to the second session of the Assembly, "in order that in the light of the experience gained the General Assembly may be able to decide whether any other procedure may be desirable for dealing with such information in future years." This proposal was adopted by a vote of 10 to 4, with 5 abstentions.[7]

When the report of the subcommittee was presented to the Fourth Committee, Cuba proposed an amendment, providing for the same type of *ad hoc* committee that had been rejected in the subcommittee. The arguments for and against this amendment were much the same as those expounded in the subcommittee. The United States delegate stated that the establishment of new machinery in the form of an *ad hoc* committee would be a "modification of the Charter." Nevertheless, the Fourth Committee adopted the Cuban amendment by a vote of 21 to 12, with 4 abstentions,[8] and decided that if the General Assembly approved the establishment of an *ad hoc* committee, the Assembly should at that time elect eight non-administering Members to the committee.[9]

The arguments on both sides were again presented at the plenary meeting of the General Assembly. The Netherlands, in addition to opposing the committee on legal grounds, stated that the welfare of dependent peoples could best be promoted by co-operation on a regional basis among administering nations and by obtaining comparative reports in fields related to improvements in living conditions. Such reports could best be prepared by expert organizations such as the specialized agencies. The United States asserted that if the *ad hoc* committee as well as the Secretary-General were

---

of the subcommittee. Further reference will be made to this later on in the discussion of relations between the Committee on Information and other United Nations organs.

[7] U.N. General Assembly, *Resolution . . . for Dealing with Information Submitted under Article 73 (e) . . .*, Doc. A/C.4/Sub. 2/22 (Nov. 25, 1946), p. 1.

[8] U.N. General Assembly, First Session, Second Part, Fourth Committee, *Official Records*, 21st Meeting (Dec. 8, 1946), p. 127.

Australia, Belgium, France, and the United Kingdom reserved the positions of their governments.

[9] U.N. General Assembly, First Session, Second Part, Fourth Committee, *Official Records*, 25th Meeting (Dec. 11, 1946), pp. 155, 157.

to handle reports on about eighty territories, nothing useful would be prepared for the next General Assembly.

Cuba claimed that the creation of an *ad hoc* committee was a procedural matter and therefore did not require a two-thirds majority of the Assembly, but no decision was made on this point. When the paragraphs of the resolution that would establish the *ad hoc* committee were put to a vote, however, they received exactly a two-thirds majority. New Zealand, which abstained, was the only administering nation that did not cast a negative vote. The entire resolution was subsequently adopted by a vote of 27 to 7 with 13 abstentions, and the Assembly thereupon elected the eight nonadministering members of the *ad hoc* committee.[10] The task of the committee under the resolution was to examine the Secretary-General's analyses of information from non-self-governing territories with the dual purpose of "aiding the General Assembly in its consideration of this information" and of "making recommendations to the General Assembly regarding the procedures to be followed in the future."[11]

Thus the first of several "temporary" committees was created for dealing with this problem. As the life of each came to an end, the nations with a strong anti-colonial bias would press for the creation of a permanent committee. Long and heated debate would ensue, with all the same arguments reiterated, but with Belgium, France, and the United Kingdom becoming more threatening in their reservations and sharper in their denunciations of such action.

On the basis of a vote taken at the second session of the Assembly in 1947, resolutions providing for the creation or extension of the life of the committee were, until the eighth Assembly, deemed important matters requiring a two-thirds majority. This fact, together with threats on the part of some administering Members to boycott the committee, has tended to prevent the creation of a permanent committee. The sentiment in favor of the committee has been strong enough, however, to ensure successive extensions of it.

In 1947, the *ad hoc* committee was replaced by the Special Committee on Information Transmitted Under Article 73(e), the life of

[10] Brazil, China, Cuba, Egypt, India, Philippines, Soviet Union, and Uruguay. U.N. General Assembly, First Session, Second Part, Plenary, *Official Records,* 64th Meeting (Dec. 14, 1946), p. 1369.
[11] Res. 66(I), Dec. 14, 1946.

which was limited to two years, but extended in 1949 for three more years. In 1952, a draft resolution providing for continuation of the Special Committee on the same basis for a further period of three years was amended by the Fourth Committee, in line with a proposal presented by twenty-one nations, to provide for the automatic continuation of the Special Committee at the end of the three-year period, unless otherwise decided by the Assembly, for as long thereafter as there were territories whose peoples had not yet attained a full measure of self-government. When this draft resolution came before the Assembly, the representatives of Belgium, France, and the United Kingdom announced that their governments would not participate in the work of the Special Committee if it were established on a permanent basis. The United Kingdom and France indicated a willingness to participate in a spirit of co-operation on a temporary basis, but they could not accept the implication that administering Members were accountable to the United Nations for the administration of their non-self-governing territories.[12]

The Indian delegate pointed out that the General Assembly had authority under Article 22 of the Charter to create the Special Committee on a permanent basis.[13] He contended that the committee was indispensable to the General Assembly and that if it were discontinued, the Fourth Committee would have to fall back on a committee of its own to discharge the same responsibilities. However, India and most of the other nations that favored a permanent committee recognized that the Special Committee could not function effectively without the participation of the principal administering Members. They therefore yielded, and the General Assembly adopted by a vote of 53 to 2, with 3 abstentions, a resolution to continue the committee on the same basis until 1955,[14] at which time it was continued for another three-year period.[15] The resolution in 1952 deleted the word "Special" from the name of the committee. Its official title became and still is the Committee on Information from Non-Self-Governing Territories, usually referred to as the Committee on Information.

[12] U.N. General Assembly, Seventh Session, Plenary, *Official Records*, 402nd Meeting (Dec. 10, 1952), pp. 341-55.

[13] Article 22 provides that: "The General Assembly may establish such subsidiary organs as it deems necessary for the performance of its functions."

[14] U.N. General Assembly, Seventh Session, Plenary, *Official Records*, 402nd Meeting (Dec. 10, 1952), p. 355. See Res. 646(VII), Dec. 10, 1952.

[15] Res. 933(X), Nov. 8, 1955.

Composition, Functions,
and Powers

The Committee on Information is composed of the administering Members and an equal number of nonadministering Members elected by the Fourth Committee for staggered terms of three years.[16] Although the administering and nonadministering Members seldom vote as a block, the balanced composition serves to protect the administering Members against the adoption by the committee of extreme measures and to encourage compromise of differing viewpoints. The General Assembly has rejected proposals to enlarge the committee or otherwise to alter its balanced membership. Furthermore, proposals have been rejected to have the General Assembly rather than the Fourth Committee elect the nonadministering Members. The administering Members have insisted that the Committee on Information be subordinated to the Fourth Committee rather than to the Assembly itself in order to minimize its importance. It serves, in effect, as a subcommittee of the Fourth Committee.

Although Belgium is entitled to a seat on the Committee on Information, it carried out its threat at the seventh session of the Assembly and did not thereafter send a representative to the meetings of the committee. Belgium contends that the powers and functions of the committee exceed the limits of competence conferred by the Charter on United Nations organs, but it has continued to transmit information on the Congo. The committee thus, in fact, has an unbalanced membership.

The functions and powers of the Committee on Information have been slightly increased with almost every renewal of its life and by separate resolutions of the Assembly, but not in ways that might reasonably be regarded as contrary to the Charter. Its principal functions and powers are:

. . . To examine, in the spirit of paragraphs 3 and 4 of Article 1 and of Article 55 of the Charter, the summaries and analyses of information transmitted under Article 73 (e) of the Charter on the economic, social and educational conditions in the Non-Self-Governing Territories, including any papers prepared by the specialized agencies and any reports or information on measures taken in pursuance of the resolutions adopted

[16] There are now seven administering Members: Australia, Belgium, France, the Netherlands, New Zealand, the United Kingdom, and the United States. There were eight until Denmark withdrew from the committee after the 1954 meeting due to the achievement of full self-government by Greenland, the only dependent territory that Denmark administered.

by the General Assembly concerning economic, social and educational conditions in the Non-Self-Governing Territories;

. . . To submit to the regular sessions of the General Assembly reports containing such procedural recommendations as it may deem fit and such substantive recommendations as it may deem desirable relating to functional fields generally but not with respect to individual Territories.[17]

It has also from time to time been assigned special tasks by the Assembly such as: (1) to examine the factors that should be taken into account in determining whether a territory is non-self-governing; (2) to make recommendations on the application in the non-self-governing territories of the Universal Declaration of Human Rights; (3) to study the means of increasing the participation of duly qualified representatives of the territorial peoples in its work; (4) to make recommendations on communications relating to the cessation of transmission of information; (5) to consider a resolution on self-determination approved by the seventh session of the Assembly; and (6) to study ways of facilitating examination of information on a regional basis.

The General Assembly, by overwhelming majorities, rejected suggestions made by the Soviet Union in the early years that the Committee on Information should examine petitions, make annual visits to the territories, and consider information from private individuals and groups. The Assembly has, by narrower margins, rejected proposals that would empower the committee to make recommendations with respect to individual territories. An attempt by India in 1955 to expand the scope of the committee collapsed more rapidly than earlier attempts, signifying perhaps the success of the tactic used by several administering Members of threatening to withdraw from the committee if its functions were enlarged.

The Committee on Information now convenes annually in the spring. Until 1955, it met a few weeks before the annual session of the General Assembly, an arrangement insisted upon by the administering Members in the belief that it would limit the activities of the committee. The meetings of the committee last about three weeks. The chairmanship of the committee is alternated each year between representatives of an administering and a nonadministering Member.

Unlike the Mandates Commission of the League of Nations or the Trusteeship Council of the United Nations, the Committee on Infor-

[17] Res. 933(X), Nov. 8, 1955.

mation does not examine the basic information transmitted on each territory. Only occasionally is it even referred to. The committee attempts to gain insights into trends, mainly through the summaries, analyses, and special studies of the Secretariat and from statements by experts, in non-self-governing territories generally. Since 1950, the committee has given special attention in rotation each year to educational, economic, and social conditions. It appoints a balanced subcommittee of six members to prepare a draft report for its consideration and ultimate submission to the Assembly. This report usually serves as the basis for one or more resolutions by the Assembly.

Information is supplied annually on each territory, with emphasis usually on those items in the Standard Form on which new information is available.[18] The Secretariat may, with the approval of the administering state concerned, utilize other official documents in preparing the summaries and analyses. In practice, such approval is obtained only when the Secretariat has some doubt about a document and then only on an informal basis. In addition, the administering Members as well as the Secretariat and the specialized agencies often submit special papers on the principal subject under consideration by the committee. As a result, an impressive collection of technical documentation is being developed by the United Nations in this field.

The purpose of the examination by the committee of the summaries and analyses and other technical documents has not been entirely clear. Few of the representatives on the committee are qualified specialists or even interested in the technical problems involved. Nevertheless, the nonadministering Members desire to make technical as well as policy recommendations. Some administering Members may agree with the recommendations in substance, but they object in principle to the nonadministering Members making them. The committee has, however, adhered to its terms of reference remarkably well. Except for routine denunciations, by doctrinaire anti-colonial nations,[19] of the administering powers for violating obligations under Chapter XI of the Charter, political questions unrelated to cessation of the transmission of information have not been

---

[18] The Standard Form is an outline approved by the Assembly for the guidance of administering Members in preparing information for transmission under Article 73 (e).

[19] Mainly by the Soviet Union when it was a member from 1950 to 1952.

discussed in the committee, and no resolutions have been directed at individual territories.

The powers of the Committee on Information, although much more limited than those of the General Assembly, have served to limit the powers of the Fourth Committee. Also because of its membership, the Committee on Information has afforded the administering Members the opportunity of laying before the Fourth Committee resolutions that are acceptable to them. The Fourth Committee has, on occasion, ignored the recommendations of the Committee on Information and has also recommended resolutions that the latter committee had not previously considered. Nevertheless, the Committee on Information has a moderating influence. If it were to be discontinued, the Fourth Committee would approach each session with a clean slate, with the Secretary-General's analyses of information, and other Secretariat suggestions serving as the principal guide for its members—most of whom are strongly anticolonial—in formulating resolutions for consideration by the General Assembly. It is a paradox that the nonadministering Members have pressed to give the Committee on Information permanent life while increasingly upsetting its recommendations in the Fourth Committee, and the administering Members, who would discontinue it, have defended with vigor its recommendations in the Fourth Committee.

Some of the administering nations are fearful that the creation of a permanent committee would in itself imply their acceptance of the principle of "international accountability" for the fulfillment of their obligations under Chapter XI of the Charter. This in turn would, they believe, diminish their sovereignty over their territories, and they are opposed to any semblance of international supervision over these territories. They regard Chapter XI as a declaration of principles, which, except for Article 73(e), involves no obligations on their part to the United Nations. Thus, while they may admit privately that the committee has value so long as the General Assembly concerns itself with the information transmitted under Article 73(e), they oppose the establishment of a permanent organ having competence in matters exclusively relating to non-self-governing territories. Furthermore, they feel that the establishment of such an organ would set a precedent that might tend to justify the granting of powers to it by the General Assembly similar to those that the Trusteeship Council exercises.

The Committee on Information can help to ensure fulfillment of the provisions of Article 73 of the Charter, and there is little likelihood that it will be discontinued. And the interests of the nations of the free world are not served, and the Organization itself is harmed, by periodic strife within the United Nations over the continuation of the committee.

Within the framework of changes that may be possible through Charter revision or otherwise, the problem in relation to Article 73 can be summarized as follows: How can a committee be constituted to avoid infringement, or threat thereof, on the authority of Members in the administration of their territories and at the same time to assist the General Assembly (1) in keeping informed of the manner in which administering Members are fulfilling their obligations under Article 73(e) of the Charter; (2) in facilitating the exchange of information and experts in technical fields; (3) in placing at the disposal of administering Members the technical resources and facilities of international agencies; and (4) in making the administering Members accountable to world opinion for any violations of their pledges under Chapter XI of the Charter?

Application of Term "Non-Self-Governing"

The General Assembly, since its earliest sessions, has been debating the respective roles of the administering Members and of the United Nations in determining the territories to which Article 73(e) applies. The question was first raised in an effort to determine the territories on which information should, in the first instance, be transmitted to the Secretary-General. An attempt to define the term "non-self-governing territory" proved unsuccessful, but it provoked little conflict because most of the Members were satisfied with the enumeration made by the administering Members of the territories on which they intended to transmit information.

Soon after this enumeration had been made, however, several administering Members announced that for various reasons they would not transmit information on some of the territories they had enumerated or on which they had previously transmitted information. The controversy then centered on questions relating to the cessation of information: When is a territory no longer non-self-governing for purposes of Article 73(e)? Does the respective administering Member have the sole and exclusive right to decide when and under what circumstances it can cease transmitting information on a territory, or should the United Nations also have a role in this decision, and if so, what should it be? There are as yet no definite answers to these questions, but how they might be answered in future cases is suggested by the debates and the actions in early cases of the cessation of transmission of information.

Definition of Non-Self-Governing Territory

The Secretary-General, in June 1946, sent a letter to each Member of the United Nations requesting its opinion on various matters, including: (1) the factors to be taken into account in determining which are the non-self-governing territories referred to in Chapter IX of the Charter; and (2) an enumeration of the non-self-governing territories subject to its jurisdiction. This letter was sent to Members to enable the Secretary-General to comply with the resolution approved by the General Assembly in February 1946, requesting him to include in his annual report a statement summarizing the information transmitted under Article 73(e).[20]

Replies were received from twenty-two governments, ten of which commented on the questions raised. In these replies or in statements made at the second part of the first session of the General Assembly, Australia, Belgium, Denmark, France, the Netherlands, New Zealand, the United Kingdom, and the United States enumerated seventy-four territories on which they would transmit information.[21] France, however, pointed out, with reference to territories it had listed, that on January 1, 1947, Martinique, Guadeloupe, French Guiana, and Reunion would receive a status equal to that of a metropolitan department of France, and added that the "juridical position" of other territories within the French system was "in process of evolution."[22]

At the same session of the General Assembly, the question which territories fell within the scope of Chapter XI of the Charter was referred by the Fourth Committee to a subcommittee. Various

[20] U.N. Secretariat, *Non-Self-Governing Territories, Summaries and Analysis of Information Transmitted to the Secretary-General During 1947* (1948), p. 14.

[21] U.N. General Assembly, *Non-Self-Governing Territories: Transmission of Information by Members Under Article 73(e)*, Doc. A/74 (Oct. 21, 1946), pp. 19-30; Doc. A/74/Add. 1 and 2 (Oct. 26 and Nov. 16, 1946).

[22] *Ibid.*, p. 29.

views were expressed by Member governments on the definition of the term "non-self-governing territories."

The United Kingdom and New Zealand felt that it would be extremely difficult, in view of the variety of conditions in the territories and the different policies of administering Members, to define the principles that should be applied in determining whether any particular territory comes within the scope of Chapter XI of the Charter. The United Kingdom stated that the terms of Article 73(e) appeared to provide a sufficient and satisfactory guide in practice. Canada suggested that Chapter XI was not "applicable to territories within the metropolitan areas of a Member state," and added that "it would appear to be a question of fact to be determined in each case whether the peoples outside the metropolitan areas of Member states in substance govern themselves."[23]

France listed three factors to be considered: "dependence in relation to a State member, responsibility exercised by that State in the administration of the territory, [and] peoples who have not yet attained a full measure of self-government." It also stated that the application of any final definition "can only be a matter for the national competence of the State entrusted with the administration of the territories."[24]

The United States suggested that Chapter XI of the Charter would "appear to apply to any territories administered by a Member of the United Nations which do not enjoy the same measure of self-government as the metropolitan area of that Member." It indicated that it had used a purely pragmatic approach in selecting the territories on which it should transmit information in the hope that the experience of the various Members would perhaps reveal more clearly the kind of criteria, if any, that could be agreed upon in making the selection.[25]

India commented in detail. It declared that: "Non-self-governing territories may . . . be defined to mean and to include territories where the rights of the inhabitants, their economic status and social privileges are regulated by another State." India claimed that a territory is not non-self-governing if it has representative executive and legislative bodies that are free to regulate "the economic conditions and social rights of their people," even though in some

[23] *Ibid.*
[24] *Ibid.*, p. 28.
[25] *Ibid.*, p. 19.

aspects, such as foreign relations, the territory might be subject to the control of another state. In the subcommittee, the Indian representative stated that the definition in the Charter of "territories whose peoples have not yet attained a full measure of self-government" was quite clear, but stated that he had no objection to the definition proposed by the United States.[26]

Egypt stated that the determining factor "should be the state of dependence of a nation in relation to another with which it has no natural ties. For this purpose, those extrametropolitan territories should be considered Non-Self-Governing, in which the people are of different language, race and culture from the peoples of the powers which rule them." It went on to exclude the Sudan from consideration as a non-self-governing territory on the ground that it constitutes "an integral part of Egypt to which it is united by close bonds of language, culture and race, and with which it forms a complete geographic unity."[27]

The Soviet Union said that sooner or later a precise definition would have to be sought. The Soviet delegate later suggested that non-self-governing territories were all possessions, protectorates, and territories that do not govern themselves and whose populations do not participate in the election of the higher administrative bodies.

In the subcommittee, Cuba stated that a formal definition might tend to restrict the Charter provisions. France and the United Kingdom also opposed any formal definition. Australia noted that if no information were submitted on a territory, any Member could call attention to this fact. The subcommittee therefore agreed not to attempt a definition of the term, but instead to enumerate the territories on which information would be transmitted.

The Fourth Committee accepted this decision, and the resolution approved by the General Assembly listed seventy-four non-self-governing territories concerning which eight governments had already transmitted information to the Secretary-General or had declared their intention of so doing.[28] The resolution also records the protest lodged by Panama that the Panama Canal Zone, for which the United States had transmitted information, should not be considered a non-self-governing territory as the Republic of Panama retained its sovereignty over the Canal Zone; and the protests of

[26] *Ibid.*, pp. 5, 22.
[27] *Ibid.*, p. 24.
[28] Res. 66 (I), Dec. 14, 1946.

Australia
  Papua
Belgium
  Belgian Congo
Denmark
  Greenland[b]
France
  Comoro Archipelago[c]
  French Equatorial Africa
  French Establishments in India[b]
  French Establishments in Oceania[b]
  French Guiana[b]
  French Somaliland
  French West Africa
  Guadeloupe and Dependencies[b]
  Indo-China[b]
  Madagascar and Dependencies
  Martinique[b]
  Morocco[b]
  New Caledonia and Dependencies[b]
  Reunion[b]
  St. Pierre and Miquelon[b]
  Tunisia[b]
Netherlands
  Curaçao (Netherlands West Indies)[b]
  Netherlands Indies[d]
  Surinam[b]
New Zealand
  Cook Islands
  Nieue Island[c]
  Tokelau Islands
United Kingdom
  Aden Colony and Protectorate
  Bahamas
  Barbados
  Basutoland
  Bechuanaland Protectorate
  Bermuda
  British Guiana
  British Honduras
  British Solomon Island Protectorate
  British Somaliland Protectorate
  Brunei

  Cyprus
  Dominica[e]
  Falkland Islands
  Fiji
  Gambia
  Gibraltar
  Gilbert and Ellice Islands Colony
  Gold Coast Colony and Protectorate
  Grenada[e]
  Hong Kong
  Jamaica
  Kenya Colony and Protectorate
  Leeward Islands
  Federation of Malaya
  Malta[b]
  Mauritius
  Nigeria
  North Borneo
  Northern Rhodesia
  Nyasaland Protectorate
  Pitcairn Island
  St. Helena and Dependencies
  St. Lucia[e]
  St. Vincent[e]
  Sarawak
  Seychelles
  Sierra Leone Colony and Protectorate
  Singapore
  Swaziland
  Trinidad and Tobago
  Uganda Protectorate
  Zanzibar Protectorate
United States
  Alaska
  American Samoa
  Guam
  Hawaii
  Panama Canal Zone[f]
  Puerto Rico[b]
  Virgin Islands
Condominium of France and United Kingdom
  New Hebrides

[a] U.N. Department of Public Information, Research Section, *Non-Self-Governing Territories: Background Paper No. 73*, Doc. ST/DPI/SER.A/73 (Jan. 6, 1953), pp. 5-8.
[b] Information has ceased to be transmitted on this territory.
[c] The separate treatment of the Comoro Archipelago and Nieue Island, formerly covered in the information transmitted on Madagascar and Dependencies and on the Cook Islands, respectively, added two to the list of Non-Self-Governing Territories.
[d] The Republic of Indonesia having become an independent state in 1950, the Netherlands continued to transmit information only on Western New Guinea.
[e] Dominica, Grenada, St. Lucia, and St. Vincent, which together form the Windward Islands, have been treated since 1948 as one non-self-governing territory.
[f] The United States transmitted information initially on the Panama Canal Zone, but after protest by the Republic of Panama, regarded the transmission as in error and did not transmit information on the Zone thereafter.

Guatemala and of Argentina, regarding British sovereignty in British Honduras and the Falkland Islands, respectively. The General Assembly has not at any session considered applying the term "non-self-governing territory" to any area that was not included among the original seventy-four that were voluntarily put forward by the administering Members themselves. Belgium contended that other Members are obligated under Article 73(e) to transmit information on areas inhabited by "natives" or tribal groups under their jurisdiction. This view has not been seriously considered, despite the fact that there are some areas actually designated and administered as "territories" that fit the definition of "non-self-governing territories" as proposed by the United States, and whose only distinguishing feature is their contiguity to the metropolitan areas of the administering states. Among these are the Northwestern Territory of Canada, the Northern Territory of Australia, the Territories of Quintano Roo and Baja California of Mexico, the Andaman and Nicobar Islands of India, and the five Federal territories of Brazil. The original enumeration settled at the time the question which territories were non-self-governing within the meaning of Article 73, but the question of defining the term "non-self-governing territory" was to arise again in connection with the cessation of the transmission of information under Article 73(e).

Cessation of Information

In 1947, a number of administering Members failed to report information on the non-self-governing territories that had been enumerated in the resolution passed by the General Assembly in 1946, and India made an unsuccessful attempt to persuade the *ad hoc* committee to call the attention of the General Assembly to this fact, but the Assembly took no action on the matter. By 1948, it had become apparent that no information would be transmitted on eleven of the seventy-four territories that had been originally enumerated. In the same year, the French representative reversed a position previously held and suggested in the Special Committee that it would be useful if the committee would define the term non-self-governing territories. He stated that inasmuch as the Assembly had never defined the term, the administering Members themselves had to determine which territories fell within the scope of Article 73(e).

In response to the French suggestion, India introduced a working paper that stated in part that in view of "information being withheld" by a certain administering power on the plea that the term "non-self-governing people" needs to be legally defined, "it is suggested that steps be taken to clarify the position so that an Administering Power may recognize the obligatory character of its responsibility under [Article] 73(e) in respect of any territory inhabited by a people of a different race, culture, and language from its own in the Metropolitan country, whose international relations and representation are under the control and direction of such a Metropolitan country and which does not enjoy the same basis of self-government as the Metropolitan Government, particularly in respect of electoral qualifications and conditions of representation in the Metropolitan legislature."[29] The Indian representative felt strongly that the decision on which territories come within the scope of Article 73(e) could not be made by the administering Member alone. He indicated that the problem of defining the term could be referred to the Fourth Committee of the General Assembly and, if necessary, the advice of the International Court of Justice should be sought.[30]

The United Kingdom delegate, however, stated emphatically that it was for the administering state alone to decide which territories come within the scope of Article 73(e), and he opposed any attempt to define the term "non-self-governing territories." He held that the Special Committee was not competent to discuss constitutional changes in various territories, and the Assembly could not define the term because it would involve a decision on constitutional relationships within the domestic jurisdiction of the metropolitan powers concerned. Nor would his government agree to have the matter referred to the International Court of Justice for an advisory opinion.[31] The Special Committee did not adopt the Indian proposal, and India then reopened the question in the Fourth Committee, which approved its proposal.

The resolution of the Fourth Committee noted that some Member governments had, without explanation, ceased to transmit information on certain territories which they had previously regarded as non-self-governing; welcomed any recent developments of self-govern-

[29] U.N. General Assembly, *Non-Self-Governing Territories: Working Paper Transmitted to Special Committee on Information by the Representative of India*, Doc. A/AC.17/W. 10 (Sept. 4, 1948), p. 2.

[30] U.N. General Assembly, Non-Self-Governing Territories, Special Committee on Information, *Summary Record of 12th Meeting.* Doc. A/AC.17/SR.12 (Sept. 10, 1948), pp. 12-13.

[31] U.N. General Assembly, Non-Self-Governing Territories, Special Committee on Information, *Summary Record of 11th Meeting,* Doc. A/AC. 17/SR.11 (Sept. 9, 1948), p. 7.

ment; stated it is "essential that the United Nations be informed of any change in the constitutional position and status of any such territory just prior to cessation"; and requested "the Members concerned to communicate within a maximum period of six months to the Secretary-General information on the constitution, legislative act or executive order providing for the government of the territory, and the constitutional relationship of the territory to the Government of the metropolitan country." In the debate that preceded the vote on this resolution, the United States stated that the action called for was "logical and proper," if it were understood that it "did not alter the right of each Administering State to determine the constitutional position and status of any particular territory under its sovereignty."[32]

Australia, Belgium, France, New Zealand, and the United Kingdom made explicit reservations on the clause in the resolution requesting information on the constitutional status of territories. They did not object to making the information available informally, as indeed it is normally available to the general public, but they vigorously opposed the implication that the General Assembly could discuss or decide whether the decision made by an administering state that a territory had ceased to be non-self-governing was an appropriate one.

The abstentions on the vote included an unusual grouping of states. Canada, Luxembourg, and the Union of South Africa joined the states that made reservations, but in addition Argentina, Bolivia, Brazil, the Dominican Republic, Greece, Lebanon, Panama, Peru, and Saudi Arabia also abstained. The resolution was adopted in the plenary meeting without opposition.[33]

In 1949, the Secretary-General distributed to members of the Special Committee on Information, the replies he had received from France, the United Kingdom, and the United States to an inquiry he had made pursuant to the above resolution. In summary, these replies were as follows:

1. France reiterated its position that the determination of the territories to which Article 73(e) applies lay exclusively within the competence of the respective administering state. This principle and the status of the territories within the French Union had, in its opinion, justified its ceasing from 1947 onward to transmit informa-

---

[32] U.N. General Assembly, Third Session, Fourth Committee, *Official Records,* 52nd and 59th Meetings (Oct. 6 and 14, 1948), pp. 10-11, 59 respectively.

[33] Res. 222 (III), Nov. 3, 1948.

tion on the Overseas Departments of Guadeloupe, Guiana, Martinique, and Reunion, the status of which was largely identical to that of departments of metropolitan France. Therefore, it "would be no more possible in their case to speak of dependence than it would be in the case of a province in relation to the State of which it formed a part." Also, New Caledonia, the French Settlements in Oceania, and St. Pierre and Miquelon were granted "a regime which on the whole closely resembles that of the Overseas Departments of metropolitan France as regards the status of the inhabitants and their method of political representation." In the case of the Associated States of Indo-China, France stated that freedom of self-government to the extent of independence within the French Union had been granted to them. Finally, France asserted that it had granted the French Settlements in India wide local liberties within a regime that enabled them to participate in the institutions of the Republic, and enabled their inhabitants to enjoy without distinction of origin or status, political rights similar to those of citizens of metropolitan France.[34]

2. The United Kingdom referred to its previous explanation in the *ad hoc* committee in 1947 that Malta had attained full responsibility for local self-government. It maintained that inasmuch as "educational, social, and economic conditions in Malta are now the exclusive concern of the Government of Malta, it would be inappropriate, and indeed, impossible, for His Majesty's Government . . . to continue to transmit information on these matters under Article 73(e) of the Charter."[35]

3. The United States, in transmitting information in 1947, had notified the Secretary-General that, in view of the protest by Panama at the first session of the General Assembly, the United States would not transmit information on the Canal Zone "pending clarification of this question with the Republic of Panama."[36] In its reply to the Secretary-General's inquiry, the United States held that the resolution did not apply to the Canal Zone because the United States had never claimed that there had been any change in its constitutional status. The United States restated its opinion that the problem of

[34] U.N. General Assembly, *Information from Non-Self-Governing Territories: Report of the Secretary-General*, Doc. A/915 (June 14, 1949), pp. 3-5.
[35] *Ibid.*, p. 2.
[36] U.N. Secretariat, *Non-Self-Governing Territories, Summaries and Analysis of Information Transmitted to the Secretary-General During 1947* (1948), p. 391.

the status of the territory was a matter for further study and consultation between the two governments concerned.

These replies were discussed in the Special Committee, where the administering Members reiterated their positions. Egypt, supported by India, disagreed with the views of administering states, but held that the Special Committee, not being competent to discuss the issues involved, should recommend to the General Assembly that they be referred to the Fourth Committee. It was decided that the Special Committee was not competent to consider such a proposal and that any delegation could put the matter on the agenda of the Assembly.

A related issue was debated in 1949, when the Soviet Union proposed the withdrawal from consideration of the information on Indonesia on the ground that the Indonesian Republic was a sovereign state. The Netherlands stated that Indonesia was still under its sovereignty; the question whether it was obligated to transmit information on Indonesia was for the Netherlands to decide and beyond the competence of the committee to discuss. Australia, Belgium, France, and the United Kingdom argued that the Special Committee had no choice but to examine the information submitted by the Secretary-General. Australia added that in view of the situation in Indonesia, the Netherlands "might have decided to refrain from submitting information" on that territory.[37]

Venezuela and the Dominican Republic agreed that the Soviet proposal was outside the competence of the Special Committee and pointed out that the question of independence for Indonesia was still a subject of controversy and on the agenda of the Security Council. India, on the other hand, took the position that although the Special Committee was not entitled to reject any information transmitted, it was surely entitled to determine whether the information on a territory was outside the jurisdiction of the committee and thus could not be considered. In the end, however, the committee voted 12 to 4 that it was not competent to consider the Soviet proposal.[38]

The vast majority of members of the Fourth Committee at the

---

[37] U.N. General Assembly, Non-Self-Governing Territories, Special Committee on Information, *Summary Record of Eighth Meeting*, Doc. A/AC.28/SR.8 (Aug. 31, 1949), p. 5.

[38] *Ibid.*, p. 7.

session of the General Assembly in November 1949 opposed the view of the administering states that the determination of which territories come within the scope of Article 73(e) is exclusively a matter for the respective administering power to decide. France and the United Kingdom were severely criticized for ceasing to transmit information on certain territories. In particular, the basis for French action with respect to New Caledonia, the French Establishments in Oceania and India, and St. Pierre and Miquelon was not convincing, nor at the time was that for the British action with respect to Malta.[39] Furthermore, the United Kingdom failed to communicate documentation bearing on its constitutional relationship with Malta.

The two governments, however, stoutly defended their action in the Fourth Committee. France referred to its constitution as uniting all units within the French Union. Both France and the United Kingdom sought protection in the phrase in Article 73(e) that makes the transmission of information "subject to such limitations as . . . constitutional considerations may require." The United Kingdom did not claim that Malta had achieved a "full measure of self-government," but inasmuch as the Government of Malta had been vested with full responsibility for economic, social, and educational matters in the territory, constitutional considerations precluded the United Kingdom Government from transmitting information on these matters. The United Kingdom was prepared to inform the Secretary-General of constitutional developments in a territory that makes the continued transmission of information on it impossible, but it was simply a matter of informing the Secretary-General. The Charter did not, in the British view, confer on the General Assembly the responsibility of determining the effect of constitutional limitations on the obligation of a Member to transmit information.[40]

The Philippine delegate stated that it was not for the administering state alone to decide whether to continue to transmit information on a certain territory, because once the territory had been included on the list of non-self-governing territories, the administering state

[39] In 1956, on request of the elected Government of Malta, Malta became integrated with the United Kingdom under constitutional arrangements that increased the powers of the Parliament of Malta, provided safeguards for the Roman Catholic Church, and granted the Maltese three seats in the British House of Commons.

[40] U.N. General Assembly, Fourth Session, Fourth Committee, *Official Records*, 117th Meeting (Nov. 5, 1949), p. 138.

no longer held the sole responsibility for making this decision. This was the crux of the position taken on this question by the nonadministering powers, and it was developed at great length in the debates on the subject.

A draft resolution presented by Egypt, which was designed to achieve a definition of the term "non-self-governing territory," was adopted with some amendments by the Fourth Committee and, subsequently, by the General Assembly. After noting the reasons given for the cessation of information on certain territories, the resolution stated "that it is within the responsibility of the General Assembly to express its opinion on the principles which have guided or which may in future guide the Members concerned in enumerating the territories for which the obligation exists to transmit information under Article 73(e) of the Charter." It then provided that the General Assembly invite the Special Committee "to examine the factors which should be taken into account in deciding whether any territory is or is not a territory whose people have not yet attained a full measure of self-government."[41]

The United States, which did not participate in the debate on the resolution, abstained from voting on it and explained its abstention in the plenary meeting of the Assembly. It "wondered who was to determine which were the Non-Self-Governing Territories referred to in Chapter XI, what were or should be the responsibilities, if any, of the Special Committee on the issue and what were the Non-Self-Governing Territories referred to in the Charter. There was also the fact that the Special Committee did not have authority to require political information." For these reasons the United States would have preferred to give the question further consideration.[42]

In 1950, the Special Committee decided to postpone consideration of a background paper that the Secretariat had prepared for its use in examining the factors that should be taken into account in determining whether a territory is non-self-governing. Its decision was based in part on the limited time available for consideration of such a complex subject. Moreover, the Communist attack had been launched in Korea, and the French delegate referred to the "inappropriateness of a discussion on so intricate a problem

[41] Res. 334(IV), Dec. 2, 1949.
[42] U.N. General Assembly, Fourth Session, Plenary, *Official Records,* 263rd Meeting (Dec. 2, 1949), p. 460.

at a time of tension in international relations."[43] France also insisted that any future study prepared by the Secretariat should comprehend all people in territories that had not yet attained a full measure of self-government and not only those in territories that were enumerated originally.

Later the same year, Indonesia was admitted as the sixtieth Member of the United Nations. The Netherlands had written the Secretary-General several months previously that it would no longer transmit information on Indonesia "since the sovereignty over these territories, with the exception of Netherlands New Guinea, was formally and irrevocably transferred" to the Republic of Indonesia. The communication also advised "that in all probability no further reports on the Netherlands West Indies and Surinam will be submitted after 1950, since both these territories will then have acquired an autonomous status and a full measure of self-government, placing them outside the scope of Chapter XI of the Charter."[44] The Netherlands also said that should it cease to transmit information on these latter territories, it would present a report to the United Nations setting forth the reasons for its action.

After the admission of Indonesia to the United Nations, India introduced in the Fourth Committee a draft resolution that, while noting with satisfaction the communication of the Netherlands on the cessation of information on Indonesia, raised obliquely the question of the competence of the General Assembly to decide the appropriateness of cessation by requesting the Special Committee "to examine such information as may be transmitted in future to the Secretary-General in pursuance of General Assembly Resolution 222(III), and to report thereon to the General Assembly."[45] It will be recalled that Resolution 222(III) requested administering Members to send to the Secretary-General of the United Nations, in advance of cessation, documentation on the new constitutional status of the territory concerned. The significance of this resolution did not escape the United Kingdom, which stated that it would abstain from voting on the second part of the resolution because it could

---

[43] U.N. General Assembly, Non-Self-Governing Territories, Special Committee on Information, *Summary Record of 25th Meeting*, Doc. A/AC.35/SR.25 (Sept. 8, 1950), p. 10.

[44] U.N. General Assembly, *Information from Non-Self-Governing Territories, . . . Report of the Secretary-General*, Doc. A/1302/Rev. 1 (Aug. 15, 1950).

[45] U.N. General Assembly, *Information from Non-Self-Governing Territories: India Draft Resolution*, Doc. A/C.4/L.115 (Nov. 24, 1950).

not agree that the Special Committee or the Assembly could discuss information submitted in accordance with Resolution 222(III). The Soviet Union also announced that it would abstain in the voting as "the status of Netherlands New Guinea and its relationship to Indonesia was not clear." The resolution was adopted by the Fourth Committee and later by a vote of 41 to 0, with 8 abstentions in the plenary meeting.[46]

Several questions were subsequently to illuminate further the arguments for and against the view that an administering Member alone is competent to decide when it can cease transmitting information on a territory under its administration. These questions, which are analyzed below, were: the study of the factors that should be taken into account in determining whether a territory is non-self-governing; the cessation of the transmission of information on Surinam and the Netherlands Antilles; and the cessation of the transmission of information on Puerto Rico. The cessation of information on Greenland provoked much the same arguments and action on the competency issue as occurred in the General Assembly in the other cases of cessation. But there was far greater unanimity among Members that cessation was justified in the case of Greenland than in the other cases, and the debate on the competency issue was much more a matter of form.

Study of Factors

In 1951, the Committee on Information undertook, on the basis of a paper prepared by the Secretariat, a study of the factors that should be taken into account in determining whether a territory is non-self-governing. Opinions by experts on interpretation of the Charter were included in this paper and in an addendum circulated by the committee, but they were of little help because they differed as widely as did the positions of the Member nations. Although little practical use has been made to date of the factors finally agreed upon, the debates reveal the constant maneuvering of nonadministering Members to establish the principle of international accountability and the varying views of Members regarding what constitutes self-government. Moreover, the United Nations may make greater use

[46] Res. 448 (V), Dec. 12, 1950. Also see, U.N. General Assembly, Fifth Session, Fourth Committee, *Official Records*, 190th Meeting (Nov. 29, 1950), p. 314; U.N. General Assembly, Fifth Session, Plenary, *Official Records*, 320th Meeting (Dec. 12, 1950), p. 601.

of the factors in the future in considering questions relating to the attainment by trust territories and dependent territories generally of self-government or independence, and also to the intermediate steps to these goals.

The committee, drawing heavily on the suggested factors contained in the paper, had little difficulty in agreeing on the factors to be considered. The controversy centered on the general statement introducing the factors. For example, the nonadministering Members wanted to state that: "there are a large number of elements which should be taken into consideration in order to lead to a decision on the applicability of Chapter XI of the Charter to any given territory." Some of the administering Members insisted that the factors "should be regarded as a guide to conclusions rather than determining such conclusions." The latter viewpoint prevailed, but the former was noted in the report of the committee.[47]

The General Assembly adopted a resolution at its sixth session creating an *ad hoc* committee consisting of five administering and five nonadministering Members to carry out a further study of the factors to be taken into account in deciding whether a territory is a non-self-governing territory. The list of factors prepared by the Special Committee, as modified by a subcommittee of the Fourth Committee of the Assembly, was to serve as a basis for the study. The resolution called on all Members to transmit their views on the problem to the Secretary-General, and asked the *ad hoc* committee to take into account all information available, including the reasons given by certain administering Members for ceasing to transmit information on certain territories. The resolution also requested Members to submit a report to the General Assembly at its seventh session.[48]

The resolution reflected compromises by both the administering and the nonadministering Member states. Some administering Members had previously objected to any formal link between the questions of factors and the cessation of transmitting information; they also objected to the creation of an *ad hoc* committee to make further study of the problem. On the other hand, the nonadministering Members had evidently been willing to drop a suggestion that a

[47] U.N. General Assembly, Sixth Session, *Official Records,* Supplement No. 14, "Report of the Special Committee on Information Transmitted Under Article 73 (e) of the Charter," (November 1951), pp. 41-43.

[48] Res. 567 (VI), Jan. 18, 1952.

committee should examine the specific cases of territories on which administering Members had stopped transmitting information.

Seventeen Members replied in substance to the request for views on this question. Most of these repeated positions already stated, some elaborated on their previous positions or made variations in them. Greece suggested that if there were no agreement between the administering Member and the United Nations, the *status quo ante* should be retained.[49] The Soviet Union and Byelorussia stated that the decision to discontinue transmitting information could be taken only if that territory had become an independent state in which the power was exercised by the indigenous inhabitants.

France and the Netherlands held that the transmission of information should cease as soon as a territory attained full autonomy in economic, social, and educational matters; otherwise, continued transmission would constitute undue interference in the internal affairs of the territory. The United Kingdom stated that:

> If a people is self-governing in the sense that it fully controls the Government of the territory it inhabits, then the international status of that territory (which is in fact what is meant by reference to "independence" or "association") is for that people, and them alone, to decide: the fact that they may decide to associate themselves with some other people, or to consent to the continuance of any such existing association, or to insist on an independent existence, or to forego some part of their sovereignty for the sake of regional etc., association, is merely a manifestation of, and not a characteristic of self-government. [Therefore] . . . a full measure of self-government . . . will provide for the totality of the people . . . to participate on a basis of freedom and equality in the selection and deposition of the executive branch of the Government of the Territory . . . the consent of the governed, and the means freely and equally to exercise, and to give and withhold that consent, is the cardinal and essential feature of a self-governing people.[50]

The United Kingdom suggested that all other factors that might be listed derived from this basic principle.

Cuba, El Salvador, and Guatemala attacked the opinions expressed by France and the Netherlands. They held that a "full measure of self-government" means primarily political self-govern-

---

[49] U.N. General Assembly, *Replies of Governments Indicating Their Views on . . . Whether a Territory Is or Is Not a Territory Whose People Have Not Yet Attained a Full Measure of Self-Government,* Doc. A/AC.58/1 (May 22, 1952), p. 17.

[50] *Ibid.,* Add. 3 (July 16, 1952), pp. 18-19. It is noteworthy that neither in the case of Malta nor in the other early cases of cessation was it established that the inhabitants chose the new status in preference to other alternatives.

ment, which is the origin of self-government in educational and other matters.

The Philippine Government agreed with this view and challenged the theory of constitutional limitation. It stated that the reference to "constitutional considerations" in Article 73(e) was intended to establish a basis for limiting the information transmitted, and not for destroying the obligation to transmit information. If a territory is not fully self-governing, it is still under the sovereignty of the administering state regardless of the matters that it controls, and there could be no constitutional bar to the state concerned from obtaining the information required by Article 73(e). By illustration, the Philippines held that acceptance of anything less than dominion status in the British Commonwealth would throw open the door to the classification of all conceivable types and gradations of self-government as a "full measure," and perhaps tend to "freeze" territories at that point in their development. It further stated that the General Assembly should ensure that association with the metropole results from the freely expressed will of the territorial population, and not from the unilateral decision of the administering authority.

Belgium and France felt that the list of factors should provide the basis for extending the obligation under Article 73(e) to those Members that, although possessing territories, had held they were not affected by Chapter XI. Belgium submitted a list of twenty-five areas inhabited by tribal peoples on which no information had been transmitted.

The meetings of the *Ad Hoc* Committee on Factors were harmonious. It was early agreed that the factors could do no more than serve as a guide in determining whether a territory is fully self-governing, and that it was outside the terms of reference of the committee to consider what authority was competent to make that determination. Many of the comments on factors made by governments not represented in the committee were adopted by it. Several delegations objected to the inclusion of certain factors, but did not press their views, inasmuch as the factors were only suggestive.

The committee decided that there should be one list of factors indicative of the attainment of independence, another for other systems of self-government, and a third indicative of the free association of a territory with other component parts of the metropole.

The report of the committee was presented to the seventh session of the General Assembly, and the Assembly adopted a resolution that approved provisionally the list of factors recommended by the committee and set up a new *ad hoc* committee of ten members, composed of five administering and five nonadministering states, to carry out a more thorough study of the factors, including: (1) "the possibility of defining the concept of self-government for purposes of Chapter XI," (2) "the features guaranteeing the principle of the self-determination of peoples" in relation to that chapter, and (3) "the manifestation of the freely expressed will of the peoples in relation to the determination of their national and international status."[51]

The second *Ad Hoc* Committee on Factors agreed that it was not possible to define the concept of "a full measure of self-government" for the purposes of Chapter XI of the Charter, although the list of factors and the statements from governments would help to indicate whether full self-government had been achieved in any particular case. With respect to the second and third points of the resolution, the *Ad Hoc* Committee, after noting that the Economic and Social Council and the Commission on Human Rights were studying self-determination, stated that some of the features of self-determination, in relation to Chapter XI, are: (1) political advancement sufficient to enable the population to decide the future destiny of their territory by democratic processes; (2) the functioning of a representative system of government under which people can exercise their free will; (3) the enjoyment of individual rights, including universal adult suffrage and freedom to join political parties; (4) absence of coercion so that the people may freely express their views on their future status; and (5) assurance that the views of the population will be respected.[52] The administering Members reserved their position on the fifth point because it seemed to assert that whenever a people declared its will, its desire must be met. The principle of self-determination, they held, should not be followed blindly with disregard for equally valid principles.

Guatemala proposed another point to the effect that when the people of a territory freely limit their sovereignty in favor of the metropole, they should be free subsequently to change their status by democratic process. The United States unsuccessfully proposed

[51] Res. 648 (VII), Dec. 10, 1952.
[52] U.N. General Assembly, Eighth Session, *Report of the Ad Hoc Committee on Factors, Non-Self-Governing Territories,* Doc. A/2428 (Aug. 4, 1953), p. 2.

amending this point to make such changes subject to existing agreements, explaining that the unqualified unilateral right of secession or altering of agreements was not a sound principle. The original text was retained, however, and Burma and the administering states reserved their positions. Guatemala further said that no metropolitan government should be able to change the political status of a non-self-governing territory while the latter was the subject of claim or litigation on the part of another state. The United Kingdom opposed this view, saying it was irrelevant to the task of the committee and that the *de facto* administering state has the duty of promoting realization of the objectives of Chapter XI of the Charter.

Debate on the list of factors centered around the question of divisibility of sovereignty. Several minor changes were made, and the list was adopted. Belgium made reservations, including one that, in effect, stated that if the factors were universally applied, Members other than those now transmitting information would find that they had obligations under Chapter XI.

The eighth session (1953) of the General Assembly adopted a resolution based on the report of the second *Ad Hoc* Committee on Factors.[53] The resolution and the factors provoked much dissension. Nineteen amendments to change the list of factors, and ten other amendments to make more explicit the competence of the General Assembly to determine the attainment of self-government by a territory were approved by the Fourth Committee. The United States, joined by a number of other delegations, reserved its position on the substance of the first group of amendments and abstained on all, declaring that the decisions being made were "hasty and ill-considered." The Assembly adopted the resolution, as amended, by a vote of 32 to 19, with 6 abstentions.[54]

The resolution recommended that: (1) the list of factors adopted by the Fourth Committee "should be used by the General Assembly and the Administering Members as a guide in determining whether any Territory, due to changes in its constitutional status, is or is no longer within the scope of Chapter XI of the Charter, in order that . . . a decision may be taken by the General Assembly on the continuation or cessation of the transmission of information"; (2) each case should be decided in the light of its particular circum-

[53] Res. 742(VIII), Nov. 27, 1953.
[54] U.N. General Assembly, Eighth Session, Plenary, *Official Records*, 459th Meeting (Nov. 27, 1953), p. 312.

stances and taking into account the right of self-determination; (3) although the way in which a territory can become self-governing is primarily by attaining independence, it can also achieve self-government by a form of association with one or more states if done on the basis of absolute equality and the freely expressed will of the people; (4) the factors should in no way be interpreted as a hindrance to full self-government; (5) the people of a territory must have attained a full measure of self-government for it to be deemed self-governing in economic, social, or educational affairs; and (6) the Committee on Information was instructed to study, in the light of the approved list of factors, documentation transmitted by administering Members setting forth reasons for ceasing the transmission of information on their territories, and the committee was invited to suggest changes that would improve the list of factors.

Thirty-four major factors, divided into three parts, were enumerated. The first comprised those indicative of independence, and includes items such as: responsibility for acts that are inherent in the exercise of external sovereignty and in the administration of internal affairs; eligibility for membership in the United Nations; right to provide for national defense; complete freedom to choose the form of government; freedom from interference in internal matters; and autonomy in economic, social, and cultural affairs.

The second part comprehends factors indicative of other separate systems of self-government. The emphasis is on self-determination: freedom of the people to choose among several possibilities, including independence or the status they desire; freedom of the people of a territory that has associated itself with a metropolitan country to modify at any time this status by democratic means; and political advancement of the people sufficiently to enable them to decide their destiny. Other factors are designed to measure the autonomy of a territory in internal and international affairs, including the extent to which the government is representative of the people.

The third part relates to factors indicative of the free association of a territory on an equal basis with the metropolitan or other country. These factors include all those in the second part with minor variations and several additional items on the constitutional relations between the metropole and the territory, on equal representation without discrimination in central legislative organs, and on the equal status and rights of citizenship with citizens of the metropole. Other items measure freedom from outside interference in elections and the extent to which the territory and its people will have the same political status and rights as other jurisdictions and people of the state with which the territory becomes associated—whether it be a federal or unitary state.

Several of the factors reflect more concern for the national self-interest of nonadministering Members than for the interests of the territorial populations. For example, if the new status accords with the freely expressed wishes of the people and meets other basic tests of self-governing status, the relevancy to self-governing status of such factors as: the geographical relationship of the territory to its metropole, the racial and cultural differences of the territorial and metropolitan populations, and whether the territory is subject to claim or litigation by another state is obscure.

Test of Theory on Factors in
Case Studies of Cessation

The cessation by the Netherlands of the transmission of information on Surinam and the Netherlands Antilles in 1951 was the subject of resolutions by the sixth, seventh, eighth, and tenth sessions of the General Assembly. The debates on these resolutions ran concurrently with those on factors and the role of the Assembly in determining when a territory has attained a full measure of self-government for the purposes of Chapter XI of the Charter. The cessation of information on these territories provided, in effect, case material that helped to test and refine the theories expounded on factors and on the respective rights of the territorial peoples, the administering Members, and the Assembly with respect to the transmission of information.

These Dutch territories were granted self-government in domestic matters under "interim regulations" approved, in 1949 and 1950, by the Netherlands Government and by the representative governments of the territories. The "interim" character of the arrangements related to relationships between the Netherlands and the territories on matters of common concern such as foreign relations and defense. In 1951 and subsequently, representatives of the governments of Surinam and the Netherlands Antilles stated emphatically at meetings of the Fourth Committee of the Assembly that continued transmission would detract from the measure of self-government their territories had already achieved, and would be unconstitutional and wholly improper. The Assembly, however, decided to withhold an opinion on whether future cessation was proper in these cases, pending conclusion of the negotiations. A resolution of the eighth session of the Assembly requested the Netherlands to continue the transmission of information under Article 73(e) "until such time as the General Assembly takes a decision that the transmission of information in regard to these territories should be discontinued."[55] The Netherlands stated that to continue the transmission of information would be an action contrary to its own laws; and it did not transmit such information after 1951. However, it kept the Assembly informed of the negotiations on final constitutional arrangements. These negotiations were concluded in 1954, and the charter for the Kingdom of the Netherlands was ratified by the freely elected governments of the Netherlands, Surinam, and the Netherlands Antilles. The charter reaffirms that local matters are solely within the jurisdiction of each country and establishes an ingenious system for joint participation in decisions on matters specified as being of mutual interest. What was a typically colonial relationship has been transformed into a free association of self-governing peoples for their mutual benefit.

The Netherlands Government communicated the details of these constitutional arrangements to the Secretary-General and stated that in the light thereof, it regarded its responsibilities under Chapter XI of the Charter in respect to Surinam and the Netherlands Antilles as being terminated. The Netherlands communication was discussed in the Committee on Information in 1955 and received the whole-hearted support of the administering Members. However, the non-administering Members wanted to study the matter further. The committee held a special meeting prior to the tenth session of the Assembly to consider the matter again. By an affirmative vote of the administering Members plus Brazil, the committee adopted a resolution complimenting the Netherlands and endorsing the cessation of information on the two territories. The tenth session of the Assembly later adopted a resolution that although expressing the opinion that cessation is appropriate, contained no complimentary references to the Netherlands and including a clause asserting the competence of the Assembly to decide whether a territory has attained a full measure of self-government, a clause taken over from the resolution of the eighth session of the Assembly on the cessation of informa-

[55] Res. 747 (VIII), Nov. 27, 1953.

tion on Puerto Rico.[56] The administering Members took strong exception to the clause, as they had in the case of the resolution on Puerto Rico. Belgium opposed the resolution, and three other administering Members abstained from voting because of it.

The cessation of information on Puerto Rico arose at the eighth session of the Assembly and was the first case of cessation to be endorsed by the United Nations. The United States advised the United Nations early in 1953 that due to changes in the constitutional status of Puerto Rico, it would cease the transmission of information on it. The Government of Puerto Rico also requested this cessation.

The basis for cessation was discussed first in the Committee on Information, and the committee adopted without objection a resolution commending the United States and Puerto Rico for the political advances made and noting with approval the cessation of information.

At the outset of the debate in the Fourth Committee, requests for oral hearings were received from the Independence Party and also from the terrorist Nationalist Party of Puerto Rico. The petitions were denied, but there were a large number of statements and votes in support of them. The request of the Independence Party was defeated 19 to 25, with 11 abstentions;[57] that of the terrorist group that had attempted to assassinate the President of the United States was defeated 17 to 29, with 8 abstentions.[58] Underlying this vote was the question whether the Assembly could hear petitioners from non-self-governing territories other than those territories under trusteeship, and undoubtedly some votes were cast more on the principle involved than on the merits of these particular requests.

The case for cessation of information on Puerto Rico can be summarized as follows: The Puerto Ricans voted in 1948 overwhelmingly for a candidate for Governor who favored commonwealth status, in preference to candidates espousing the cause of

[56] U.N. General Assembly, Tenth Session, Plenary, *Official Records,* 557th Meeting (Dec. 15, 1955), p. 462.

[57] U.N. General Assembly, Eighth Session, Fourth Committee, *Official Records,* 321st Meeting (Sept. 30, 1953), p. 34.

[58] *Ibid.,* 343rd Meeting (Oct. 26, 1953), p. 178.

Those voting in favor of the Nationalist Party petition were: Czechoslovakia, Egypt, Guatemala, India, Indonesia, Iraq, Lebanon, Mexico, Poland, Saudi Arabia, Syria, Ukraine, Soviet Union, Yugoslavia, Bolivia, Burma, and Byelorussia. Those abstaining were: El Salvador, Ethiopia, Iran, Liberia, Uruguay, Venezuela, Afghanistan, and Argentina.

statehood or of complete independence. The basis for relations between the United States and Puerto Rico was set forth in a law
passed by the Congress,[59] and adopted by the people of Puerto Rico
in a referendum held in 1950. The act states that it is "in the nature
of a compact." Delegates were elected to a constitutional convention, and the constitution drawn up there was approved by the
people of Puerto Rico. The United States Congress approved this
constitution subject to the acceptance by the constitutional convention of certain amendments, which would eliminate a section on
economic and social rights, make clear that education in nongovernmental schools will be allowed, and place restrictions on the
substance of future amendments.[60] When these amendments were so
accepted, the Governor proclaimed the Constitution of the Commonwealth of Puerto Rico. The constitutional amendments were
then approved by the people of Puerto Rico at the next general
election.[61]

The constitution establishes the political sovereignty of the people
of Puerto Rico. They have exclusive authority to amend the constitution, with certain restrictions, as noted, on the substance of amendments. Puerto Rico is for the most part tied into the web of federal-
state relations (*e.g.* federal functions and grants-in-aid apply there
as in the states), but there are important differences. Puerto Ricans
do not participate in national elections, and their only representative in Congress is a nonvoting commissioner. Although most federal laws apply to Puerto Rico, those imposing taxes normally do
not. Moreover, commonwealth status is not a static concept, a point
that was not brought out in the discussion in the General Assembly.
The relations between the United States and Puerto Rico are set
forth in a compact and are not limited by the division of powers
between the United States and the states under the Federal Constitution. By mutual consent, the United States could perform certain
functions in Puerto Rico that are reserved to the states, and Puerto

[59] 64 Stat. 319 (July 3, 1950).
[60] 66 Stat. 327 (July 3, 1952).
[61] See U.N. General Assembly, *Non-Self-Governing Territories: Communication
from the Government of the United States . . . Concerning Puerto Rico,* Doc.
A/AC.35/L.121 (Apr. 3, 1953) for the text of the Constitution of the Commonwealth of Puerto Rico (Annex I); Memorandum of the United States Government
giving the history of the Constitutional development of Puerto Rico under United
States Administration, as well as the development and adoption of the Puerto
Rican Constitution (Annex II); and Communication from the Governor of
Puerto Rico to the President of the United States (Annex III).

Rico could perform functions that are prohibited to states under the Federal Constitution. There is thus ample scope for commonwealth growth.

The United States delegate stated in a plenary meeting of the General Assembly that he was authorized to state on behalf of the President of the United States that if, at any time, the Legislative Assembly of Puerto Rico adopted a resolution in favor of more complete or absolute independence, he would immediately recommend that such independence be granted. Following this event, he would also welcome adherence by Puerto Rico to the Treaty of Rio de Janeiro and the Charter of the United Nations.[62]

Members of the United States delegation, including the elected commissioner from Puerto Rico who appeared before the Committee on Information and the Fourth Committee, expected the Soviet bloc to object to the cessation of information on Puerto Rico. Statements made, however, by such nations as Burma, Guatemala, Honduras, Indonesia, and Mexico, which felt that Puerto Rico had not yet achieved full self-government, came as a surprise to some United States delegates.[63] The delegate from Mexico hoped that the case of Puerto Rico would emphasize the need to ensure that no peoples in the world are ever forced to sacrifice their dignity in order to live. He declared that politically Puerto Rico had less self-government than when under Spanish domination.

India suggested that the committee was witnessing a new form of colonialism and offered proposals calling for future investigation of the whole Puerto Rican question. The United States said it would be helpful to know why India regarded the Commonwealth of Puerto Rico as less self-governing than the Andaman and Nicobar Islands. The Indian delegate replied that those islands had representatives in the Indian Federal Parliament. Questioning by the United States, however, brought out the fact that these representatives were appointed by the Indian Government and not elected by the people in those territories.

A clause in the resolution asserting "the competence of the Gen-

[62] U.N. General Assembly, Eighth Session, Plenary, *Official Records*, 459th Meeting (Nov. 27, 1953), p. 311. It should be noted that in January 1954, the Puerto Rican Legislature rejected a resolution calling for complete independence from the United States.

[63] House Committee on Foreign Affairs, *Report on the Eighth Session of the General Assembly of the United Nations by the Hon. Frances P. Bolton and Hon. James R. Richards,* H. Rept. 1695, 83 Cong. 2 sess. (May 28, 1953), pp. 82-83.

eral Assembly to decide whether a Non-Self-Governing Territory has or has not attained a full measure of self-government," provoked a long and heated debate. It caused the United States to abstain in the vote on the resolution in the Fourth Committee and to make a specific reservation with respect to this clause in voting for the resolution in the plenary meeting of the Assembly. The other administering powers and certain other states, which stated that they would have supported the resolution without the clause, either opposed the resolution or abstained from voting, and some made specific reservations regarding the clause.[64] The clause itself might have been defeated had its approval required a two-thirds vote. However, on the basis of a highly confusing earlier vote, the President ruled that it was the will of the Assembly that questions in regard to Chapter XI be decided by a simple majority. The inclusion of this clause caused about ten nations to oppose or to abstain from voting on the final resolution.

The Assembly adopted the resolution, by a vote of 26 to 16 with 18 abstentions.[65] In addition to asserting the competence of the General Assembly to decide whether a territory is non-self-governing, the resolution recognized the achievement by democratic means of the new constitutional status of the Commonwealth of Puerto Rico; expressed the opinion that this association between Puerto Rico and the United States was a mutually agreed association; recognized that Puerto Ricans had effectively exercised their right to self-determination, and that Puerto Rico had become an autonomous political entity; considered that Chapter XI of the Charter no longer applied to the territory; noted the opinion of the United States on ceasing the transmission of information on Puerto Rico and considered it appropriate that the transmission should cease; and expressed the assurance of the Assembly that due regard would be paid to the will of both the Puerto Rican and the American peoples in the event either of the parties might desire any change in the terms of the association.[66]

Contrasting the willingness with which Member states were prepared to accept the cessation of information on Greenland and Indonesia with their reluctance in the cases of Puerto Rico, Surinam,

---

[64] *Ibid.,* pp. 85-86.
[65] U.N. General Assembly, Eighth Session, Plenary, *Official Records,* 459th Meeting (Nov. 27, 1953), p. 320.
[66] Res. 748 (VIII), Nov. 27, 1953.

and the Netherlands Antilles, it would appear that many Members regard with suspicion expressions of self-determination by dependent people that fall short of complete integration or complete independence. They seem to believe that arrangements providing for voluntary association have been contrived by the administering states to continue colonialism while escaping the obligations of Chapter XI of the Charter; and some cannot believe that a dependent people would prefer voluntary association with their metropole to independence. A measure of skepticism is both understandable and desirable in view of some of the earlier instances of cessation of information by France and the United Kingdom. Moreover, the unwillingness of the General Assembly to endorse the cessation of information on Surinam and the Netherlands Antilles until final arrangements were concluded might well have caused the parties concerned to seek a greater measure of perfection than might otherwise have been the case. Whether United States officials might have sought more earnestly to remove imperfections in the Federal Relations Act when it was being drafted, if they had been similarly aware of the close international scrutiny to be given the status of the new commonwealth of Puerto Rico, is a matter for speculation. However, once the self-governing status of these territories had clearly been approved by the peoples concerned, it seems regrettable that so many Members of the United Nations were unwilling to recognize that status. Indeed some Members seemed willing to substitute their judgment or that of the General Assembly for the freely expressed will of the peoples concerned. Rather than opposing forms of voluntary association by dependent territories with their metropoles or other independent states, the United Nations should be prepared not only to expect such arrangements but also to make them more attractive by providing a dignified place in international life for the self-governing community.

The question of the role of the Assembly in determining whether a territory has attained full self-government is becoming somewhat academic. Although the question is still capable of provoking long and heated debate, a measure of equilibrium has been achieved. The Assembly has established a precedent for not regarding its votes with respect to cessation of the transmission of information as "important," a simple majority having been sufficient to adopt all resolutions relating to non-self-governing territories since the eighth session of the Assembly, including those relating to cessation. Some administering members now want the Assembly to examine first all documentation bearing on cessation, *i.e.,* to by-pass the Committee on Information. In any case, the nonadministering Members have the votes and are determined to assert the authority of the Assembly to make, or at least to participate in, the final decision on cessation of information. The administering Members all challenge this assertion, but none is willing to seek an opinion from the International Court of Justice on it. Furthermore, the vigilance of nonadministering Members in this field is such as to discourage premature cessation of information in the future. Finally, when the administering Members decide in the future to cease transmission of information, they are likely to be on such firm ground that the Assembly will either confirm their action, or it will be unwilling to test its position regarding cessation in specific cases by seeking an advisory opinion from the International Court of Justice. Despite the equilibrium presently achieved, the question of cessation of information under Article 73(e) is likely to consume time in the Assembly, and unless a formula is found to minimize conflict, it will provoke much dissension among the free nations as new cases and new procedural questions arise in the future.

Type of Information To Be Transmitted

Some issues relating to Chapter XI of the Charter were not in themselves contentious when they were raised in the early years, and they might not have become "issues" if the Member states had been reasonable in their approach to them. The fact that they have become issues indicates that on the one hand, the more doctrinaire anti-colonial Members press points until they have "drawn blood" and that on the other, some administering nations "bleed" too easily.

It is taken for granted now that most of the nonadministering and administering Member states are hostile and suspicious toward one another, but they were not actively so in the early years. The situation has developed gradually, and part of the fault lies with those administering Members that have opposed every suggestion that seemed to go beyond the letter of Article 73(e) of the Charter. Their theory has been that every such suggestion had to be opposed, or it might advance them toward the "steep and slippery slope" of international supervision. Their precautions in terms of the situation today are understandable, but the situation itself may be due in part to their own exaggerated precautions in the early years.

For example, an issue developed over whether the transmission of information on matters pertaining to political and human rights is obligatory, optional, or excluded under Article 73(e). After the administering Members had transmitted information in 1946, it became apparent that if the Secretary-General was to make comprehensible summaries and analyses of the information, as requested by the General Assembly,[67] the information should, in so far as practicable, conform to some agreed form. The nature of the information first transmitted varied not only between territories of different Members but also between territories under a single administration. Some transmittals included political information, other did not.

The United States, recognizing this as a problem, suggested the adoption of an outline that would serve as a guide to administering Members in transmitting information under Article 73(e) and to the Secretary-General in summarizing and analyzing the information. The United States made it clear, however, that the suggested outline should not be binding on the Members.[68] The first section of the outline, which was entitled "optional category," included points to elicit general information on the geography, history, people, and government of a territory. The other major headings followed the terminology of Article 73(e): social conditions, educational conditions, and economic conditions. Among the items under social conditions was one relating to human rights, another to race relations, and another to penal conditions.

The outline was discussed in the *ad hoc* committee on information in 1947. It was agreed that although conditions varied between territories, a general guide of this nature was desirable. Representatives of various specialized agencies suggested changes, and there was considerable discussion whether "political information" should be obligatory. The committee agreed that it should be optional and that it should be summarized but not analyzed by the Secretary-General. The items on human rights and penal administration were, without much debate, placed in the optional category. No question was raised about moving the item on race relations from the section dealing with social conditions. The outline, the full title of which was "Standard Form for the Guidance of Members in the Preparation of Information to be Transmitted under Article 73(e) of the Char-

[67] Res. 66(I), Feb. 9, 1946.
[68] The administering Members were insistent on the word "outline" rather than "questionnaire" because questionnaires are used as a means of international supervision of trust territories.

ter" (referred to as Standard Form), as amended, was adopted unanimously.

The second session of the General Assembly adopted without objection a resolution incorporating the Standard Form as an Annex and expressing the hope that it would be followed to the fullest extent in the preparation of information in the future.[69] The Assembly also agreed that the voluntary transmission of political information was entirely in conformity with the spirit of Article 73 of the Charter and should therefore be encouraged.[70]

It soon became apparent, however, that despite the fact that the Secretary-General's analyses of information did not comprehend political and other information voluntarily transmitted, some Member states were not transmitting such information on any of their territories, or only on some of them. The United States was among the few Members that included political information on all of its territories. A resolution of the fourth session of the Assembly expressed the hope that administering Members that had not done so might voluntarily include details on the government of non-self-governing territories in their transmissions under Article 73(e).[71]

The sixth session of the Assembly adopted without objection a resolution to which was annexed a much more detailed Standard Form to replace the previous one.[72] The resolution merely invited the administering Members to undertake all necessary steps to render information as complete and up to date as possible and for that purpose "to take into account" the sections of the revised Standard Form. The Standard Form itself retained items under the heading of "Government" in an optional category and restored to the heading under "Social Conditions" items on human rights and penal administration.

At its seventh session, the Assembly strengthened its request by "recommending" that administering Members include in the information transmitted under Article 73(e) details on the extent to which the right of peoples and nations to self-determination "is exercised by the peoples of those territories," including the steps taken to satisfy their aspirations and to promote the progressive development of their free political institutions.[73] This recommendation was

---

[69] Res. 142 (II), Nov. 3, 1947.
[70] Res. 144 (II), Nov. 3, 1947.
[71] Res. 327 (IV), Dec. 2, 1949.
[72] Res. 551 (VI), Dec. 7, 1951.
[73] Res. 647 (VII), Dec. 10, 1952.

embodied in a resolution on self-determination previously approved by the Commission on Human Rights, the Economic and Social Council, and the Third (Social, Humanitarian, and Cultural) Committee of the Assembly. The preamble states that the United Nations should possess official information on the government of dependent territories in order to facilitate United Nations action to promote respect for the right of self-determination of the people in these territories. The Assembly decided to place this resolution on the agenda of the 1953 session of the Committee on Information.

The administering Members opposed this resolution, partly on the ground that the United Nations should be concerned with self-determination not only in dependent territories, but also in territories that have lost their independence or are in danger of losing it. They strongly opposed, and in some cases made reservations regarding, the submission of the information requested and the propriety of discussing this highly political subject in the Committee on Information. Belgium referred to this resolution in explaining its refusal to participate in the 1953 session of the committee. Actually, the Committee on Information subsequently gave no more than perfunctory attention to the resolution after France and the United Kingdom made clear their intention not to participate in any discussion of it.

Resolutions have also been approved by the Assembly requesting the administering Members concerned to submit documentation of a political nature in each instance in which there has been cessation in the transmission of information. The question was raised at the tenth session in connection with a resolution calling on the Secretary-General to advise the eleventh session on the main points that might usefully be covered in an examination of the progress made since the establishment of the United Nations toward attaining the goals set forth in Chapter XI.[74] Although the administering Members made the record clear that only information transmitted pursuant to Article 73(e) should be included in any such examination, it is quite likely that the question of political information will be raised again in this context as the measurement of progress toward full self-government is clearly one of the purposes of the resolution.

The question whether the transmission of "political information" is or should be obligatory has been overshadowed by other issues,

[74] Res. 932 (X), Nov. 8, 1955.

but it is not dead. It underlies the repeated requests for voluntary transmission of information, the latest being that of the ninth session of the Assembly, which the United States opposed as it had in previous sessions. At present, Belgium, France, and the United Kingdom do not transmit political information on any of their territories. The other administering Members, including the United States, transmit political information voluntarily on all of their territories. So long as some administering Members fail to transmit political information voluntarily, the pressure on them to do so will persist and will seek various outlets—as in the case of the resolution of the Assembly on self-determination. In fact, the Commission on Human Rights has adopted a highly controversial proposal to establish still another United Nations commission to "examine any situation resulting from alleged denial or inadequate realization of the right of self-determination" that would come within the scope of Article 14 of the Charter, and that has been brought to the attention of the commission by any ten Members of the United Nations.[75] The Economic and Social Council has transmitted this proposal to the Assembly along with an alternative proposal of its own for the creation of an *ad hoc* committee to study the problem.[76]

Despite the desire of many Members to use the Fourth Committee as a forum for debating political issues, both the Committee on Information and the Fourth Committee, except in cases involving cessation of the transmission of information, have, to a remarkable extent, observed the rule that the political information transmitted under Article 73(e) will not be analyzed, discussed, or made the subject of recommendations. The rule is explicit only in the case of the Committee on Information, but the Fourth Committee has generally adhered in practice to the same limitation. The nonadministering Members know that if they violate this rule, those Members that have voluntarily transmitted such information will discontinue doing so. The administering Members, therefore, have quite favorable conditions under which to supply this information.

It is true that there is no mention in Article 73(e) of the word "political" in specifying the information required, but that it "had been considered at San Francisco and had been rejected" as the

[75] U.N. Commission on Human Rights, *Report of the Tenth Session*, Doc. E/2573 (April 1954), pp. 37-38.
[76] For a more detailed discussion of the resolutions and draft covenants relating to self-determination, see the monograph in this Brookings series, *The United Nations and Human Rights*.

United Kingdom and others have contended is not entirely clear.[77] At the San Francisco Conference, the following reportedly took place in the drafting committee that was considering Article 73(e), of which the United States representative was the chairman:

> The Representative of the Union of Soviet Socialist Republics stated that it would be useful to add the word "political" before "economic" in line four, in order to make it consistent with the earlier sub-paragraph. The Chairman observed that in the United States "political" would be taken to refer to politics and political parties. The United Kingdom representative suggested the addition of a phrase which would make it clear that only such information as might be available to Parliament could be expected.[78]

Despite this bit of legislative history, the nonadministering Members have not attempted to use it in order to establish that the transmission of information on governmental institutions or other political matters is obligatory under Article 73(e). Some have argued that because the word "political" appears in paragraphs (a) and (b), it can reasonably be implied in paragraph (e). However, they have not pressed the point, and the administering Members have strongly opposed such interpretations. Although the request by nonadministering Members for the voluntary transmittal of this information may be politically motivated—that is, to embarrass those administering Members who refuse to supply it—there are also some practical reasons to justify their request. For example, information on educational programs is more meaningful if accompanied by a description of the governmental framework within which educational laws and policies are formulated and carried out. But, until means are devised to ensure that political information on dependent territories will not be the subject of future discussion and recommendations by the Assembly, some administering Members will probably be unwilling to transmit it.

Relations Between the Committee on Information and the Inhabitants of the Territories

The General Assembly at its first session considered a proposal by the Philippines urging that the Economic and Social Council call

[77] U.N. General Assembly, Second Session, Fourth Committee, *Official Records,* 36th Meeting (Oct. 3, 1947), pp. 32-33.
[78] Cited in U.N. Secretariat, *Non-Self-Governing Territories: Summaries and Analysis of Information Transmitted to the Secretary-General During 1947* (1948), p. 8.

a world conference of representatives of dependent territories. This was later revised, limiting it to a recommendation that the administering Members convene conferences of representatives of territorial inhabitants.[79] Such conferences had been convened by the Caribbean Commission and are now held periodically by both the Caribbean Commission and the South Pacific Commission.

In recent years, a conscious effort has been made by nonadministering Members to establish direct relations between the United Nations and non-self-governing territories. The sixth and seventh sessions of the General Assembly adopted resolutions to explore the possibility of creating an associate membership status for dependent territories on the Committee on Information, as has been established by some specialized agencies, and of otherwise arranging for representatives of the territories to participate in discussions of the committee.[80] The administering authorities were also invited to transmit reports and resolutions of the United Nations regarding non-self-governing territories to the legislative and executive branches of territorial governments. These resolutions were supported on various grounds, the main ones being that in territories where representative bodies control economic or other matters within the scope of Article 73(e), representatives of the inhabitants rather than of the administering Member should discuss such matters with the committee; also, as some territories are moving rapidly toward independence, their association with the United Nations would be mutually beneficial.

The administering Members objected strenuously to the concept of associate membership in a committee of the Assembly and regarded such a step as contrary to the Charter. In their view, such membership would constitute "dual representation" in the United Nations. Moreover, although administering Members have included territorial representatives on their delegations, some of them regard resolutions requesting them to do so as interference by the Assembly in the composition of their delegations. The eighth session of the Assembly, apparently persuaded by the arguments of the administering Members, recognized that the principle of unity of representation must be maintained, but it then proceeded again to invite administering Members to attach to their delegations qualified indigenous representatives from politically advanced territories

---

[79] Res. 67 (I), Dec. 14, 1946.
[80] Res. 566 (VI), Jan. 18, 1952; Res. 647 (VII), Dec. 10, 1952.

and to ask the Committee on Information to continue studying the means of increasing the direct participation of territorial representatives in its work.[81] The latest suggestion in this field, made in 1955 by India in connection with the renewal of the Committee on Information, would have authorized the committee, with the consent of an administering Member, to admit as observers persons appointed by the territorial governments concerned. This suggestion was rejected, but the invitation to administering Members to include indigenous persons on their delegations was renewed.

Functions of Other United Nations Organs

The work of the United Nations in relation to Chapter XI of the Charter is concentrated in the Fourth Committee of the General Assembly, the Committee on Information, and the Secretariat. Almost all United Nations organs and agencies, however, including the specialized agencies, concern themselves to some extent with non-self-governing territories.

The Security Council, for example, took action in the case of Indonesia when the latter was a dependent territory. The Trusteeship Council keeps a watch on administrative unions involving trust and neighboring territories. The Economic and Social Council and its subsidiary organs, particularly the Commission on Human Rights, are concerned with dependent territories as well as independent nations in almost everything they do.

All of the committees of the General Assembly, not just the Fourth Committee, may consider proposals relating directly or indirectly to non-self-governing territories. For example, in the tenth session of the Assembly, the First (Political and Security) Committee took note of negotiations by France with political leaders in Morocco, and between the Netherlands and Indonesia regarding their dispute over the sovereignty of Western New Guinea. The *Ad Hoc* Political Committee considered a report on a matter of interest to a few former colonies and to territories approaching independence, namely the admission of new Members to the United Nations. The Second (Economic and Financial) Committee made recommendations on international technical assistance programs that bear incidentally on non-self-governing territories. The Third

[81] Res. 744 (VIII), Nov. 27, 1953; Res. 745 (VIII), Nov. 27, 1953.

(Social, Humanitarian and Cultural) Committee adopted, after prolonged and heated debate, an article on self-determination for incorporation in the draft covenants on human rights that mentions specifically the obligation to promote self-determination in trust territories and non-self-governing territories. The Fifth (Administrative and Budgetary) Committee dealt indirectly, through the budgets for the Secretariat and other matters, with the dependent area activities of the United Nations. The Sixth (Legal) Committee, at a previous session, formulated a protocol to a convention to eliminate slavery, under which the United Nations will assume the functions previously exercised by the League of Nations.

In addition to the activities noted earlier in this study, some specialized agencies have co-operated directly in the implementation of Article 73(e).[82] The Food and Agriculture Organization, International Labour Organisation, United Nations Education, Scientific and Cultural Organization, and World Health Organization have participated in the meetings of the Committee on Information and its subcommittees, have offered substantive comments on information transmitted and on the Standard Form, and have prepared excellent technical studies for the use of the committee. Some administering Members tried to have these studies made world-wide in scope, but they were unsuccessful in this as they were also in insisting that the Secretary-General compare conditions in dependent territories with those in neighboring independent countries in analyzing the information transmitted under Article 73(e).

The relations between the Committee on Information and the specialized agencies are progressively improving and proving mutually helpful. Even the United Kingdom, which has been most skeptical of the committee, defended its discussion of technical subjects on the ground that the committee formed a link between the Assembly and the specialized agencies. This was in reply to a statement by India urging caution in the use of experts by the committee.

Although an effort has been made to avoid duplication in the requests of international agencies for information from dependent territories, there is still room for improvement. Officials in some territories feel burdened by reporting requirements, due in part to the numerous and somewhat overlapping inquiries from interna-

[82] See above, Chap. II.

tional agencies. Also, only a beginning has been made in using specialized agencies to provide technical assistance to dependent territories and in encouraging the more advanced non-self-governing territories to participate in the work of specialized agencies as associate members.

So far there seems to have been no need for special machinery to co-ordinate the work of United Nations organs and specialized agencies on non-self-governing territories. This is done to some extent informally within the Secretariat, by the delegations themselves, and in the plenary meetings of the Assembly. The proliferation of United Nations activities in this field is, however, politically significant. It facilitates and aggravates attacks on colonialism. Similar issues can be raised in various organs simultaneously, and if one is deemed not competent to consider an issue, another can perhaps be found which is, or may be claimed to be, competent.

The role of the Secretariat and its relations with the Committee on Information and the Fourth Committee of the Assembly provide good material for a case study in the political dynamics of international organization. The Secretariat has provided more than just staff services in this field. Its analyses of information transmitted under Article 73(e) and its special studies requested by the United Nations organs concerned often have political overtones. Furthermore, it has actively participated, directly and indirectly, in the substantive work of the two committees.

Initiative by the Secretariat in shaping United Nations work in this field was particularly noticeable during the early years. It was noted earlier that in the memorandum prepared by the Secretariat for consideration by the Fourth Committee at the first session of the Assembly, it was suggested that an *ad hoc* committee on information might be established. But a subcommittee of the Fourth Committee, in taking up the memorandum, agreed to delete the reference to an *ad hoc* committee in accepting items in the memorandum for consideration. At a subsequent meeting, however, the *rapporteur* of the subcommittee suggested that a draft resolution prepared by the Secretariat, which provided for the Secretary-General to convene an *ad hoc* committee, be used as a basis for discussion, and his suggestion was adopted. Cuba congratulated the Secretariat on the "constructive, impartial and progressive spirit manifested" in its text, but the United Kingdom pointed out that the subcommittee had agreed to delete any mention of an *ad hoc* committee, and that although delegates might revert to the question, it was not for the Secretariat to reopen the discussion by drafting a text itself.

The Assistant Secretary-General in this field felt constrained to justify the action of the Secretariat. He pointed out that the Secretariat had previously initiated papers, that confusion sometimes resulted if there were no documents to serve as a basis for discussion, that the powers of the Secretary-General had changed since the days of the League of Nations, and that the international staff should not bear the burden of political responsibility but rather should be given explicit instructions on what they can and cannot do. He then answered French and Belgian arguments against establishing an *ad hoc* committee.

Other instances have arisen reflecting uncertainty and conflict over the role of the Secretariat. During the meeting of the Special Committee in 1949, several administering Members criticized a working paper prepared by the Secretariat for suggesting that the committee invite administering Members to make changes in their policies in non-self-governing territories, an action that they would regard as improper. They also doubted that the members of the committee had sufficient knowledge to endorse the recommendations proposed by the Secretariat. The paper was defended by several Members, and a Secretariat official pointed out that it was designed to carry out a resolution of the Assembly calling for analyses of information, and that for future reference, the Secretariat would welcome guidance from the committee. In the Assembly that year, several administering Members attacked the analyses of information prepared by the Secretariat as "mischievous."

The Secretariat, although disclaiming that any of its actions have been improper, has become increasingly cautious. Its position is a difficult one. The administering Members criticize it for excessive zeal and interference. They contend as do some other Members that the function of the Secretariat is to serve the committee as a whole and not individual Members; that if the latter practice were followed, it would destroy the impartiality of the international staff. However, most nonadministering Members do not have colonial specialists on their staffs, and they seek information and guidance from the Secretariat in order to give expression to their anti-colonial views. Secretariat experts sometimes provide the assistance requested; they assert that they cannot, for example, refuse to assist

in the drafting of a resolution requested by a Member simply because the resolution is anti-colonial. Secretariat experts resent criticism of favoritism, because they have, in fact, helped to persuade nonadministering Members not to adopt extreme anti-colonial resolutions such as those that would have provoked the discussion of political issues in the Fourth Committee. Moreover, the Secretary-
General was severely criticized by nonadministering Members at the
tenth session of the Assembly for advising the deletion of specific
references to trust territories and non-self-governing territories in the
self-determination articles of the draft covenants on human rights.

The Secretariat performs essential functions in connection with
the work of the United Nations relating to Chapter XI of the
Charter. It prepares much of the documentation considered by the
Committee on Information. It has done a remarkable job each year
in analyzing the great mass of information transmitted by administering members. In view of the sharp differences among Member
states on colonial issues, it is to the credit of the Secretariat that it has
not more often offended one side or the other. Nevertheless, the
instances that have occurred suggest the need for public clarification
of what the role of the Secretariat is and should be in this highly
controversial field.

The Committee on Information is, in effect, a subcommittee of
the Fourth Committee. Ironically, the limited terms of reference of
the Committee on Information have served to limit in practice the
scope of the Fourth Committee. Although Article 10 of the Charter
enables the Assembly to discuss whatever it wishes, the administering
Members have thus far succeeded in their efforts to restrain the
Fourth Committee from discussing political questions in dependent
territories not under trusteeship, except in cases involving cessation
of the transmission of information. Moreover, both committees have,
at the insistence of administering Members, cast their recommendations relating to Chapter XI of the Charter in general terms and not
addressed them to situations in individual territories.

It has not been easy to hold the line. At the sixth session of the
Assembly, for example, the French delegation walked out of the
Fourth Committee when it appeared that the committee was ready
to adopt an Iraqi resolution to assert the competence of the committee "to discuss political matters and political aspects" in regard
to non-self-governing territories. The resolution followed protests
made by France in the committee against an attack by Iraq and

Egypt on French administration of Morocco and Tunisia. A vote on the draft resolution was postponed for twenty-four hours and the chairman opened the next meeting by pointing out that he could not be accused of restricting freedom of speech in the committee; he had tried, however, to restrict the exercise of that right to the items under consideration. He recognized that there were some economic problems that could not be discussed without reference to political matters, but he asked speakers to confine their remarks to essential points and to deal with political questions only if they were related to educational, economic, or social questions. The representative of Iraq said that the statement of the chairman contained the substance of what he wished to say in the draft resolution, and although he was unwilling to withdraw the resolution, he did not want it put to a vote at that time. A showdown on the competence of the Fourth Committee to consider political questions was thus avoided.

The Moroccan question was revived, however, at the seventh session of the Assembly, by which time the political unrest in the territory had increased, and the question was referred to the First Committee. Despite the strongest protests by France that consideration of the question would constitute violation of Article 2(7) of the Charter and that France would therefore be unable to participate in the discussion, the First Committee proceeded with a heated debate on the question. It approved a mild resolution on the subject, which the Assembly amended, to make it more palatable to France, and then adopted.[83] Subsequently, efforts made in 1953 to place the Moroccan issue on the agenda of the Security Council failed, but the issue was later referred to the First Committee and was the subject of resolutions at the eighth, ninth, and tenth sessions of the Assembly.

In the eighth session of the Assembly, the United Kingdom threatened to walk out of the Fourth Committee if the committee adopted a proposal by India to discuss the effect of the Central African Federation on the future obligations of the United Kingdom under Article 73(e). The United Kingdom opposed the proposal because it was not on the agenda and because it was beyond the competence of the committee, involving the constitutional relations of the United Kingdom with its Central African territories, and the examination of a petition concerning non-self-governing territories. A motion by the United Kingdom for the closure of

[83] Res. 612(VII), Dec. 19, 1952.

debate was defeated. India then proposed that the debate be adjourned with the understanding that the delegations could later revert to the discussion. This motion was adopted.[84] At the last meeting of the Fourth Committee, in the eighth session, India asked the United Kingdom again for assurances that the creation of the Central African Federation would not remove these territories from the scope of Article 73(e). The United Kingdom said it would not comment on a matter outside the competence of the committee and the matter was dropped.

Perhaps the most significant development in relations between the Committee on Information and the Fourth Committee was the vote in the plenary meeting of the eighth session of the Assembly to regard the resolution on Puerto Rico and other significant as well as minor questions relating to Chapter XI of the Charter as subject to a simple majority vote and not as important matters requiring a two-thirds vote. The two-thirds rule had, since the vote in 1947 on the continuation of the Committee on Information, been applied to all resolutions relating to Chapter XI. On several occasions between 1947 and 1953, the question whether specific resolutions in this field should require a two-thirds majority for adoption was raised, and in each case it was assumed that the two-thirds rule applied. Moreover, prior to the eighth session of the Assembly, no resolution in this field was adopted by less than a two-thirds vote. At that session, however, the delegate of Mexico opened the debate on seven resolutions relating to Chapter XI by challenging the practice in previous years of regarding all questions relating to Chapter XI as important and therefore, pursuant to Article 18 of the Charter, requiring a two-thirds vote. The application of the two-thirds rule to the pending resolutions was important from the standpoint of the administering Members because three of the resolutions contained clauses asserting the competence of the Assembly to decide whether a territory has attained full self-government and therefore when the Member responsible for its administration may properly cease transmitting information on it. The President put the motion of the delegate of Mexico "that the draft resolution may be carried by a simple majority," before the Assembly. It passed by a vote of 30 to 26.[85] Confusion developed over whether the motion applied

[84] U.N. General Assembly, Eighth Session, Fourth Committee, *Official Records,* 343rd Meeting (Oct. 26, 1953), pp. 176-77.

[85] U.N. General Assembly, Eighth Session, Plenary, *Official Records,* 459th Meeting (Nov. 27, 1953), p. 309.

to all the pending resolutions or only the first one as the verbatim record seemed to indicate. The President ruled that the motion applied to all of the resolutions, and a vote by the Assembly affirmed that ruling.

The previous assumption that the two-thirds rule applied to all resolutions in this field had served to offset somewhat the heavy numerical advantage of the nonadministering Members in the Assembly. The nonadministering Members, in discovering that this rule can be successfully challenged, have acquired a new source of power, which they probably will be unwilling to give up in the future. It will give them further cause to by-pass the Committee on Information. For example, recent suggestions that the Fourth Committee rather than the Committee on Information should first examine documentation on constitutional changes in territories in cases of cessation of information may be due in part to the increased confidence of nonadministering Members in their voting strength. They are not likely, however, to abuse it to the extent that administering Members will feel compelled to walk out of the Fourth Committee, join Belgium in boycotting the Committee on Information, or seek relief from the International Court of Justice. Thus, a measure of equilibrium, tenuous though it be, may be maintained despite the great increase of voting power of the nonadministering Members in the Assembly with regard to questions involving Chapter XI of the Charter.

The record of United Nations activities in relation specifically to Chapter XI of the Charter is seemingly more one of conflict among Member nations than of accomplishment on behalf of dependent peoples. This has been due largely to ambiguities in the Charter, and to the conflicting national and regional interests of Members, which too often overshadow the interests of the United Nations in the advancement of dependent peoples as set forth in the Charter.

The direct benefits to dependent peoples from the work of the Committee on Information, the Fourth Committee, and the Secretary-General are difficult to trace. Except for discussions on the cessation of transmitting information in specific cases, few of the issues relating to Chapter XI have directly affected, or even been widely noted in, the territories. That is true also of the Secretary-General's summaries and analyses of information; the reports of the Committee on Information; the studies done by specialized agencies; and the resolutions of the Assembly on economic, social, and educational conditions and on racial discrimination in the territories. It does not seem too hazardous to state that, despite the circulation given these documents, few are read by governmental leaders in the territories.

The activities of these organs have nevertheless benefited dependent peoples indirectly in important ways. They have contributed greatly to the knowledge of Member nations and of international agencies about dependent territories. They have discouraged premature cessation of the transmission of information and thus held the administering Members to more complete fulfillment of their pledges under the Charter. They have contributed to the international atmosphere that has spurred administering Members to greater effort in their territories and thereby indirectly fostered development in all fields. They have stimulated research on problems of dependent areas and encouraged greater provision and use of international technical assistance in dependent territories—perhaps the most constructive contributions of the United Nations in this field.

Little more could be asked of the United Nations in connection with Chapter XI than that it perform these tasks well and that it do so in ways that will provoke the minimum of hostility among its Members. As the agitation of colonial issues seems to serve the national interests of many Member states and to some extent appears necessary to accelerate the efforts of administering Members on behalf of dependent peoples, it is unrealistic to expect the United Nations to discharge its duties in this field in an atmosphere of serenity. Nevertheless, it is essential that correctives be sought to the current situation, which makes of each new issue a potential crisis involving the possible collapse of the system of examining information from non-self-governing territories.

The Committee on Information serves the interests of the administering Members as well as those of the nonadministering Members that insist on its continuation. The transmission of information under Article 73(e) would be relatively meaningless without its examination by the United Nations. The administering Members would be well advised to agree to the establishment of the committee on a permanent basis, provided its present terms of reference are maintained.

The request of nonadministering Members that political information be voluntarily transmitted on all territories is a reasonable one so long as it is understood, as it has been in the past, that this information will not be analyzed, discussed, or made the subject of recommendations. Political information is essential to an understanding of educational, economic, and social problems in the territories. It has value to almost everyone concerned even if its use is restricted. The administering Members would in no circumstance regularly transmit such information if it were to be made the subject of debate and recommendation in the United Nations. Moreover, it is doubtful whether it would generally be helpful to the dependent peoples to have the evolution of their constitutional relationship subject to influences as alien to them as are the interests of many Member states.

The early cases of the cessation of transmission of information were founded on such equivocal bases that the question of participation by the General Assembly in future decisions on cessation was bound to be raised. A measure of equilibrium has been achieved as a result of the storm then raised, despite the lack of agreement on a definition of non-self-governing territories or on the competence of the Assembly to decide whether cessation is appropriate. The study of factors has helped to establish among many nonadministering Members the fact that there are legitimate alternatives to independence and to serve notice on the administering Members that changes in status should be founded on the freely expressed wishes of the peoples concerned. The administering Members have reserved, as they must, the right to interpret their constitutional relations with their territories. Where legal issues are involved, the General Assembly, in the event it cannot confirm the cessation of information on a given territory, might consider requesting an advisory opinion of the International Court of Justice rather than condemning prematurely the action of an administering Member.

The administering Members gain prestige by attaching indigenous officials to their delegations in the Committee on Information. In the case of advanced territories, whose internal affairs are largely directed by elected representatives, such participation is particularly appropriate. Nonadministering Members should recognize the practical limitations, particularly the cost involved, of bringing officials from the territories. An understanding in this matter might help to settle other issues involving the establishment of relationships between the United Nations and the territories that are unacceptable to the administering Members.

The terms of reference of the Committee on Information have served generally to limit in practice the scope of the Fourth Committee, but only by virtue of shrewd negotiations and by reason of the threats of administering Members concerned to withdraw from discussions that, in their opinion, would intrude on their domestic jurisdiction. This is a highly precarious basis on which to found the work of a committee of the Assembly. It is essential that the non-administering Members agree that the Fourth Committee must in general confine itself to the terms agreed upon for the Committee on Information. It is a price that they know they must pay for continued participation by some of the administering Members in the Committee on Information and the Fourth Committee.

Political and other issues relating to dependent territories should be handled in other committees of the Assembly on exactly the same basis as issues relating to Member nations. It is neither possible nor desirable to insulate dependent territories from the normal subject matter competence of the various United Nations organs.

The precedent set by the eighth session of the Assembly in adopting important resolutions relating to Chapter XI of the Charter by a simple majority vote aggravates the political problems within the United Nations in this field. In view of the statements made by nonadministering Members emphasizing the importance of United Nations activities relating to Chapter XI, and of the provision, in Article 18 of the Charter, for regarding trusteeship questions as important matters, the practice should be established by amendment of the Charter or the rules of procedure to include questions relating to Chapter XI of the Charter among the important matters on which decisions by the Assembly require a two-thirds vote.

The Secretariat, if it maintains complete impartiality, can play an important role in this field. Many delegations that lack both specialists and strong interests in colonial matters look to the Secretariat for information and guidance, but there is both opportunity and danger inherent in this situation. The danger lies principally in the twilight zone between service to individual Members on request and complicity with individual Members in the formulation of statements or resolutions critical of other Member states. It would be well to impress upon the staff that adventures in this delicate field can seriously injure the United Nations and impair its role in the advancement of dependent peoples. The Secretariat can help to bring about the desired understandings and to guide United Nations actions along sound lines, but to minimize the risks involved, this effort should only be undertaken by or with the knowledge of top officials.

There is thus a broad basis for agreement. Some of the demands of nonadministering Members appear reasonable. It should be possible for administering Members to meet them if simultaneously they are given safeguards against subsequent demands that would complicate their task of administration or impair their constitutional relations with the territories. Such a formula would, it is believed, contribute toward removing the threat to United Nations activities in this field and, by reducing the number of crises, enable a majority of Member states to work more effectively in the interests of the peoples of non-self-governing territories.

CHAPTER IV

The International Trusteeship System

T HE experience of the United Nations in carrying out the objectives and provisions of the Charter relating to the peoples of territories under the international trusteeship system differs substantially from the experience of the Organization in dealing with the problems of the peoples in other non-self-governing territories. The Charter spells out in considerable detail the powers and functions of the Organization under the international trusteeship system. Thus an analysis of the operation of this system should be helpful in determining not only what, if any, changes should be made to enable the system to function more effectively, but also what guides might be used in reassessing the role of the United Nations with respect to dependent peoples in general. As a preliminary to such an analysis, however, it is necessary to understand how the international trusteeship system was set into motion.

Establishment of the Trusteeship System

Chapters XII and XIII of the Charter provided for an international trusteeship system, but the system could not be established until a sufficient number of trusteeship agreements were approved.[1] The approval of agreements was required to place territories under international supervision and also to enable the Trusteeship Council to be formed of an equal number of Members that administer trust territories and of those that do not. Under Article 79 of the Charter, trusteeship agreements must be approved by the "states directly concerned," including the mandatory power in the case of territories held under mandate, and subsequently approved by the General Assembly or, in the case of strategic areas, under Articles 83 and 85, by the Security Council.[2]

[1] For general background, see Elizabeth H. Armstrong and William I. Cargo, *The Inauguration of the Trusteeship System of the United Nations,* U.S. Department of State Publication 2795 (1947).

[2] At a meeting in October 1945 of the Executive Committee of the Preparatory

At the first session of the General Assembly in 1946, Australia, Belgium, France, New Zealand, and the United Kingdom named the mandated territories on which they would submit draft trusteeship agreements. All of the territories formerly under League of Nations mandate were named, except Syria and Lebanon, which had already achieved independence; Transjordan, which was in process of becoming independent; Palestine, out of which later was to be created the independent state of Israel and, in theory, an international regime for certain parts of Jerusalem; South-West Africa, on which the Union of South Africa reserved its position pending consultation with the people of the territory; and the Pacific Islands formerly under Japanese mandate, which were then under United States military government.

The Assembly welcomed the statements made by the mandatory powers and invited them to take steps together with other states directly concerned to negotiate trusteeship agreements. It also regarded the intention of the mandatory powers to continue administering their territories for the well-being of the peoples concerned as being in accord with their obligations under the terms of the mandates, which would continue until other arrangements between the United Nations and the respective mandatory powers had been agreed upon.[3]

The respective mandatory powers circulated draft trusteeship agreements to certain interested powers, including the United States, which was the only state that suggested amendments during these preliminary consultations. Its amendments were directed primarily at specifying in greater detail the civil rights of the inhabitants, the obligations of the administering authority to ensure their political, economic, social, and educational advancement, and the guarantees of equal economic treatment for all Members and their nationals. Most of these amendments found their way into all of the agreements that have been approved by the United Nations.

Commission of the United Nations, it was decided that a temporary trusteeship committee should be established as an interim "subsidiary organ" under Article 22 of the Charter until a sufficient number of trusteeship agreements should be concluded. There was considerable opposition, however, to this proposal in the commission, and it was not recommended to the Assembly. For further details of this proposal, see the volume in this Brookings series, *The Organization and Procedures of the United Nations.*

[3] Res. 9(I), Feb. 9, 1946.

Debate on Draft Agreements

Eight trusteeship agreements were considered at the second part of the first session of the General Assembly: for British Togoland, British Cameroons, and Tanganyika submitted by the United Kingdom; for French Cameroons and French Togoland submitted by France; for Ruanda-Urundi by Belgium; for New Guinea by Australia; and for Western Samoa by New Zealand. The debate on these draft agreements centered on four issues, all of which were either satisfactorily resolved by the Assembly, or which for other reasons are no longer of practical significance.[4]

First, the United States wanted to restrict the grant of private monopolies in trust territories. The United Kingdom and Belgium agreed to include in their agreements a provision to prevent discrimination on grounds of nationality in the granting of private monopolies and declared that such monopolies would be granted only when essential for economic development of interest to the inhabitants. France declared that under French law private monopolies were prohibited in trust territories to be administered by France.

Second, strong opposition was voiced to the provisions in most of the agreements authorizing the administering authority to administer the trust territory as an "integral part" of its territory. Although such provision was contained in the terms of the mandates, most Members felt it revealed "annexationist tendencies." The United States was among those pressing for the deletion of the provision or its modification, as in the New Guinea draft, to "as if it were an integral part." New Zealand agreed to delete the provision, and Belgium, France, and the United Kingdom stated that it was intended only for administrative convenience and not to imply their sovereignty over the territories involved.

Third, the power of the administering authority to establish military bases and to station forces in the trust territory, as provided in all eight agreements and which reversed the policy under the mandates system, was one of the most heatedly debated issues. The Soviet Union, India, and China strongly opposed such a provision. They felt that to grant this power would be an extension of Article 84 of the Charter, and that unless military bases were declared strategic trust areas under Articles 82 and 83, they could be estab-

---

[4] Another issue over a clause authorizing administrative unions between trust territories and neighboring dependent territories has been revived on several occasions and is discussed later.

lished only pursuant to agreements made with the Security Council under Article 43.

The administering powers, supported by the United States, held that the philosophy of the Charter, unlike that of the Covenant of the League of Nations, made it not only their right but also their obligation to ensure that trust territories play their part in the maintenance of international peace and security. They said that Article 84 of the Charter was especially designed to protect the inhabitants as well as the rest of the world community, and the duty it imposes exists notwithstanding any delay in negotiating the special agreements under Article 43. The suggested provision, they felt, was consistent with the Charter and would give the administering authorities the necessary discretion in fulfilling their obligation. The Soviet Union and India carried the fight on this question to the plenary meeting of the General Assembly where they lost by a vote of 34 to 6 with 11 abstentions.[5]

The final major issue arose over the method of fulfilling the requirement under Article 79 that the terms of trusteeship be agreed upon by the "states directly concerned," as well as approved by the United Nations. There was nothing in the legislative history of this provision that would shed light on its meaning or on the method by which such states should be determined. There were political overtones in the resolution of this issue, because under the Charter not only the approval of the agreements but also their subsequent amendment is subject to the concurrence of such states.

The United States, which had originally suggested the phrase to make sure that it would have a voice in the disposition of the mandated territories, including the former Japanese mandated islands, conceived an ingenious formula for avoiding the impasse that seemed imminent. Under this formula, which was adopted by the Fourth (Trusteeship) Committee, every state interested, whether technically a "state directly concerned," would have a chance to present its views on each agreement but (1) would forego, without prejudice to its rights, any formal classification of being or not being among the "states directly concerned." (2) would not be formal signatories of the preliminary agreements, and (3) would accept the verdict of a two-thirds vote in the General Assembly on the adoption of the agreements. This formula was vigorously opposed

[5] U.N. General Assembly, First Session, Second Part, Plenary *Official Records,* 62nd Meeting (Dec. 13, 1946), p. 1286.

by the Soviet Union, which wanted to be recognized as a "state directly concerned" in connection with every trusteeship agreement. When the agreements came before the General Assembly in plenary meeting, the Soviet Union introduced a resolution to reject the draft agreements as contrary to the Charter on the grounds that the "states directly concerned" had never been specified, that the agreements made trust territories integral parts of administering states, and that they did not provide for approval by the Security Council of the military arrangements. This resolution was defeated. Then, by more than the required two-thirds vote, the eight trusteeship agreements were approved by the General Assembly.[6] The Soviet Union, still contending that the agreements were illegal, did not attend meetings of the Trusteeship Council until the latter part of its second session. The Council was formed in December 1946 after these eight trusteeship agreements were adopted.

Other Territories under Trusteeship

Three more territories—Nauru, Somaliland, and the former Japanese mandated islands—were later placed under trusteeship, the agreements for each containing special features.

The General Assembly, in 1947, approved a trusteeship agreement for Nauru. The agreement, like the terms of the League of Nations mandate, designated Australia, New Zealand, and the United Kingdom jointly as the administering authorities, with Australia acting on behalf of the three governments in administering this Pacific island. This is the first and only use thus far made of the provision of the Charter permitting more than one state to be designated as an administering authority.

In breaking the deadlock among the four major powers on the disposition of the former Italian colonies, the General Assembly, in 1949, provided that Somaliland should be placed under the international trusteeship system for a ten-year period ending in 1960, when it would become independent. Italy was asked to be the administering authority, assisted and advised by an advisory council composed of representatives of Colombia, Egypt, and the Philippines.[7] Pursuant to this action of the Assembly, the Trusteeship

---

[6] For the texts of the eight agreements as approved on December 13, 1946, see U.N. General Assembly, First Session, Second Part, *Official Records,* Supplement No. 5.

[7] Res. 289(IV), Nov. 21, 1949.

Council and the Government of Italy negotiated a draft trustee-ship agreement, which the Council adopted on January 27, 1950. Italy assumed provisional administration of the territory, accepting the transfer of authority from the United Kingdom whose forces had occupied the territory since early in the Second World War. The General Assembly approved the trusteeship agreement on December 2, 1950. For the first time, a state not a Member of the United Nations became an administering authority, the Trusteeship Council negotiated a trusteeship agreement on behalf of the Assembly, an advisory council consisting of three Members was created to advise and assist the administering authority on the spot,[8] a definite time limit was set for the achievement by a trust territory of independence, and a Declaration of Constitutional Principles was attached to the agreement prescribing the basic structure and princi-ples on which the independent government should be founded. Perhaps most significant of all was the fact that the major world powers, victorious in war and unable to decide among themselves on the disposition of the colonies of the vanquished, had turned the power of decision over to an international agency. The chronically serious economic difficulties of Libya and Somaliland have been of continuing concern to the United Nations.[9] Until a reasonable meas-ure of economic stability is assured for both areas, the wisdom of the decision of the Assembly will remain in doubt.

The United States submitted a draft trusteeship agreement for the former Japanese mandated islands (the Marshall, Caroline, and Northern Mariana Islands) to the Security Council in February 1947. The submission was made to the Security Council in accord-ance with Article 83 of the Charter because the draft agreement pro-vided that the territory would be designated as a strategic area. During the course of the discussions on the agreement, members of

[8] During its first three years, nine different persons served on the council—only the Colombian serving continuously. The full representation in the council was present in Somaliland during the year ending March 31, 1954 for a period of only twenty-eight days and there was a quorum of two members during a period of only twenty-three days. Recent reports indicate that absenteeism is no longer a problem. There have been reports on various occasions of tenseness in the relations between the Advisory Council and the administering authority, dis-harmony among council members, and confusion among the inhabitants regard-ing the position of the Advisory Council vis-à-vis the administering authority. The experiment, on the whole, appears not to have been successful but bears watching for the lessons it may afford.

[9] Res. 924(X), Dec. 9, 1955, on assistance to Libya and Res. 855(IX), Dec. 14, 1954, on financing economic development plans in Somaliland.

the Far Eastern Commission that were not members of the Security Council were invited to participate in the debate. The draft agreement was, generally speaking, comparable to the other trusteeship agreements with two notable exceptions:

First, Article 8 of the agreement would give the United States the right to confer on its nationals and companies treatment preferential to that accorded the nationals and companies of other nations. The United States threatened to withdraw the agreement if the Council had adopted a proposed amendment that would have removed the clause conferring this preferential treatment. Its representative made it clear that the United States had no intention of taking advantage for its own benefit of the meager resources in these islands and that the clause was dictated by the "strategic" nature of the trusteeship. The amendment was not approved.

Second, Article 13 of the agreement would in effect make the regular trusteeship functions of the United Nations (*i.e.*, with respect to annual reports, petitions, and periodic visits) applicable to this strategic trust territory, "provided that the Administering Authority may determine the extent of their applicability to any areas which may from time to time be specified by it as closed for security reasons."[10] Its purpose was to ensure protection of United States strategic interests while affording the inhabitants the protection of international supervision over the administration of their affairs and manifesting respect for the principles of international trusteeship.

Several minor amendments to the agreement were adopted, and the agreement was then approved unanimously. It seemed strange to find the United States and the Soviet Union in accord on this important matter. The Soviet Union, however, might have considered that a veto would probably have induced the United States to take steps toward annexing the islands. It might also have welcomed the opportunity of recognizing United States interests in the Pacific Islands in the belief that the United States would then not question Soviet claims under the Yalta agreement to the Kuriles and certain other Japanese islands.

When the agreement was approved by the President on authorization of Congress, it entered into force, and the United States became the first and only administering authority of a strategic trust territory. Two atolls, Bikini and Eniwetok, have since been closed to visits by United Nations missions. Otherwise the Trusteeship

---

[10] Louis B. Sohn, ed., *Cases and Other Materials on World Law* (1950), p. 624.

Council has carried out its functions relating to this particular trust territory in the same manner as it has elsewhere, except that its reports thereon are sent to the Security Council instead of to the General Assembly.

By virtue of the approval of these trusteeship agreements, the following eleven territories are now under the International Trusteeship System:

Trust Territory	Estimated Population[11] (In thousands)	Administering Authority
Cameroons (British)	1,460	United Kingdom
Togoland (British)	429	United Kingdom
Tanganyika	8,196	United Kingdom
Cameroons (French)	3,065	France
Togoland (French)	1,070	France
Ruanda Urundi	4,252	Belgium
New Guinea	1,207	Australia
Nauru	3	Australia[12]
Western Samoa	93	New Zealand
Somaliland	1,269	Italy
Pacific Islands	61	United States
	21,115	

South-West Africa

Of the mandated territories under the League of Nations, only South-West Africa has not been placed under the international trusteeship system or transformed into an independent state. The Union of South Africa at the outset interpreted local opinion in the mandated territory as favoring integration with the Union. Despite the most severe criticism in the General Assembly, and resolutions at almost every session of that organ urging the Union of South Africa to place its mandated territory under trusteeship, it has refused to do so. In addition to the general feeling that the Union was morally if not legally obligated to place the territory under trusteeship, was the belief, supported by oral hearings in the Fourth Committee of the Assembly, that the administration of the territory by the Union of South Africa was oppressive and generally violative of the terms of the mandate. Running concurrently with the debates of South-West Africa were the debates on racial discrimination in the Union of

[11] U.N. Department of Economic and Social Affairs, Statistical Office, *Demographic Yearbook, 1955.*
[12] On behalf also of the United Kingdom and New Zealand.

South Africa itself. These combined to make the Union the symbol for many nations of all that was offensive in prewar colonialism and in racist doctrines and practices.[13]

The Assembly has gradually developed a system for supervising the administration of South-West Africa, backed by advisory opinions of the International Court of Justice issued in 1950, 1955, and 1956. This system, although less effective than the trusteeship system, helps to maintain the international status of the territory. The opinion in 1950 stated that although the Union of South Africa is not legally obligated to place South-West Africa under the United Nations trusteeship system, it cannot modify the international status of the territory without the consent of the United Nations. The opinion held that South-West Africa was still a territory under the League mandate and that the Union of South Africa continues "to have the international obligations stated in Article 22 of the Covenant of the League of Nations and in the mandate for South-West Africa as well as the obligation to transmit petitions from the inhabitants of that territory."[14] The Court advised that the supervisory functions were to be exercised by the United Nations, to which the Union should submit annual reports and petitions.

The Assembly, in 1950, created an *ad hoc* committee consisting of five Members to work out, in consultation with the Union of South Africa, procedures for implementing the opinion of the Court and to undertake an examination of reports on the administration of the territory, including petitions transmitted by the mandatory power. Although the Union consulted with the committee, it was subsequently unwilling to accept the terms the committee proposed for supervision by the United Nations, and it refused to transmit reports and petitions.

A new committee was created by the Assembly in 1953, consisting of seven Member governments, to examine information within the scope of the questionnaire adopted by the Permanent Mandates Commission of the League of Nations, to examine reports and petitions conforming as closely as possible to the Mandates Commission procedure, and to negotiate with South Africa on the means of implementing the advisory opinion of the Court. The rules of pro-

[13] For an account of the debates in the Assembly on racial discrimination in South Africa, see the monograph in this Brookings series, *The United Nations and Human Rights,* Chap. IV.

[14] International Court of Justice, "International Status of South-West Africa," Advisory Opinion, July 11, 1950, *I.C.J. Reports, 1950,* p. 19.

cedure of the committee are similar to those under the Mandates Commission with one notable exception. If the mandatory power fails to provide the required information, the committee will examine such information as may be available in respect of the territory, and which the committee may consider necessary for the preparation of its report to the Assembly. In the absence of an annual report from the mandatory power, the Secretariat of the United Nations, beginning in 1954, has prepared, primarily on the basis of official publications, annual reports on South-West Africa for the consideration of the committee. The committee has examined written petitions and, on the basis of an opinion of the International Court in 1956, will be able to grant oral hearings to petitioners on matters relating to South-West Africa.

Although the Union of South Africa has refused to participate in the work of the Committee on South-West Africa, it has participated in some debates on the territory in the Fourth Committee. At the ninth session of the Assembly, the Union opposed a proposal to regard questions on South-West Africa as important ones, within the meaning of Article 18 of the Charter, to be decided by a two-thirds vote. It contended that under the 1950 opinion of the Court, the Assembly cannot adopt a resolution on South-West Africa that the Union opposes because the unanimity rule must in such a case apply as it did in the Council and the Assembly of the League of Nations. A stormy debate on this issue was resolved by the Assembly finally deciding to seek an opinion from the Court on the matter. The Court in 1955 issued a unanimous opinion stating that questions relating to reports and petitions on South-West Africa should be decided by a two-thirds vote of the Assembly, *i.e.,* without special weight to the vote of the Union.[15]

The resolutions of the Assembly have been rather moderate in view of the antagonism of many Members toward the Union of South Africa. The failure of the Union to co-operate has handicapped the effort of the Assembly to discharge its responsibilities with respect to the territory. That, together with reports of unsatisfactory conditions in the territory, such as the denial of political participation to 400,000 Africans and other non-Europeans, has spurred other Members to use all means legally and practically possible to supervise the territory.

[15] International Court of Justice, "Voting Procedure on Questions Relating to Reports and Petitions Concerning the Territory of South-West Africa," Advisory Opinion, June 7, 1955, *I.C.J. Reports, 1955,* p. 67.

The system for the international supervision of South-West Africa is sufficiently different from that established by the Assembly for the implementation of Chapter XI of the Charter and from the international trusteeship system to merit continuous study in the effort to improve international organization in this field. It might have been more in consonance with the opinion of the International Court for the Committee on South-West Africa to have been composed—like the Mandates Commission—of nongovernmental specialists instead of governmental representatives. This would also have afforded a more useful basis for comparison between the two systems.

The Trusteeship System in Operation

The Charter provides that the Trusteeship Council shall consist of the Member states administering trust territories, the permanent members of the Security Council, and as many other Member states elected for three-year terms by the General Assembly as are necessary to ensure that the number of nonadministering Members is equal to that of the administering authorities. Thus, at the outset, two nonadministering Members were elected to the Council. Although the United States started out as a member of the Council by virtue of its being a permanent member of the Security Council, it became an administering Member when its trusteeship agreement was approved in April 1947. In order then to restore the balance between administering and nonadministering members, two more Members were elected to the Council. Italy participated without vote in sessions of the Council after it became the administering authority for Somaliland in 1949. It became a member of the Council when it was admitted to membership in the United Nations in December 1955. Another nonadministering Member state was then elected to the Council. Thus, the Council now consists of fourteen members—the seven administering authorities; China and the Soviet Union, the permanent members of the Security Council that are not administering authorities; and five other Members elected by the General Assembly.

The Charter provides in Article 86(2) that each member of the Council shall designate "one specially qualified person" to represent it therein. Although some of the administering authorities have selected persons with special knowledge or experience in territorial administration, few of these, and none of those designated by the nonadministering Members, have been experts approaching the stature of the members of the Permanent Mandates Commission under the League of Nations. Furthermore, the persons serving on the Council, regardless of whether they are experts, are subject to instructions from their respective governments. Consequently, they are not regarded as being objective or impartial in their approach to trusteeship questions as were the members of the Mandates Commission. The fact that the Council is a political, not an expert, organ and the feeling in the Assembly that the nonadministering states are not adequately represented on the Council underlie the most critical problem that has arisen in the trusteeship field—namely, the conflict between the Trusteeship Council and the General Assembly on trusteeship matters.

Although most representatives on the Council are not experts, they acquire in due course a familiarity with major problems in the trust territories by participating in visiting missions and other functions of the Council. This accounts in part for the greater understanding between the administering and nonadministering Members in the Council than in the Assembly.

With the help of provisional rules drawn up by the Preparatory Commission of the United Nations and suggested revisions made by the Secretariat, the Council adopted at its first session the rules of procedure to guide its deliberations and to carry out its functions.[16] The Council holds two sessions annually, one in the winter beginning in January and another in the summer convening in June. A new president is elected each June, the office by custom being alternately held by an administering and a nonadministering Member. All votes in the Council are by simple majority. The Council submits a report each year to the General Assembly and also one to the Security Council with respect to the Trust Territory of the Pacific Islands. In the General Assembly, votes on trusteeship questions require a simple majority in the Fourth Committee and, as specified in the Charter, a two-thirds majority in the plenary meetings.

Examination of Annual Reports

Articles 87 and 88 of the Charter require the administering authorities to submit annual reports for each of their trust territo-

[16] For the text of the rules, see U.N. Trusteeship Council, First Session, *Official Records*, Supplement, Annex 2, pp. 2-11.

ries on the basis of a questionnaire drawn up by the Trusteeship Council. The Council now examines the reports on six of the trust territories in Africa at its winter session and the reports on Somaliland and those in the Pacific at its summer session.

A large part of each session is devoted to these reports. A special representative of the administering authority, usually a high official of the territory under review, is questioned by members of the Council not only on matters referred to in the reports but also on items contained in petitions and in reports of the visiting missions of the Council. A general debate is held, in which each member presents his views, ending with a final statement by the administering authority, which usually includes comments on the views expressed by other delegations. A committee is then appointed, consisting normally of two administering and two nonadministering Members, to draft, principally on the basis of views presented in the final debate, detailed conclusions and recommendations on the territory for consideration by the Council. The Soviet representative has rarely served as a member of a drafting committee, perhaps because his views are almost always distinctively and amply recorded along with other minority views in the final report of the Council to the Assembly.

The annual reports and their examination by the Council constitute the backbone of the system of international supervision. They ensure that recent information is available in comprehensible form, and provide the basis for review by the Council of conditions in trust territories and of the manner in which the administering authorities are fulfilling their trusteeship obligations. It is largely through the annual report and its examination that the Council follows up on general questions raised in petitions, on the findings of its visiting missions, and on the steps taken by the administering authorities to carry out recommendations of the Council and the Assembly. Certain problems have arisen, however, in connection with this important function.

The Council follows in its examination procedure a set pattern with respect to each territory each year, involving a somewhat tedious round robin in which questions or remarks are solicited from each member separately on political, economic, social, and educational matters. It then attempts to render a verdict on all aspects of administration in a territory, with the result that observations on important items tend to become buried.

The ninth session of the Assembly agreed that the report of the Council to the Assembly should include comprehensive information on a trust territory only every third year coinciding with the examination by the Council of the report of the visiting mission to the territory, with the account in intervening years limited in the main to developments and progress made during the year. This has not, however, changed perceptibly the procedure of the Council for examining annual reports.

Despite the expansion of the questionnaire of the Trusteeship Council and the efforts of the United Nations to avoid overlapping inquiries from international agencies, administering authorities still receive detailed inquiries from the specialized agencies. Substantial staff time is required to answer these. Recognizing the primary interests of the Trusteeship Council in obtaining information from trust territories, an evaluation should be made of the need for the information requested by other agencies, and a renewed attempt should be made to minimize such requests.

The time lag between the year reported on and the examination by the Council of the report has extended as long as eighteen months. Although the special representative has usually referred in his opening statement to noteworthy events since the year reported on, the Council decided, in 1954, that it should have such a statement in writing a month in advance of its examination of the report. This has apparently worked out satisfactorily.

Although Article 88 of the Charter requires the Trusteeship Council to formulate a questionnaire for "each trust territory," one very detailed questionnaire has heretofore served as the basis for the annual report on all trust territories.[17] The eighth session of the Assembly, however, expressed dissatisfaction with the questionnaire and created a subcommittee "to study such changes as may be necessary to adapt it to the special conditions of each territory, and to submit its conclusions to the Trusteeship Council."[18] The elected members of the Council constituted the subcommittee, partly because the administering members were skeptical of the practicability of preparing separate questionnaires. Moreover, Belgium expressed a desire that the administering members not be made mem-

[17] The Mandates Commission of the League started out with two almost identical questionnaires—one for "Class B" and another for "Class C" mandates. Later the commission adopted a more comprehensive questionnaire applicable to both classes of mandates.

[18] Res. 751(VIII), Dec. 9, 1953.

bers so that they would not be blamed for any failure to prepare the questionnaires.

In July 1956, the subcommittee suggested numerous revisions of the questionnaire as applied to New Guinea. It expressed the view that separate questionnaires were not necessary for British Togoland, French Togoland, Somaliland, British Cameroons, French Cameroons, and Western Samoa because the objectives of trusteeships are expected to be fulfilled there at an early date. It had previously started and then dropped work on the Somaliland questionnaire. As the deficiency in the omnibus questionnaire from a practical standpoint has never been demonstrated, it seems reasonable to assume that the subcommittee has suggested reducing the number of separate questionnaires to be prepared mainly because the effort involved is not worth it. In any case, the creation by the Assembly of this subcommittee represents an unnecessary proliferation of United Nations activities and adds to the confusion in relationships between the Assembly and the Council.

Examination of Written Petitions

Article 87(b) of the Charter provides that the General Assembly, and under its authority the Trusteeship Council, may "accept petitions and examine them in consultation with the administering authority." Petitions cover a vast range of subjects. For example, the following were among the petitions before the Council in 1956: (1) complaining against differences in pay and allowances between African and European employees of commercial firms; (2) challenging the authority of a chief and characterizing his rule as "despotic"; (3) charging that unless the petitioning group is represented in the police force, the next political election cannot take place in an atmosphere of freedom; (4) complaining that Europeans are encroaching on their land; (5) appealing a court order banishing the petitioner from specified communities; (6) charging that the police tried to prevent a group from hearing the report of a person's mission to the United Nations; (7) charging that the petitioner was fired from his job for no other reason than his political activities; (8) seeking renewal of an employment contract to teach; (9) complaining that health, educational, and economic conditions in their community are deficient; and (10) complaining that the taxes are oppressively high, particularly the head tax.

The action of the Council on almost all such petitions is to send the petitioner the views of the administering authority thereon. Occasionally, it will advise the petitioner of the proper procedure to follow in pursuit of his objective. Seldom does the Council "express the hope" that the administering authority will take a certain action and rarely does it "urge" or "recommend" a certain action.

The petition by the people of the Marshall Islands following injury to inhabitants of two atolls from the fall-out resulting from a hydrogen bomb explosion illustrates the type of petition on which the Council recommends action. The Marshall Islands form part of the Trust Territory of the Pacific Islands, which the United States administers. The fall-out from the explosion at Bikini on March 1, 1954 contaminated two islands, causing burns, nausea, and other injury and necessitating evacuation of the inhabitants to Kwajalein for observation and treatment.

In May 1954, members of the Holdover Committee of the Marshall Islands Congress and one hundred other Marshallese petitioned the United Nations. They asked that the experiments with lethal weapons be stopped or, if the continuance of the tests was adjudged absolutely necessary for the eventual well-being of all the peoples of the world and could not be carried out elsewhere, that certain precautions be taken. They stated that the petition should not be regarded as a repudiation of the United States as the governing agency because its administration was the most agreeable one in Marshallese memory.

The Council, after receiving explanations and reassurances from the United States, passed a resolution, with which the United States concurred, recommending that if further tests were necessary, the United States should take all precautions necessary to ensure that no inhabitants of the territory are again endangered. The Council urged the United States to give prompt and sympathetic attention to all claims for damage and to assist evacuees in resettling in their homes as soon as possible.[19]

In response to another petition that the Marshallese presented to the visiting mission in 1956, the Council reaffirmed its previous position.[20] During the discussion of the petition in the Council, India stated that it would ask the eleventh session of the Assembly to seek an opinion from the International Court of Justice on whether

[19] Res. 1082(XIV), July 15, 1954.
[20] Res. 1493(XVII), Mar. 29, 1956.

the conduct of nuclear tests in the trust territory is consistent with the terms of trusteeship.[21]

The number of written petitions from trust territories has grown enormously in recent years from less than fifty in the early sessions of the Council to about five hundred in recent sessions.[22] This growth has been stimulated in part by visiting missions and in part as a result of the fact that the people concerned have become aware of their right to petition the United Nations. There has also been a tremendous increase in the number of communications from trust territories—some 33,000 having been received in fiscal 1954-55 as a consequence of disorders in the Cameroons under French administration.[23] The petition procedure has brought the inhabitants of trust territories into direct contact with the United Nations, and although it has served to some extent to safeguard and to advance the interests of the inhabitants, it has also created various problems.

As the number of petitions has increased, so has the delay or cursoriness of the examination of them by the Council. Despite some improvements, the machinery is inadequate to cope with this problem. At its first session, the Council created an *ad hoc* Committee on Petitions, which met during the session of the Council to consider the admissibility of petitions and to group the petitions for more expeditious examination by the Council. The Council then examined the petitions in the presence of a representative of the administering authority. After several sessions, a series of form replies to the petitioners emerged, which provided easy refuge from the numerous problems posed. The substantive action by the Council on petitions was often postponed for long periods due to delays

[21] For a comprehensive analysis of both sides of this question, see Emanuel Margolis, "The Hydrogen Bomb Experiments and International Law" and M. S. McDougal and M. A. Schlei, "The Hydrogen Bomb Tests in Perspective: Lawful Measures for Security," *The Yale Law Journal* (April 1955), pp. 629-710.

[22] Moreover, at its eleventh session in 1952, the Council revised its procedure to authorize its visiting missions to decide whether petitions they receive are intended for their information or for presentation to the Council. Previously, almost all the communications the missions received were passed on for consideration by the Council. Thus, fewer petitions now appear on the agenda of the Council than would otherwise be the case. For example, the 1955 Visiting Mission to the Togolands received over 200,000 communications, of which only 63 were passed on to the Council.

[23] U.N. Trusteeship Council, *United Nations Visiting Mission to the Trust Territories of the Cameroons under British Administration and the Cameroons under French Administration, 1955: Report on the Cameroons under French Administration,* Doc. T/1231 (Feb. 17, 1956), p. 47.

in the receipt of information or views from the administering authorities.

Concern developed among nonadministering Members in both the Council and the Assembly that the right to petition the United Nations would fall into disrepute among people of the trust territories unless remedial action was taken. This culminated in the adoption by the General Assembly in 1950 of a resolution, which indirectly criticized the Council on its examination of petitions. It stated that the right of petition is one of the fundamental human rights and one of the most important features of the trusteeship system. It regarded the improvement of the petition examination procedure as essential to the interests of the inhabitants, and recommended that the Council consider: constituting the *ad hoc* Committee on Petitions as a standing committee to meet if necessary between sessions of the Council; requesting administering authorities to submit such observations as they desire on petitions within two months after they receive such petitions; studying all other measures to improve the procedure for petition examination; and requesting administering authorities to submit each year special information on the action they have taken on the recommendations of the Council with respect to petitions, except in cases where the Council does not think it necessary.[24]

The *ad hoc* Committee on Petitions during the ninth session of the Council (June-July 1951) considered this resolution. France, the United Kingdom, and Australia were opposed to having a standing committee meet between Council sessions. On the basis of the report of the committee, the Council made several changes in the petition procedure at that session, the most important one being to request the administering authority concerned to submit to the Secretary-General written observations on petitions within two months after the date on which it receives them. It modified the resolution of the Assembly by requesting administering authorities to submit, when the Council deems it necessary, special information on actions they take on recommendations of the Council. Finally, it asked Members to suggest means of perfecting the examination of petitions.

In 1952, the Council created a Standing Committee on Petitions and made further revisions in the petition examination procedure. The Standing Committee consists of three administering and three

[24] Res. 435(V), Dec. 2, 1950.

nonadministering Members, which the Council appoints at the end of each session to serve until the close of the ensuing session. Its meetings usually start several weeks prior to a Council session and continue through the session. At its fourteenth session, the Council decided that the committee should meet as often as necessary, depending on the volume of its work.

New procedures were adopted to avoid duplication in the work of the Council and the committee and to enable the Council to devote more of its time to substantive issues. The Secretary-General circulates to members of the Council all petitions and other communications bearing on trusteeship that contain grievances or requests, with the exception of the manifestly inconsequential, which he lists with a summary of contents for the Council. Visiting missions, which are a prolific source of petitions, now decide which of the communications they receive are intended for their own information, and which are petitions to be transmitted to the Secretary-General together with any observations they wish to make after consultation with territorial officials.

The Standing Committee screens the petitions and performs a variety of other tasks in connection with them. It identifies the petitions concerning general problems to which the attention of the Council had already been called and on which the Council had previously made decisions. These petitions are not considered individually by the Council, but are called to its attention when these general problems are again discussed.

Between sessions of the Council, the Standing Committee conducts, in consultation with representatives of the administering authority concerned, a preliminary examination of those petitions on which written observations by the administering authority are available. It attempts to complete its preliminary examination of those petitions that the administering authority agrees to have examined without the presence of the special representative. It formulates questions for submission to the administering authority or its special representative, when necessary, and instructs the Secretariat to make such studies as may be needed.

The committee prepares a report to the Council on each petition to which the established petition procedure should be applied, together with recommendations for action by the Council in each case. The Council acts on these petitions individually, usually approving without discussion the recommendations of the committee.

Finally, the Council acceded to the requirements of the Assembly for special information from administering authorities on the action they have taken pursuant to recommendations of the Council on petitions. The Standing Committee brings to the attention of the Council those petitions on which such information should not be required.

Contrary to the opinions expressed by most administering authorities in opposing the establishment of the Standing Committee on Petitions, the committee has improved the examination of petitions by the Council. It ensures that individual attention is given each petition by at least a few members of the Council. Although the present system allows the Council to handle a larger number of petitions each year than before, it is already overburdened, and the system will prove inadequate if the number of petitions continues to increase.

The Council has wisely refused to consider petitions on matters that have been or are subject to adjudication in courts of law, unless such petitions challenge the compatibility of territorial laws with the Charter or the terms of trusteeship. At least two other changes would, it is believed, make the role of the United Nations in connection with petitions coincide more closely with its authority and responsibility under the trusteeship system.

First, the Council should not examine petitions seeking special favors for individuals or groups. Although the Council might properly urge measures to speed full employment or to expand educational facilities, its intercession on behalf of an individual seeking a job or a group appealing for a school tends to be self-defeating. If the petition is successful, it could have results detrimental to the public interest in a territory and increase the number of such petitions. If unsuccessful, the prestige of the United Nations might suffer.

Second, the Council should re-examine the information now sent to petitioners to avoid its serving the propaganda interests of the Soviet Union or any other Member state. The record of discussions and actions on a petition, in both the Standing Committee and the Council, is now transmitted to the petitioner. The Soviet Union has been a member of the Standing Committee throughout most of the life of that body, and almost invariably supports the indigenous petitioners and ensures that the records of its comments will serve its propaganda ends when read by the petitioner. No purpose would be served by removing the Soviet Union from the committee because it would only fill the time and record of the Council even more than it now does with its comments on petitions.[25] Further study is needed to design measures to prevent this abuse of the petition system.

In fact, the petition system generally merits far more analytical study than it has received. It seems to be an effective instrument for international supervision because it keeps the Council more intimately informed than it would otherwise be of conditions in the territories. It also seems to provide a useful means of communication between the petitioner and his government. The average petitioner probably gets a more complete statement of the position of his government on a matter by petitioning the United Nations than he could otherwise. Finally, the existence of the system may make the administering authorities more alert than they would be to situations that could give cause for complaint, and it probably speeds the redress of serious grievances.

However, case studies are needed to gain deeper insights into the effects of the present system. For example: What effect do petitions have on the decision-making process of a territorial government? Are persons more likely to obtain what they seek by petitioning the United Nations? What effect do petitions have on the relationships between the administering authority, the United Nations, and the inhabitants of the territories? How valid are the actions of the Council generally on petitions? Answers to these and other questions might help to improve the system of international trusteeship.

Examination of Oral Petitions

The conflict between administering and nonadministering Members on trusteeship questions and its effect on relations between the Trusteeship Council and the General Assembly are clearly revealed by the United Nations experience in handling oral petitions. Under Article 87(b) of the Charter, the General Assembly and, "under its authority," the Trusteeship Council may accept and examine petitions; and the Council decided this authorization applies to oral as well as written petitions. It also determines in each case whether

[25] For an analysis of the manner in which the Soviet Union attempts to use the Trusteeship Council for propaganda purposes see D. Vernon McKay, "Communist Exploitation of Anti-Colonialism and Nationalism in Africa," in *The Threat of Soviet Imperialism*, C. Grove Haines, ed. (1954), pp. 258-78.

it will hear petitioners. The Trusteeship Council heard the first oral presentation of a petition at its second session. It has heard oral petitions at some of its subsequent sessions, but neither the number nor the handling of such petitions has constituted a problem. The problem lies in the possible increase in the number of oral petitions addressed to the General Assembly, in the attempt by petitioners to play off the General Assembly against the Trusteeship Council and the administering authority, and in the disposition of the Fourth Committee of the Assembly to hear petitioners before they have been heard by the Trusteeship Council and to reach somewhat different conclusions from those of the Council on the same petitions.

The Fourth Committee began hearing oral petitioners at the fifth session of the Assembly. Prior to that time, the nonadministering Members did not seem to be aware that the Assembly could, under the Charter, exercise the same functions that the Trusteeship Council had been performing. However, it was not until the seventh session, in 1952, that the problem of oral petitions became apparent. At that session, the Fourth Committee devoted ten meetings to hearing representatives of various groups in British Togoland and French Togoland on the unification of the Ewe people and of the two Togolands. The committee spent six meetings hearing representatives of the Wa-Meru tribe in Tanganyika, who had previously been heard by the Council, charge that three thousand members of the tribe had been evicted by force from their lands in 1951 to permit allotment of these lands to white settlers. The Council had previously expressed regret at the eviction of the group and had asked the administering authority to relieve hardships sustained by the tribe and to compensate them generously for their losses. The Fourth Committee recommended that the Assembly approve a resolution regretting that the steps taken by the Council to solve the problem had proved inadequate and inviting the administering authority to return the lands from which the tribe had been evicted. The resolution failed, although only narrowly, to receive the necessary two-thirds majority in the plenary meeting of the Assembly, and thus two conflicting recommendations from the United Nations on this matter were prevented. Rejection of the resolution also avoided a showdown on the effect of recommendations by the Assembly relating to trust territories, because the United Kingdom had stated categorically that it would not implement the resolution if it were adopted.

Although the Fourth Committee has devoted an increasing amount of time to hearing oral petitioners, including petitioners who have not previously been heard by the Trusteeship Council, the majority of the members in the committee at the seventh, eighth, and tenth sessions refused even to consider establishing criteria for determining the kinds of petitions the committee should hear. The most complete discussion of this problem was at the eighth session, at which the United Kingdom proposed the creation of a subcommittee to study it. The subcommittee was to consist of eight members— four of whom should be members of the Trusteeship Council. The administering Members, the Dominican Republic, Canada, and the Union of South Africa spoke in favor of the proposal. The Dominican delegate, who had sought adoption of a general procedure at the seventh session, said that "while the right of petition should be safeguarded, the Committee must not allow itself to be inundated by frivolous or merely personal petitions."[26]

The United States agreed that the Fourth Committee should hear petitioners from the trust territories, but it was concerned over the practical problems involved in the indiscriminate granting of requests for hearings in a committee of sixty states. It suggested the following principles as a guide in deciding whether to grant a hearing: (1) the problem raised by the petition should be specifically stated and of sufficient importance to merit a hearing; (2) the petitioner should be a person who could provide useful information and should normally be an inhabitant of the territory concerned; (3) lawyers who are residents of the territory might advise but should not speak on behalf of petitioners; (4) petitioners should normally be heard in the Trusteeship Council before they are heard in the Fourth Committee; and (5) the Fourth Committee should take into account the past actions of the Council and the Assembly in connection with the problem raised by the petitioners. The United Kingdom suggested that another criterion might be the establishment of a time limit for the submission of requests, such as two weeks before the beginning of the session.

Other administering authorities pointed out that refusal by the committee to grant an oral hearing did not constitute a restriction on the right of petition, as that right did not necessarily include an oral presentation of a complaint. The question was whether an oral

[26] U.N. General Assembly, Eighth Session, Fourth Committee, *Official Records*, 318th Meeting (Sept. 28, 1953), pp. 11-12.

hearing would advance the work of the committee or enable it to make wise decisions. Unless petitions concerned urgent and important matters already examined by the Trusteeship Council, they should not come before the Fourth Committee. The Trusteeship Council had developed rules of procedure for accepting and examining petitions, and the Assembly should do likewise. They also criticized the tendency of the Fourth Committee to usurp functions of the Council instead of looking to the Council for "expert" advice.

Other delegations vigorously opposed most of these views. India for example, stated that persons with grievances against administering authorities had a right to be heard by the General Assembly, and that the people of the territories were in a better position than the committee to decide which requests were urgent and important. Although the possibility that oral hearings might be used for propaganda purposes was not excluded, it was believed that the question was not whether a right was used or abused, but whether such a right as a right should be allowed. Yugoslavia stated that the United Nations was legally, politically, and morally bound to find time to hear petitioners. It suggested that perhaps there had been a loss of confidence in the Council, which, in its opinion, did not always act in accordance with the wills of the United Nations as expressed in decisions of the Assembly.

Indonesia felt that the Fourth Committee was receiving requests for hearings because the Council had failed to carry out its duties. Other representatives believed that the hearing of petitioners helped greatly in establishing a link between the Fourth Committee and the peoples of trust territories.

There was also opposition by a number of states to the requirement that half of the subcommittee be composed of members of the Trusteeship Council. In view of this opposition, the United Kingdom amended its proposal by deleting this requirement. Nevertheless, the proposal was rejected. The vote to grant hearings to all seven groups petitioning the eighth session of the Assembly was by overwhelming majorities.[27]

At the ninth Assembly, the Fourth Committee again devoted much time debating whether a hearing, which the Trusteeship Council had denied the petitioners, should be granted, and it decided, as it had at the seventh session, to hear them. At the ninth session also, Israel suggested that a committee composed of five mem-

[27] *Ibid.*, pp. 27-28.

bers be created to study the advisability of establishing procedures for accepting and examining oral petitions in the Fourth Committee, but the suggestion was rejected.

Thus, the Fourth Committee has not yet established criteria to guide it in deciding whether to grant oral petitioners a hearing. On the basis of action to date, it would appear that almost any trust territory inhabitant with a complaint—whether legitimate or doctrinaire, important or trivial—can command the attention of one of the great committees of the Assembly if he can meet the cost of transportation to New York. Oral petitions have been received from non-self-governing territories other than trust territories, but only those relating to South-West Africa and Libya have thus far been granted hearings by the Fourth Committee.

Many of the issues presented at oral hearings have been important ones, and many of the petitioners have been extremely able. Moreover, the knowledge of the Member states is enriched by being able to hear and question outstanding local leaders in the trust territories. But if the present system is continued, it might further weaken the Trusteeship Council and involve the Assembly in local issues that it does not have either the responsibility or the authority to settle. Once the Assembly grants an oral hearing on a subject, it must hear all interested parties; otherwise it gets a distorted picture and might aggravate a problem. As noted later, the Assembly acted without all the facts in the early stages of the Ewe unification question. The administering authorities involved were subsequently as desirous as were the nonadministering Members of having other interested parties heard by the Assembly in order to bring out all relevant facts and views. Although the Trusteeship Council functions under the authority of the General Assembly, it is a separate organ of the United Nations, and it is not clear what weight should be given by the administering authorities to the recommendations of each should the recommendations conflict. This problem has not as yet created any apparent difficulty, but it could in the future, if remedial measures are not taken.

If the number of petitioners to the Assembly for oral hearings increases, that organ will be compelled to develop a more orderly procedure for examining them. Unless the Assembly refuses to grant hearings to petitioners until after they have been heard or been denied a hearing by the Council, and then only if they can establish cause for such a hearing, the Council will be completely by-passed by future petitioners, and its role in the trusteeship system will be undermined. The Council received only one request for an oral hearing during its sessions in 1956, an evidence of its waning prestige.

Use of Visiting Missions

Article 87(c) of the Charter states that the General Assembly and, under its authority, the Trusteeship Council may "provide for periodic visits to the respective trust territories at times agreed upon with the administering authority." The authority to visit trust territories is one of the outstanding innovations of the United Nations trusteeship system. This authority can be a constructive force, but it can also be sterile or even harmful. It serves as a check on the accuracy of statements contained in the annual reports of the administering authorities. It enables the Council to become more familiar with conditions in the territories, to observe specific need for changes in policies and programs, and to assess progress being made. It places the United Nations in direct contact with the people of the trust territories and their leaders. It serves to "educate" those who participate in the mission, so that they learn of the practical problems of administration and the complexity of political problems confronting the administering authorities.

During the early years, the Council and the Assembly discussed the composition of the visiting missions. The United States and most other Members felt that the Council must be certain of the competence and integrity of the members of the missions and should therefore designate specific individuals as members of them. The Soviet Union argued that the Council was composed of states, not individuals, and visiting missions must be similarly constituted, with states designating the persons to serve on them.

The Council has fallen into the practice of selecting states that are members of the Council to nominate persons who will serve on a mission, and later giving *pro-forma* approval to the individuals nominated. There were minor but unimportant variations in this procedure during the early years, but there is now relatively little discussion even of the states to be represented on a mission. The selection is usually based simply on the availability for this purpose of members of the Council or their colleagues. The states submit brief biographical sketches of their representatives, and the Council almost invariably approves these designations without discussion. It is an extremely delicate matter for the Council to question the designation of a Member government, and only in one instance has there been a change of designation that could be attributable to informal discussions with the government concerned by members of the Council.

There was early recognition of the desirability of having the representatives on the Council serve on the missions so that they could become better informed of conditions in the territories and allow the Council as a whole to benefit from their experience. Of the first forty-three persons who served as members of visiting missions, ten were representatives on the Council, fifteen were alternate representatives, ten were advisers on the delegations of their governments on the Council, and eight were associated in no continuing way with the work of the Council. The sixth session of the Assembly reaffirmed the desirability of having representatives sitting on the Council participate in visiting missions, but it recommended that when these representatives were unable to participate, the Council should consider inviting states not members of the Council to nominate suitably qualified candidates. No effect has been given to this recommendation.

Despite general agreement on the theory that members of missions do not represent their governments, there has been virtually no opposition to the idea of equal representation on each mission of administering and nonadministering states. The principle of balanced membership is frequently extended even to mission working parties, although some parties have consisted of a single member, and in one case the representatives of administering states formed one working party and those of nonadministering states another. The Council has thus recognized that persons serving on missions cannot help but reflect to some degree the policy of their respective governments.[28]

Various delegations have suggested that experts be included on visiting missions as members or in a staff capacity. Only the special mission to Western Samoa, however, has included, apart from Secretariat employees, a nongovernmental expert. He served, however, as a consultant to, not as a member of, the mission.

[28] The Soviet Union has never been a member of a visiting mission. It has indicated a desire to become a member on various occasions, but has not made a formal proposal to that effect, perhaps because of foreknowledge that the administering authorities would oppose it.

The size of missions has also been debated at length. The special mission to Western Samoa consisted of representatives of two non-administering states, of which the United States was one, and one administering state. Every mission since then has been composed of representatives of two administering and two nonadministering states. At first there was considerable feeling, which the United States shared, that the missions should consist of six members. However, the cost to the United Nations, the limitation of transportation and living facilities in some territories, and the difficulty encountered in finding representatives on the Council who could serve as members have reconciled the Council to a mission of four members accompanied by about six members of the United Nations Secretariat and by one or two local officials of the territories concerned. An administering authority is never a member of a mission that visits a territory it administers.

At its first session, the Council discussed at length the frequency with which visiting missions should be dispatched to the territories. Belgium, France, and the United Kingdom favored sending one mission each year to one of the three general areas—East Africa, West Africa, and the Pacific—and the Council agreed, by a vote of 5 to 3, to their proposals.[29] France and the United Kingdom have since expressed the view, however, that major changes do not occur in such a short period and that visits every four or five years would be sufficient. The United States suggested that each territory be visited every two years, and China wanted a flexible agreement that would permit the Council to visit some territories more often than others, but other members seem generally satisfied with the three-year cycle of visits to each territory.[30]

The duration of mission visits was the subject, in the early years, of much study by the Council and of criticism by the Assembly, but there has been little change in the time spent in the territories since the first regular missions. The duration of the missions to East Africa and to the Pacific Islands, for example, has usually been about three months and to West Africa about two months. The Assembly tried unsuccessfully to persuade the Council that it should lengthen these visits or, after Somaliland became a trust territory,

[29] U.N. Trusteeship Council, First Session, *Official Records,* 26th Meeting (Apr. 28, 1947), p. 729.
[30] The Council sent two visiting missions to West Africa in 1956, at the request of the ninth session of the Assembly. The Assembly felt that political developments in Togoland merited study by a special mission.

that it should send two missions to East Africa. The criticism of the Assembly was partly in response to a statement made by the first mission to East Africa after a two-month visit that it encountered "tremendous difficulty" in completing its report by the prescribed date, and also to a statement by the second mission to West Africa that it did not have enough time to find out precisely which unification proposal enjoyed the widest support in British Togoland and French Togoland—a task that the Assembly had specifically asked it to perform.

The Council was not defiant of the Assembly. It studied the problem as it had been repeatedly asked to do by the Assembly. But, it was confronted by some practical difficulties that it was unable to communicate fully to the Assembly. One was that although the Assembly wanted the representatives on the Council to serve on the visiting missions, it was difficult to find representatives to constitute them, and to increase the number or duration of visits would have aggravated the problem. Another difficulty was the lack of understanding of what a mission can and should accomplish on a regular visit. This is illustrated in the account of the Ewe and Togoland unification question, which is discussed below.

The terms of reference of visiting missions contain a general section, which is more or less the same for all missions, and a specific section instructing the mission to investigate questions that have arisen out of the examination by the Council of annual reports and petitions. The mission has, however, wide latitude to concentrate on such matters as seem important to it.

The work load of a mission may be substantially affected by the petitions it receives, and there is no way of predicting the number or the time they will require. The mission is expected not only to receive written petitions and to grant oral hearings but also to examine, if possible, petitions that are addressed to the Council.

Since the first mission, however, the number of petitions has increased tremendously, and it has been impossible for a mission to investigate each one—a fact that has disturbed many members of the Assembly as well as the Council. The 1952 and 1955 missions to West Africa received thousands of petitions and communications. The missions could do little more than take account of these in preparing their reports.

The great increase in the petitions to visiting missions reveals the extent to which petitioners believe the United Nations to be the arbiter of their future. The missions have the insuperable task of weighing the extent to which the petitions and other manifestations of sentiment reflect public opinion generally in the territory.

The charge has on occasion been made by petitioners, and by some nonadministering Members who were represented on a mission, that the mission was shepherded too closely by the administering authority. Although the administering authorities probably do not call the attention of a mission to unsatisfactory situations that the mission might overlook, they make such arrangements as the mission desires for visits within the territories, for open hearings at which inhabitants can present their grievances or views, and for meetings with specific persons or groups. The United Nations pays for almost all costs incurred by the mission, and the mission can go anywhere in a territory, except to military installations, if travel facilities are available. None of the visiting missions has criticized an administering authority for lack of co-operation; on the contrary, they invariably express warm appreciation for the co-operation received.

Far from seeing too few people, the missions are often so worn out by their effort to hear everyone who desires an audience that they have little time or energy for independent study of general problems. Nevertheless, the fact that representatives of the administering authorities normally accompany the mission and its working parties on tours and at meetings, although essential from a practical standpoint, probably serves to restrain local inhabitants in some territories. Although local inhabitants have a measure of protection through the petition process against retaliation by administering authorities, there is no way of making such protection effective or of convincing the inhabitants that it is effective.

For their part, the administering authorities have, on the whole, been pleased with the conduct of the missions. Some have felt, however, that on occasion some members of mission parties, including the Secretariat staff, have tried to induce local persons to express dissatisfaction and have thereby provoked more petitions than might otherwise have been presented. Secretariat staff on one or two missions have also been charged with having slanted the mission report in a way that would subject the administering authority to criticism from nonadministering Members in the Council and the Assembly. Despite this occasional criticism of the staff serving the visiting missions, a large measure of the success of the missions is attributable to the ability and hard work of members of the staff.

The missions accumulate a considerable amount of information from the administering authorities, from petitions, and through their own observations. This information is sifted and organized, with the help of the Secretariat staff, into a draft report on each territory. The members of the mission then consult with the administering authorities or in some cases with territorial authorities before the mission returns to New York where the final report is usually drafted. This consultation serves to clarify questions of fact, to gain the benefit of the reaction of the administering authorities to proposed recommendations, to obtain early rectification of some situations noted by the missions, and to enable the mission to make certain suggestions that can be conveyed more effectively unofficially.

Although the reports of the various missions have differed substantially in tone, they follow the same general pattern. There are separate chapters on political, economic, social, and educational conditions, and separate chapters on special problems—such as the administrative union involving New Guinea under Australian administration. References to petitions of a general nature are often included in the body of the reports. The visiting missions to West Africa have also prepared special reports on the question of Ewe or Togoland unification.

The reports of the visiting missions usually contain conclusions and suggestions, generally phrased to avoid giving offense. Their purpose is to draw the attention of the administering authorities and the Council to the changes deemed advisable. Although the administering authorities are mindful of the observations of the mission and often act directly on the basis of them, the reports of the visiting missions are addressed to the Council.

The Council discusses the reports of the missions at the next regular examination of the annual reports on the territories concerned. The administering authorities tend to be somewhat defensive in their observations on the report of a mission, seeking to correct errors of fact and explaining in detail the practical reasons certain recommendations cannot be carried out or would be inadvisable. For example, the United Kingdom took a sharp, aggressive stand against the report of the first mission to East Africa, and some members of the Council in turn assumed a hostile attitude toward the British position. The reaction of the United Kingdom to subsequent reports of missions that have visited its territories, except for the report of the 1954 mission to East Africa, has been more conciliatory, even to the point of expressing approval, and the tone of the reports has also become more diplomatic.[31] Generally speaking, the nonadministering Members on the Council tend to emphasize critical items in the reports, while the administering Members stress the complimentary items and tend to support one another's policies. The Council refers to the findings of the respective missions in discussing conditions in the territories in its annual report to the Assembly.

The General Assembly has been somewhat critical of the handling by the Council of the mission reports, especially the delay involved in its action on them. The fourth session of the Assembly took the unusual step of instructing missions to report fully on the measures taken toward realization of the political, economic, social, and educational objectives set forth in Article 76(b) of the Charter, and in particular, on the steps taken toward self-government or independence.[32] The administering authorities objected both in the Assembly and later in the Council to the final clause of this resolution, feeling that it placed undue weight on one of several trusteeship objectives. The Council finally reached a compromise solution by directing its next visiting mission to investigate and report as fully as possible on the steps taken toward the realization of the objectives set forth in Article 76(b) of the Charter, taking into account the terms of the above-mentioned resolution of the General Assembly.[33] This solution was not entirely satisfactory to some of the nonadministering Members of the Council, which felt that the Council was disrespectful of the Assembly in failing to instruct the mission as the latter stipulated.[34]

There is no way, of course, for the Assembly to compel the Council to take specific action. The Council is composed of governments. The administering Members, as might be expected, refuse to vote in the Council for a measure, simply because the Assembly requests

---

[31] The United Kingdom and Belgium were particularly critical of the recommendations of the 1954 mission that a rigid timetable be set for constitutional development.

[32] Res. 321(IV), Nov. 15, 1949.

[33] U.N. Trusteeship Council Res. 115(VI), Jan. 31, 1950.

[34] The Assembly, in December 1954, again requested the Council to instruct

it. If they oppose a measure in principle and have voted against it in the Assembly, it is unreasonable to expect them to support it in the Council.

Despite the criticism by the Assembly of certain missions and of the Council in relation thereto, the missions have proved an effective means for international supervision of trust territory administration. The value of these periodic visits is, of course, enhanced when the representatives sitting on the Council, or persons closely associated with them, serve on the missions. It is wasteful for governments to designate subordinate officials, who will have no continuing association with the work of the Council. Moreover, it tends to lower the prestige of the missions in the eyes of the administering authorities and of the territorial peoples. All those serving on missions, including the Secretariat staff, must have a sensitive regard for their proper role in relation to the Council, the administering authorities, and the inhabitants, if the missions are to continue serving a constructive purpose under the trusteeship system. Finally, an awareness of what can reasonably be expected of a regular visiting mission is also essential.

Major Conflicts Between the Trusteeship Council and the General Assembly

The dissatisfaction of the General Assembly with the manner in which the Trusteeship Council has carried out the trusteeship functions has led it to become increasingly involved in the details of the activities of the Council and to exercise certain trusteeship functions itself, notably the examination of oral petitions. The conflict between the two organs has extended to some of the most serious substantive issues that have arisen in the trusteeship field. Two of these, the question of the political future of the Ewe people and the territories they inhabit and the problem of administrative unions,

---

its visiting missions to give special attention, in their reports to the Council, to the questions of attainment by the trust territories of self-government or independence. (Res. 858(IX), Dec. 14, 1954.) There was doubtless knowledge at the time that the 1954 mission to East Africa would break new ground by suggesting target dates for full self-government or independence for Tanganyika and Ruanda Urundi. The provision of the "attainment" resolution referred to above should therefore be viewed not as criticism of the Council, but as support for the practice started by the East African mission.

are described below. Also cited are examples of other issues that shed light on the relations between these organs and the administering authorities.

The Ewe or Togoland Question[35]

In 1947, some Ewe leaders petitioned the United Nations for the creation of a united Eweland. These petitions set in motion a series of events over the next nine years that caused the United Nations successively to appear to favor unification of the Ewe people, unification of British Togoland and French Togoland, and, finally, integration of British Togoland with the Gold Coast, at the same time manifesting uncertainty regarding the future of French Togoland. There was obvious conflict between the Trusteeship Council and the General Assembly in the process, with local political leaders playing off the Assembly against the Council. United Nations involvement in the case had profound political repercussions in the respective territories. But the changes in attitude in the United Nations were due more to the greater familiarity of Member states with opinion in the territories than to any fundamental change of opinion among the people concerned. An analysis of the record in this case sheds light on means of improving the trusteeship system and on problems that are likely to be encountered in terminating the trusteeship status of other trust territories.

As indicated in the table below, the Ewe people, numbering about 691,000, live in a fairly compact area that cuts across the boundaries of three territories.[36]

Territory	Total Population (In Thousands)	Ewe-speaking People (In Thousands)	Percentage of Total Population	Percentage of Total Number of Ewes
Gold Coast	4,000	376	9.4	54
Trust Territory of British Togoland	423	139	32.9	20
Trust Territory of French Togoland	1,070	176	16.4	26

The problem of the Ewe people arose out of the peace settle-

[35] For a comprehensive account of the Ewe problem, see James S. Coleman, "Togoland," *International Conciliation* (September 1956).

[36] U.N. Trusteeship Council, *Special Report of the United Nations Visiting Mission to the Trust Territories under British Administration and Togoland under French Administration*, Doc. T/1206 (Oct. 30, 1955). Of the 376,000 Ewe people in the Gold Coast, 300,000 live in an area adjoining the Ewe-inhabited portion of British Togoland.

ments following the First World War. The former German colony of Togoland was divided, one portion being mandated to the United Kingdom and the other to France. This partition facilitated the political unification of certain tribes in the northwestern portion of Togoland with their kin in the Northern Territories of the Gold Coast. It also, however, divided several tribes in the southern part of Togoland, notably the Ewe. Prior to the Second World War, the demand of the Ewe to be reunited was intermingled with the demand of various local organizations in the territories for unification in one form or another. The Second World War widened the political gulf separating the people of the two territories, with French Togoland under Vichy control and British Togoland on the side of the allied powers. Postwar economic dislocation aggravated the difficulties.

The question of unification was not raised when trusteeship agreements for the respective portions of Togoland under French and British administration were considered and approved by the General Assembly. Soon thereafter, however, various Ewe groups sent petitions to the United Nations protesting that the division of the Ewe people was an injustice and that placing the territories under two different administering authorities with differing policies impeded the development of a united Eweland.

The Trusteeship Council was inclined at first to accept the view of the administering authorities that co-operation between the British and French governments to solve border and other problems would alleviate the difficulties underlying the petitions. Its visiting mission in 1949 reported that the joint effort of the administering authorities was a step forward but was not enough. The mission also described divergent views on unification questions and observed that unification movements were widespread in the south of both territories, assuming "the character of a popular nationalistic movement."[37] It felt that the desire for unification had to be met to an appreciable degree, but had no suggestions regarding how unification should be accomplished. The mission believed that this should be left to the Council, and, above all, should await an expression of the attitude of the administering authorities.

The Council in 1950 and 1951 focused its efforts on strengthening

[37] U.N. Trusteeship Council, *Special Report of First Visiting Mission to the Trust Territories of Togoland under British Administraton and Togoland under French Administration on the Ewe Problem,* Doc. T/463 (Feb. 17, 1950), p. 34.

the machinery for joint consultation between the two territories. This later proved a digression, although an important one, from the main direction in which political forces were moving. The administering authorities were convinced that unification of the Ewe people or of the two Togolands would be unacceptable to the great majority of the inhabitants and would be impracticable economically, but they responded to United Nations pressures to strengthen machinery for co-operation between the two territories. The administering authorities created first a consultative commission and later, on the urging of the Trusteeship Council, proposed to transform the commission into a larger, more representative Joint Council. The representation on the Joint Council was to be based on population, with fifteen members from French Togoland and six from British Togoland. The administering authorities initially planned to have the Joint Council seek ways of satisfying the wishes of the people within the prevailing political framework. They later agreed, however, that the Joint Council would not be precluded from considering proposals for unification of any parts of the territories.

The proposed composition and terms of reference of the Joint Council provided a focus for local political controversy, causing those with definite views regarding the future of the Ewe people or the two Togolands to rally supporters and to maneuver for position. The principal contenders were those favoring (1) a united Eweland, (2) unification of the two Togolands, (3) integration of British Togoland with the Gold Coast and permanent association of French Togoland with the French Union. There were also those who believed in unification of the two Togolands as a step toward integration with the Gold Coast or toward association with the French Union. Although the controversy over the Joint Council provided evidence of this wide divergence of local opinion, most nonadministering Members of the United Nations seemed so opposed to administrative unions and so inclined to regard the Ewe petitions and the reaction thereto of administering authorities as reflecting the classical conflict of dependent peoples with their rulers that they were unable to appreciate the full range of local opinion until late in 1953. This was particularly evident in the General Assembly.

The sixth session of the Assembly was drawn into the Ewe or Togoland question as a result of petitions it received shortly after the Trusteeship Council endorsed the establishment of the Joint

Council.[38] The Fourth Committee decided to grant oral hearings to several petitioners holding different views. For example, a former president of the representative assembly in French Togoland charged that every means had been used to crush the unification movement, including fraudulent elections. He opposed the Joint Council because its membership would be hand-picked.

The Assembly urged the administering authorities to arrive at a prompt and equitable settlement, to consult with various groups before creating the Joint Council and to extend the powers of the Joint Council to enable it to make recommendations on the question of the unification of Ewe people and Togoland. The Assembly also asked the Trusteeship Council to devote more attention to this problem and to arrange for the next visiting mission to spend sufficient time on it, including the functioning of the proposed Joint Council.[39]

The second visiting mission to West Africa spent one month in the two Togolands in 1952. It concluded that, except for the northern and a few other parts of British Togoland, the people in both territories favored in principle unification of Togoland. Almost 2,500 of the 2,899 communications received by the mission requested immediate unification. It cautioned, however, that this should not be interpreted to mean that there was wide support for any one form of unification that would be acceptable to the majority in both territories because some viewpoints were so diametrically opposed as to make it impossible to satisfy them. The mission said that in the time available, it was not able to find out precisely which unification proposal enjoyed the widest support, but expressed the opinion that no single proposal enjoyed wide enough support to warrant alteration of the existing administrative arrangements.

The mission found that only twelve of the twenty-one members were participating on the Joint Council. All twelve were opponents of unification from French Togoland. The Comite de l'Unite Togolaise decided not to appoint a representative because he would be in a minority on the Council. In British Togoland, only four of the six representatives were elected because the people of two

[38] Res. 345(IX), July 24, 1951. In 1950, the General Assembly received petitions from French Togoland, but it only asked the Trusteeship Council to include a special section in its next report setting forth the steps taken on the Ewe question.
[39] Res. 555(VI), Jan. 18, 1952.

areas would have nothing to do with the Council. Furthermore, the Convention People's Party, which is the strongest political party in the Gold Coast, the All-Ewe Conference, and the Togoland Union refused to participate in the elections, objecting to unequal representation of the two territories on the Joint Council. When a motion of the British Togoland delegates to obtain parity of representation was strongly opposed, they and two pro-unification representatives from French Togoland withdrew.

Some of the difficulties encountered in establishing the Joint Council might have been due to the limited time available to the administering authorities under the resolution of the Assembly, which asked the mission to report on the functioning of the Joint Council. Also, the mere fact that the visiting mission was scheduled to visit the territory caused some groups to feel that they would gain more at the time by appeals to the United Nations than by assuming a minority role in the Joint Council.

The mission said that it did not have time to study the basis on which agreement might be reached to reconstitute the Joint Council. It did, however, suggest indirectly ways of countering the main objections to it. It suggested the desirability of greater equality of representation for the two territories by noting that the composition of previous joint bodies was not proportionate to population. Perhaps in the hope of influencing the selection process in French Togoland, the mission noted that elections in British Togoland were carried out on the basis of universal adult suffrage. Finally, regarding the absence of specific authority for the Joint Council to discuss political as well as other matters of common concern, the mission expressed its belief that the Joint Council possessed the possibility of forming the nucleus of a legislative body for the two Trust Territories once they achieved self-government. The second mission to West Africa, unlike the first, made no references to the urgency of the whole question.

The Trusteeship Council, in early December 1952, endorsed the report of the mission and invited the administering authorities to consult with each other and with local leaders regarding possible modification in the composition, powers, and functioning of the Joint Council. The administering authorities were invited to seek help from the United Nations Technical Assistance Program in their efforts to promote development of the territories. Some dismay was expressed by members of the Council at the statement of the mission that it did not have time to ascertain which form of unification was desired by the majority in the two territories, and this statement was noted in the resolution.[40]

The seventh session of the Assembly granted oral hearings to four representatives from the two Togolands and considered the recommendations of the Trusteeship Council and its visiting mission. The petitioners had little to say that had not been previously presented to the Trusteeship Council, but the Assembly was more disposed to accept the word of the petitioners. A representative of the All-Ewe Conference charged French authorities with forceful repression of the Ewe unification movement, including the beating and unwarranted searches and arrests of its leaders. These charges were refuted by France. The petitioner then turned his fire on the Trusteeship Council. They had come to the end of their patience, he said, with this "machine," which took their petitions and grievances and turned out resolutions that accepted as final the word of the administering authorities. Another petitioner claimed that the majority of people in both territories opposed unification of the Ewes. The United Nations had to share some of the blame for the continued problem as the Togolanders became agitated only when the United Nations got interested in their problems.

The Fourth Committee of the Assembly adopted a resolution, after heated debate, reiterating in more forceful terms the recommendations of the Trusteeship Council and adding several new ones of importance. It called for the reconstitution of the Joint Council, or a similar organ, by direct elections on the basis of universal adult suffrage exercised by secret ballot, and declared that the terms of reference of the Council should enable it to consider and make recommendations on all common matters, including unification. The resolution also called for the revision of the trusteeship agreements for the two Togolands, with the object of unifying the territories under a single trusteeship administration, and the final clauses of it requested the administering authority and the Council to report to the next session of the Assembly on the steps taken to implement the resolution. The Assembly adopted the resolution in plenary meeting after deleting the provision calling for revision of the agreements.[41] This provision was opposed on the ground that it prejudged the political future of the territories without affording the people an opportunity to express their wishes.

The Ewe issue was again on the agenda of the Assembly at its eighth session, and many meetings were devoted to hearing petitioners, some of whom had been heard previously. Before the hearings were over, it become evident that many states were at last becoming aware of the complexity of the problem. The Belgian delegate said there was one consoling aspect in the debate: the moderate, reasonable, and objective tone of some statements. Many delegations had come to realize that the problem was not as simple as had been believed, and that delay in solving it was not due "solely to bad faith" on the part of the administering authorities. The fact was that the people of the two Togolands were sharply divided on the question of unification of the Ewe people and Togoland.[42]

The attention of the Assembly was focused, more than at previous sessions, on the status of British Togoland. For the first time, the Assembly realized that the achievement of independence by the Gold Coast would force a showdown in the United Nations as well as in British Togoland on the future status of the territory and the unification issue. A resolution consequently was adopted by the Assembly on the unification of Togoland. The first part was directed toward reconstituting the Joint Council by direct universal adult suffrage, ensuring freedom of speech and assembly, and fostering public discussion and information on the unification problem. The second part itemized the steps that should be taken to register voters on the basis of personal identification and to ensure free, universal, and secret balloting. The third part asserted that further constitutional changes in the Gold Coast might necessitate revision of the trusteeship agreement for British Togoland. In view of the effect that this would have on unification of the two Togolands—a goal which, according to the resolution, the majority in both territories favored—the Council was asked to re-examine the problem of achieving the political objectives of trusteeship in both Togolands and to submit a special report to the ninth session of the Assembly.[43]

[41] Res. 652(VII), Dec. 20, 1952.
[42] For the record of this extensive debate see U.N. General Assembly, Eighth Session, Fourth Committee, *Official Records*, 365th–377th Meetings (Nov. 13-23, 1953).
[43] Res. 750(VIII), Dec. 8, 1953.

The Council was informed at its fourteenth session of the results of recent elections in the Gold Coast and British Togoland. Fourteen members of the Gold Coast legislature were elected from British Togoland, and all eight from the northern section favored integration with the Gold Coast. Of the six seats in the Ewe area of British Togoland, three were won by candidates of the Convention People's Party which supported integration with the Gold Coast, two were won by candidates of the Togoland Congress Party, which favored unification of the two Togolands, and one by an independent candidate. The fact that the candidates of the Convention People's Party received several thousand more votes in the Ewe area than the candidates of the Togoland Congress Party seemed to indicate that the majority of the Ewe in British Togoland favored integration with the Gold Coast.

The United Kingdom made known its intention to ask the ninth session of the General Assembly to consider the political future of British Togoland. It stated that the Gold Coast was soon to achieve its independence, and that British Togoland was too small to be administered as a separate unit. It thus seemed proper to remove the territory from the trusteeship system and incorporate it into the Gold Coast. The United Kingdom wanted the Assembly to ask the Trusteeship Council to suggest, for the consideration of the Assembly, procedures for ascertaining the wishes of the people of the trust territory regarding their political future. The Council subsequently adopted a resolution deferring further consideration of the Togoland unification problem in view of this development and suggested that the General Assembly take up the United Kingdom proposal along with the item already on its agenda relating to Togoland unification.[44]

The ninth session of the Assembly heard fifteen petitioners representing the principal points of view on the unification issue. Ten were from British Togoland. It became even more evident than at the eighth session that the turning point had been reached in the approach of Member states and in the relations between the Assembly and the Council as a result of the widespread recognition of the inherent complexity of the question and of the desire of the United Kingdom to be guided by the freely expressed wishes of the peoples concerned. The United Kingdom also made it clear that if unification with the Gold Coast were agreed upon, it would occur simul-

[44] U.N. Trusteeship Council, Thirteenth Session, *Official Records*, p. 195ff.

taneously with the achievement of independence by the Gold Coast, thus avoiding any question of territorial gains for the United Kingdom. Member states had sharply differing views, particularly over whether termination of the trusteeship would be premature, whether a plebiscite should be held only in British Togoland or in the two Togolands simultaneously, and whether annexation of a trust territory to an independent state would be compatible with trusteeship principles. The search for the proper course of action was more careful than in previous years, and the lines between administering and nonadministering Members were less evident. The resolution that was finally adopted by the Assembly at the ninth session, after separate votes on almost every phrase, stated "that steps should be taken, in the light of the particular circumstances of the Trust Territory [of British-administered Togoland], to ascertain the wishes of the inhabitants as to their future, without prejudice to the eventual solution they may choose."[45] The Council was asked to consider what arrangements were necessary for this purpose and to send a special visiting mission to the two territories.[46]

The Council dispatched a visiting mission to the Togolands in 1955. The mission suggested first a plebiscite for the people in British Togoland to choose between integration with an independent Gold Coast or separation from the Gold Coast and continuation of trusteeship. Then, if the latter course were chosen by the people of the whole territory, or either the northern or southern sections of it, the mission suggested that their final determination should wait until the political future of French Togoland had been decided. The mission noted that the situation in the latter territory might permit a plebiscite soon. The Council passed this report to the tenth session of the Assembly.

The Assembly decided, after petitioners from all principal political groups were again given a hearing, that the question posed by the mission should be presented without delay to the people of British Togoland in a plebiscite conducted by the administering authority and supervised by a United Nations Commissioner, the latter to be assisted by observers and staff appointed by the Secretary-General.[47]

[45] Res. 860(IX), Dec. 14, 1954.
[46] *Ibid.*
[47] Res. 944(X), Dec. 15, 1955.

In the plebiscite, held on May 9, 1956, over 80 per cent of the eligible voters voted, 93,365 favoring union with the Gold Coast and 67,422 favoring separation from the Gold Coast and continuation of trusteeship. In the two southernmost voting districts, where most of the Ewes in the territory live, the vote was about 3 to 2 in favor of separation.

Two months later general elections were held throughout the Gold Coast that established beyond doubt the desire of the people to transform the Gold Coast into the independent state of Ghana. This election also emphatically confirmed the results of the earlier plebiscite in British Togoland. Whereas parties favoring integration received a majority of 58 per cent of the vote in the plebiscite, they received 73 per cent of the vote in the general election. Their opponents in the general election favored greater autonomy for British Togoland under a federated arrangement with the rest of the Gold Coast.

The United Kingdom advised the Trusteeship Council of the results of these elections. It stated that continuation of a fragment of British Togoland under trusteeship would be prejudicial to the interests of the peoples involved and would create serious administrative problems for an administering authority and for the new state of Ghana. The Trusteeship Council recommended that the whole of British Togoland be united with the Gold Coast when the latter attains its independence.[48] At the same session, the Trusteeship Council by a tie vote rejected an invitation to observe a referendum that France planned to conduct in French Togoland. The eleventh Assembly thus is confronted by the question of the geographic area to be used in applying the principle of self-determination in British Togoland and the value to be assigned to a referendum conducted without United Nations approval in French Togoland. Its answers to these questions will have a profound effect on the peoples immediately concerned and, because of the precedents being set, on the inhabitants of other trust territories.

Several conclusions can be drawn from the handling of this whole issue in the United Nations.

1. Involvement of the United Nations in an issue has political significance within the territories concerned. Local politicians will attempt to make use of the United Nations not only to advance their cause but also to enhance their personal prestige in the terri-

[48] Res. 1496(XVIII), July 31, 1956.

tories. Whatever the merits of Ewe unification, the world stage that was afforded its proponents through oral hearings before the General Assembly intensified unification sentiment and became an important factor in local politics. The defeated parties in British Togoland whose prestige was enhanced by being heard by the United Nations are now hurling invective at the United Nations and are threatening war to achieve their ends—ends that the United Nations encouraged them to pursue.[49]

2. The General Assembly should await distillation by the Council of complex issues and act on general policy questions posed. Direct involvement of the Assembly in the case during the early years tied the hands of the Council. In so doing, the Assembly denied itself the value of constructive work that the Council might have done and burdened itself with hearing petitioners and other details that could have best been left to the Council. Indiscriminate hearing by the Fourth Committee of oral petitioners exposes the Assembly to serious errors, because the Assembly tends to act only on the testimony it hears, disregarding other available information. For example, by listening at the outset mainly to proponents of Ewe unity, the Assembly minimized the strength of sentiment in British Togoland for integration with the Gold Coast. Although it may have been misled also by hedged conclusions of the second visiting mission that the majority in the Togolands favored unification, it took a much firmer stand than was warranted by the report of the mission, before the people had a chance to express themselves through the ballot box. Also the resolution of the sixth session of the Assembly provoked undue haste in creating the Joint Council—although other reasons contributed to its failure—by asking the visiting mission to study the functioning of the Joint Council, which was still just an idea.

3. The General Assembly undermines the Trusteeship Council in the trust territories when it condones and even pampers oral petitioners who make unfounded attacks against the Council. The representative of the All-Ewe Conference spoke disrespectfully of the Council because it failed to act according to his desires, and he skillfully played on the lack of confidence of the Assembly in the Council to win the Assembly to his cause.

4. The Trusteeship Council encourages the administering authority to take all the desirable steps it is willing to take, but the

[49] Coleman *op. cit.,* p. 88.

Council—unlike the Assembly—seems unwilling to extend the threshold of acceptance of the administering authority. The Council should have pressed for universal adult suffrage and direct elections in French Togoland. Its second mission to West Africa hinted that such would be desirable, but it was left to the Assembly to recommend it. Most of the administering authorities opposed this recommendation in the Assembly.

5. Visiting missions, as heretofore constituted, are not a suitable means for assessing and reporting on local sentiment in trust territories. They are not staffed and do not remain long enough to perform such a task. It would seem desirable for the Trusteeship Council to form special missions composed of nongovernmental specialists when similar needs arise in the future.

6. The respective responsibilities of the United Nations and of the administering authorities for guiding the political evolution of trust territories is unclear. The Assembly seemed predisposed at the outset toward a united Eweland, and later, as evidenced by its pressure to create a Joint Council by direct election, toward unification of the Togolands. On the other hand, the United Kingdom and France, although professing a willingness to consider unification, favored, respectively, incorporation of British Togoland with the Gold Coast and development of French Togoland within the French Union. Recognizing that the views of the administering authority can influence the will of the inhabitants, the question arises whether the United Nations should manifest predispositions toward a solution that differs from that of the administering authorities.

7. The General Assembly can exert powerful influence on final constitutional arrangements in trust territories. The decisions on when a plebiscite is to be held and what questions are to be posed are bound to influence substantially the outcome of a plebiscite. This places a great responsibility on the General Assembly to see that the wishes of the people concerned are expressed as freely and also as precisely as possible. It also suggests that it is desirable for the Assembly to avoid taking sides in local political controversies so that its later actions will not be suspect. It should also use its influence to set the stage for people to express their opinions freely, as it has done with considerable success in urging France to institute adult universal and secret suffrage in French Togoland. The role of the Assembly is not to determine the political future of trust territories, but rather to see that the people concerned do.

In summary, all the normal powers and functions of the United Nations under the trusteeship system and some new ones—for example, ordering and supervising a plebiscite to determine the wishes of the people—were brought to bear on the question of Ewe and Togoland unification. These proved adequate as a means of eliciting the information needed as a basis for United Nations action, for checking the veracity of this information, and for giving the United Nations freedom of action to ensure that the inhabitants of the trust-territory freely express their wishes with respect to their political future. The deficiencies noted in the handling of the question by the United Nations have been due not to any lack of authority, but to the manner in which this authority has been allocated to and exercised by the Assembly and the Council, respectively.

Administrative Unions

Administrative unions had existed under the League of Nations, but they did not raise any question of white settler domination. Soon after the trusteeship system of the United Nations was set in motion, however, Tanganyika, Kenya, and Uganda were joined for the administration of common services through the East African Territorial Organization, and New Guinea was joined with Papua in an administrative and legislative union.[50] Many Member states expressed concern over these unions, particularly over the former, which was established without prior consultation with the inhabitants of Tanganyika or the Trusteeship Council. The question has also been the subject of lively debate in both the Trusteeship Council and the General Assembly.

In 1949, the General Assembly on the basis of a United States proposal, adopted a resolution setting forth the following principles in connection with administrative unions: that the Trusteeship Council be notified before new unions are established or old ones extended; that the unified administration be supervised as the Council deems necessary if separate data on the trust territory are

[50] Three other trust territories are involved in some form of administrative union: the political integration of British Togoland with the Gold Coast; the political integration of the British Cameroons with Nigeria; and the loose association of Ruanda Urundi with the Belgian Congo. Two others, the Cameroons and Togoland under French administration were assigned a status, not clearly defined, under the French constitution of 1946 as Associated Territories in the French Union. In 1956, French Togoland was declared to be an autonomous republic" within the French Union.

not available; that a separate judicial organization and a separate legislative body be established for each territory; and that the freely expressed wishes of the people be taken into account before establishing or broadening an administrative union.[51] The resolution called on the Council to complete the study of administrative unions requested by the Assembly at its third session, paying particular attention to these principles, and to submit a report thereon including references to any safeguards that should be instituted.

The Trusteeship Council had set up a Committee on Administrative Unions at its fourth session in 1949, and in 1950, it established a Standing Committee on Administrative Unions and spelled out four safeguards that the committee later looked for in its examination of administrative unions: (1) the existence of clear, precise, and separate data on the trust territories; (2) access of visiting missions to information on the unions; (3) maintenance of separate boundaries, status, and identity of the trust territories; and (4) public expenditures in a trust territory not to be less than revenues in the same year.[52]

Despite some initial reservations, the administering authorities concerned have co-operated in subjecting their administrative unions to scrutiny by the United Nations, but they opposed some of the principles set forth in the resolution of the General Assembly, which they regard as an intrusion on their legal authority. They emphasize the advantages to the trust territories from administrative integration with neighboring territories. They also point out that the "balkanization" of Africa could have serious consequences, as the creation of small, independent states, lacking economic viability, would hardly benefit the people concerned or contribute to the well-being of the world. Many Members, however, have contended in the past, and a few still do, that some administrative unions, such as those involving Togoland and Cameroons under British administration, are incompatible with Article 76(b) of the Charter because the integration is so complete that it denies the people of the trust territory any real choice of their political future. They expressed dissatisfaction with the Standing Committee because

[51] Res. 326(V), Nov. 15, 1949.
[52] U.N. General Assembly, Seventh Session, *Official Records*, Supplement No. 12, "Special Report of the Trusteeship Council on Administrative Unions Affecting Trust Territories and on the Status of the Cameroons and Togoland under French Administration Arising Out of Their Membership in the French Union," p. 3.

it had based its work on the four "safeguards" drawn up by the Council rather than the more exacting principles laid down by the Assembly. Also, the Standing Committee had limited itself to brief comments on the unions affecting only four territories, and no mention was made of those affecting the two Togolands, presumably because they were being considered in conjunction with the unification question.

Over the objections of the administering authorities, the Assembly, in 1952, adopted another resolution, which created its own Committee on Administrative Unions, consisting of two administering and two nonadministering Members. The resolution called for a special report from the Council analyzing each administrative union from the standpoint of the principles laid down by the Assembly and asked its committee to review this report and present its observations thereon to the seventh session of the Assembly.[53] This was done, and the Assembly then adopted another resolution reiterating some of the principles contained in previous resolutions of the Assembly and the Council. Unlike the resolution of the Assembly in 1949, no mention was made in the resolution of 1952 of the desirability of separate legislative and judicial bodies for trust territories that form parts of administrative unions. The Soviet bloc was defeated, as it had been previously, in its effort to require the establishment of separate legislative and executive organs in all trust territories affected by administrative unions. The vote was 21 to 5 with 24 abstentions—the abstentions being indicative of the misgivings of many Members.[54]

The concern of the General Assembly with administrative unions, although embarrassing to the Trusteeship Council at first, helped the Council produce several concrete results. The administering

[53] Res. 649(VII), Dec. 20, 1952.

[54] Another proposal by Iraq and Brazil to ask the International Court to give an advisory opinion on the compatibility of the administrative unions with the Charter and the relevant trusteeship agreements was withdrawn for lack of support. India had favored such a proposal in the Committee on Administrative Unions of the Assembly, but it may have been persuaded not to complicate further the question of the integration of British Togoland with the Gold Coast or of the integration of British Cameroons with Nigeria. Some opposition may have been induced by the confidence of administering authorities, such as Belgium, that the Court would only confirm the legality of the union of Ruanda Urundi with the Congo. Another theory is that the proposal called for the Trusteeship Council to formulate the questions to be put to the Court, and the Soviet bloc, in particular, would prefer the Assembly itself to formulate the questions.

authorities have made a determined effort to provide separate
financial and other data on the trust territories involved in administrative unions, even at the cost of reorganizing accounting
and statistical reporting methods. Although the Council has not
attempted to dissolve the unions that existed at the time the United
Nations was established, it has scrutinized critically proposals for
creating new unions or for extending existing ones. This was particularly evident in the case of New Guinea, in which the Council
reviewed in detail the Australian legislation calling for joint administration of the territory with Papua,[55] and in so doing, may
have helped to ensure that the identity of the trust territory was
maintained, and the interests of the inhabitants were not subordinated to those of European settlers. Finally, the Members of the
United Nations have a better appreciation of the value, in some
cases, of administrative unions to the inhabitants of trust territories.

The doctrinaire opposition in the Assembly to administrative
unions may also, however, discourage the creation of unions that
would benefit the peoples concerned. For example, the United States
has authority under the trusteeship agreement for the Trust Territory of the Pacific Islands to constitute the territory into an administrative union or federation with Guam, an island possession
of the United States that is located in the heart of the Trust Territory. Guamanians have cultural and kinship ties with the people of
other Mariana islands that are under trusteeship. Guam serves as
headquarters for the Trust Territory and is the transportation, commercial, and cultural center for the whole territory. It is reasonable
to assume that if any of the inhabitants of this trust territory ever
attain full self-government, it will only be through some form of
political association with Guam. However, the specter of international criticism that is raised at the suggestion of any such
association has discouraged serious study of its possibilities.

Other Principal Issues

In order further to illuminate the relations between the General
Assembly, the Trusteeship Council, and the administering authorities, it is well to consider some of the other controversial issues that
have arisen in the trusteeship field: the flying of the United Nations
flag in all trust territories; the relationships between the United

[55] Papua and New Guinea Act, 1949.

Nations and the people of the trust territories; the abolition of corporal punishment in the trust territories; and time-tables for independence.

When the fourth session of the Assembly passed a resolution asking the Trusteeship Council to recommend to administering authorities that the flag of the United Nations be flown in all trust territories, the proposal received enthusiastic support from non-administering Members, despite objections from most of the administering authorities, who held that they are not agents of the United Nations, that the General Assembly does not have power to direct the Trusteeship Council, which is also a major organ of the United Nations, and that flying the United Nations flag would have an unsettling effect in some territories.[56] The Council debated the issue at its next two sessions and finally adopted a resolution recommending that the United Nations flag be flown side by side with the flag of the administering authorities and the territorial flag should there be one.[57] The resolution, however, gave the administering authorities latitude to handle any practical difficulties that this might create. The United States was the only administering authority that voted for the resolution, the others opposing it or abstaining. No further action has been taken by the Assembly in this matter, but several delegates felt that the Council "flouted" the will of the Assembly. The views expressed by the administering authorities on this resolution of the Assembly probably gave impetus to subsequent resolutions by the Assembly requesting information on the implementation by administering authorities of resolutions adopted by the Assembly and the Council.

The establishment of closer relations between the United Nations and the inhabitants of trust territories has been sought by many non-administering Members. Some administering Members, including the United States, have acquiesced in the request of the Trusteeship Council that suitably qualified inhabitants form part of their delegations or otherwise participate in the work of the Council when the report for the respective territory is being reviewed. The Assembly has not been satisfied with such participation and has called for "active participation" of indigenous inhabitants in the work of the Council. The ninth session of the Assembly adopted a resolution asking the Council to take the initiative in seeking out public

[56] Res. 325(IV), Nov. 15, 1949.
[57] Res. 301(VII), July 21, 1950.

opinion and to elicit local views on the annual report.[58] Perhaps the most extreme proposal was one to have the United Nations designate one or two United Nations representatives for an initial period of two years for each trust territory to maintain liaison with United Nations agencies and to provide "good offices" for settling trusteeship matters. This proposal, which would have caused great confusion in the territories, was adopted by a vote of almost three to one in the Fourth Committee at the eighth session and fell short by only one vote of attaining the required two-thirds majority in the plenary meeting.

In regard to the abolition of corporal punishment in the trust territories, there was agreement on objectives. Lack of agreement on the facts involved, however, caused or aggravated conflict between the administering authorities and other Members of the United Nations and between the Assembly and the Council. The Trusteeship Council noted in the report of its first visiting mission to East Africa, and in annual reports from administering authorities, that corporal punishment is used in several African territories and in New Guinea, and it called for the abolition of this practice. The visiting mission also deplored illegal whipping in Ruanda Urundi. The issue, an easy one on which to render moral judgment, was seized on by nonadministering Members in the fourth session of the Assembly to criticize the administering authorities concerned. The latter explained that corporal punishment was applied in their trust territories as it is in many parts of the world in only particular kinds of cases. They agreed that it was wrong in principle, but they felt that it could not be abolished with the stroke of a pen. They contended that it accords with local custom and can be changed only gradually if harmful results are to be avoided. Nevertheless, the Assembly adopted a resolution recommending the adoption of "strong and effective measures" for the immediate abolition of corporal punishment, and asking the Council for a special report on the implementation of this resolution.[59]

In subsequent years, the administering authorities have reduced the number of offenses to which corporal punishment can legally be applied, but the practice still exists in some territories. The Assembly has continued to call for complete abolition of the practice, and at its fifth session, it recommended "immediate meas-

[58] Res. 853(IX), Dec. 14, 1954.
[59] Res. 323(IV), Nov. 15, 1949.

ures" looking toward complete abolition.[60] The sixth session of the Assembly by-passed the Council by recommending directly to the administering authorities that legislation be immediately enacted to replace corporal punishment in all cases by modern methods of penology.[61] This was the first, but not last, resolution of the Assembly addressed directly to administering authorities.

The United Nations deserves credit for the reduction in offenses subject to corporal punishment. In view of the common agreement among all concerned on objectives, however, the United Nations might have arranged, when the issue was first raised, for a study by nongovernmental specialists to ascertain the validity of the contention of the administering authorities that corporal punishment could not be abolished immediately. Better results might thereby have been achieved, and the conflict between the Assembly and the Council and between Member nations on this issue avoided.

Finally, on the question of a time-table for independence, persistence by the Assembly in calling for such a timetable is beginning to produce results in the Trusteeship Council. The sixth session of the Assembly in 1951 adopted a resolution inviting administering authorities to include in their annual reports information on the steps to be taken toward self-government or independence and the estimated time required for such steps and for the attainment of the ultimate objective. Information on the means whereby the freely expressed wishes of the people were to be ascertained was also requested.[62] Only New Zealand responded in the form desired by the Assembly, and it reported that it planned to convene, in 1954, a constitutional convention representative of all sections of the Samoan community, to formulate plans for the establishment of a self-governing state. The resolution of the Assembly, being addressed directly to the administering authorities, was virtually ignored by the Trusteeship Council.

The eighth session of the Assembly reaffirmed this resolution and asked the Council to include in its subsequent reports a separate section on measures taken or contemplated in each territory to carry out the resolution and specified the items to be covered in the report of the Council.[63] Most of the administering Members strongly

[60] Res. 440(V), Dec. 2, 1950.
[61] Res. 562(VI), Jan. 18, 1952.
[62] Res. 558(VI), Jan. 18, 1952.
[63] Res. 752(VIII), Dec. 9, 1953.

opposed this resolution, contending that it is neither possible nor desirable to attempt to set dates for political advances, especially for the final attainment of self-government or independence. In its report to the ninth session of the Assembly, the Council stated that none of the annual reports contained information responding directly to the terms of the resolution of the Assembly. Nevertheless, the Council included a section in its report on attainment of political objectives as the Assembly had requested of it, drawing on the information regularly presented in the annual reports of the administering authorities for this purpose, but it did not make any recommendations.[64]

Despite a renewed request by the ninth session of the Assembly, the Council failed to include in its report to the tenth session a special section on attainment. It did, however, decide on a procedure for preparing the information desired by the Assembly. The tenth session noted this decision of the Council and again called the attention of the Council to the importance the Assembly attached to the information.[65]

The sharp division between administering and nonadministering Members on the question of setting target dates for steps toward and final achievement of full self-government has, however, been broken. In mid-1954, the United States representative on the Trusteeship Council, who served on the East African Visiting Mission, joined the Indian and El Salvadoran members of the mission in expressing as the majority view "faith in the possibility of Ruanda Urundi . . . becoming self-governing in 20 to 25 years" and the belief that "self-government is within reach of the people of Tanganyika much earlier." Other factors might intervene to speed up the progress they believed, but "even at the present pace of development, the people [of Tanganyika] can be developed to become self-governing within a single generation."[66] The New Zealand member of this visiting mission, expressing a minority view, considered it neither possible on the evidence available nor helpful to the people to attempt to set a limit in years to the process of attaining self-government. The United Kingdom and Belgium,

[64] U.N. General Assembly, Ninth Session, *Official Records,* Supplement No. 4, "Report of the Trusteeship Council," p. 279.

[65] Res. 946(X), Dec. 15, 1955.

[66] U.N. Trusteeship Council, Fifteenth Session, *Official Records,* Supplement No. 3, "United Nations Visiting Mission to Trust Territories in East Africa, 1954: Report on Tanganyika" (1955), pp. 67-68.

the administering authorities concerned, were highly critical of the efforts of the mission to set target dates.

In 1956, the United States disassociated itself from the position taken by its representative on the East African Mission and announced a new position in the Trusteeship Council. It stated that it did not believe that it would be generally useful or practical to lay down long-range time limits, but it did think that the setting of intermediate target dates for political, economic, social, and educational advancement could give a sense of purpose and direction to peoples who were on their way to the final goal.[67] The United States thus distinguished between intermediate and final goals for attainment of full self-government or independence, and in doing so, may have established a basis for constructive effort and for co-operation on this vital matter between the Assembly and the Council and between moderate administering and nonadministering states. It may provide the framework within which the most significant work of the Council and the Assembly on trusteeship matters will be carried out.

Relations Between United Nations Organs, Specialized Agencies, and Administering Authorities

The General Assembly and the Trusteeship Council are separate organs of the United Nations, but the Charter grants both organs concurrent functions with respect to trust territories, other than those designated to be strategic, and makes the exercise of these functions by the Council subject to the authority of the General Assembly. This arrangement could work effectively only so long as the General Assembly had confidence in the Trusteeship Council. But with the administering authorities in a position to block in the Council actions favored by the nonadministering Members that are in a majority in the Assembly, the basis for such confidence has been lacking.

Consequently, the Assembly has increasingly exercised directly United Nations functions under the trusteeship system, by-passing the Council or attempting to use the Council solely as its agent, somewhat as it would use one of its own subsidiary organs. It hears oral petitioners who have not been heard by the Council and issues directives to the Trusteeship Council on procedural as well as sub-

[67] U.N. Trusteeship Council, Sixteenth Session, *Official Records* (1956), p. 268.

stantive matters. Furthermore, it makes substantive recommendations directly to the administering authorities, and these sometime differ from those made by the Council to them. The Assembly is increasingly seeking to make visibly evident the authority of the United Nations within the trust territories, to establish direct relations between the Assembly and the inhabitants of the trust territories, and to substitute its own judgment for that of the administering authorities on relatively minor matters. The only positive checks on the actions of the Assembly in trusteeship matters are the requirement of a two-thirds vote in plenary meetings, and, although not used, resort to the International Court of Justice for moral backing. The two-thirds rule has been helpful but not sufficient to enable the system to function effectively.

The Trusteeship Council has resisted dictation by the General Assembly, but it is helpless legally and politically to assert the role conceived for it under the Charter. Its prestige is at a low ebb not only among the majority of Member states but also among leaders in some of the trust territories. Furthermore, the administering authorities, regarding the Council as a necessary evil, have not done what they might to make it an effective body. Despite the good that it has done, the Council can lay claim neither to technical competence nor to impartiality. Most nations regard its decisions as being influenced too much by the administering authorities, which it was established to supervise. Although the situation has improved slightly during the last year or two, the status of the Council had so deteriorated that almost any change would have been an improvement.

Leadership in the Assembly on trusteeship matters is not centered in any single nation or bloc of nations, but shifts according to issues. A pattern of joint sponsorship of resolutions by nations in the various blocs, excluding that of the Soviet Union, has developed, however, and this has increased greatly the power of the non-administering Members. Until recently the Soviet Union has had negligible influence in the trusteeship field, and its sponsorship of a resolution virtually ensured its defeat. Its initial boycott of the Council, its subsequent role in the Korean conflict, and its implacable opposition to everything the administering powers do, isolated it and its satellites. However, during the last year or two the Soviet Union has more frequently joined with other nonadministering Members in initiating or supporting measures.

Those nonadministering Members who serve on the Council tend to reflect greater understanding of the position of the administering authorities than others in the Assembly, although this varies, depending on their anti-colonial biases. Even the moderate elected members prefer, however, to abstain on resolutions in the Council with which they agree so that their delegations in the Assembly will be free to oppose the resolution if it is politically expedient to do so, and will be free also of the taint of association with the views of the colonial powers. The United States tried hard in the early years to prevent a sharp division between administering and nonadministering Members. Due to positions taken by the nonadministering group, which the United States felt it could not support, the United States increasingly became identified with the traditional colonial powers, and its influence as a mediator thereupon declined. Australia and to a lesser extent New Zealand have even more markedly abandoned their former independent positions.

The administering authorities find themselves in an unenviable position. Under the trusteeship agreements that the United Nations has approved, they exercise full jurisdiction—legislative, executive, and judicial—in the trust territories, but both the Council and the Assembly address recommendations to them. Although legally they may not be bound to carry out these recommendations, politically they must or face international criticism. They sympathize with one another in the Council and try to reconcile their views with nonadministering Members there, but increasingly their compromises in the Council are only the prelude to more extreme measures in the Assembly, in which they are hopelessly outnumbered.

The administering Members resent criticism from some governments whose peoples have fewer political and other civil rights than the inhabitants of their trust territories and whose programs are less oriented toward improving the welfare of the people. They are sometimes embarrassed, and their task of government is made more difficult when the Assembly hears oral petitioners. They are occasionally helped by recommendations of the United Nations to do what they feel must be done—for example, opposing special privileges of white settlers—but have difficulty doing for political or other reasons. In some cases their national interests clash with trusteeship objectives, but these account for only a fraction of their difficulties with the United Nations.

The Trusteeship Council has relatively little contact, however, with the United Nations organs other than the General Assembly. It has, of course, extensive relationships with the Secretariat, which provides supporting services for the Council.[68] Despite occasional complaints from administering authorities of the substantive role played by Secretariat personnel in the trusteeship field, particularly of the staff of visiting missions, the relationship of the Secretariat to the Council has on the whole been highly satisfactory.

Although in the early days of the United Nations, it was envisaged that the Security Council would play an important role in connection with strategic trust territories, it has neither discussed reports of the Trusteeship Council relating to United States administration of the Trust Territory of the Pacific Islands, the only area under strategic trusteeship, nor taken action on them. As a result, this trust territory is supervised by the Trusteeship Council in much the same way as other areas under trusteeship, but without further review by any other organ. The United States has been mindful of the resolutions of the General Assembly directed to administering authorities, but the Assembly has not exercised trusteeship functions in relation to this strategic area despite the fact that Article 13 of the trusteeship agreement might be viewed as empowering it to do so. The United States has, therefore, been subject to less pressure than the other administering authorities.

The relationships of the Trusteeship Council with the Economic and Social Council and the specialized agencies have not been systematically developed. A committee was established to facilitate liaison, but the relationship between the two councils has been confined almost entirely to an exchange of resolutions, with the Trusteeship Council asking the Economic and Social Council to include conditions in the trust territories in any studies that the latter makes, and the Economic and Social Council asking the Trusteeship Council to bear in mind certain general problems in its study of conditions in trust territories. There has also been a somewhat superficial exchange of views on substantive proposals.

Similarly, there have been few contacts between the Trusteeship Council and the International Court of Justice. In fact, the only trusteeship questions referred to the International Court have related to South-West Africa.

The relationships of the Trusteeship Council with several special-

[68] See the volume in this Brookings series, *The Organization and Procedures of the United Nations.*

ized agencies have been fairly close but could be more fruitful. A few specialized agencies send representatives to sessions of the Trusteeship Council and have helped on such technical tasks as the preparation of the questionnaire by the Council. The United Nations Educational, Scientific, and Cultural Organization submits comments on those sections of the annual reports on trust territories within the scope of its interest, keeps the Trusteeship Council informed of scholarship opportunities, and has submitted comments on a draft five-year plan for educational development in the Trust Territory of Somaliland.

The Trusteeship Council could make better use of the advice and research facilities of specialized agencies in formulating conclusions and recommendations in technical fields. There may also be occasions when it would be useful for experts from specialized agencies to accompany the visiting missions of the Council or to make studies within the territories for the information of the Council. The Council could perhaps also be more active in urging greater application of international technical assistance resources to trust territories and in seeing that the burden on territorial authorities for preparing reports for international agencies is reduced to the minimum.

The fact that the Charter sets forth the machinery and functions of the international trusteeship system enabled the system to be set in operation as soon as a sufficient number of trusteeship agreements had been approved. Unlike the experience of the United Nations in connection with Chapter XI of the Charter, most of the time spent by the United Nations on trusteeship matters has been devoted to substantive rather than organizational and other constitutional questions.

Fewer territories have been placed under trusteeship than was expected by the San Francisco Conference. The Union of South Africa has failed to place the mandated territory of South-West Africa under trusteeship and, of the territories detached from enemy states, only Italian Somaliland has been placed under the system. The Soviet Union and the United States exercise jurisdiction over areas formerly under Japanese control, but this jurisdiction, except for the former Japanese mandated islands, is exercised outside the trusteeship system. None of the prewar colonies of the Member states has voluntarily been placed under trusteeship. Although the Charter permits the United Nations itself or a combination of states to serve as the administering authority of a trust territory, neither of these types of administering authority has been used except in the case of Nauru, for which the administering authority is Australia, New Zealand, and the United Kingdom, on whose behalf Australia actually administers the territory.

The Trusteeship Council has become excessively bound by routine in its examination of annual reports and petitions. By attempting every year to pass judgment on a wide range of matters pertaining to the territories and on most petitions, it has overburdened itself with detail. One way of dealing more effectively with annual reports and petitions would be for the Council to undertake a comprehensive examination of annual reports every three years in conjunction with the review of the reports of visiting missions, with more emphasis given to problems requiring special attention, including those arising from petitions, during the intervening years. This would tie in nicely with the recent arrangement under which the Council reports to the Assembly comprehensively on each territory only once every three years when the report of the visiting mission is examined by the Council.

It would be desirable for the General Assembly to hear only those oral petitioners that have been previously granted a hearing by the Trusteeship Council and to hear them only on matters with respect to which they have previously testified before the Council. Other criteria should also be established as a guide for deciding whether an oral petitioner will be granted a hearing in the Fourth Committee. Careful prescription of such criteria can lessen conflict between the Assembly and the Council and reduce debate on whether oral petitioners should be granted a hearing.

Petitions, both oral and written, should in most cases be viewed by the Assembly and the Council as sources of information to sharpen their insight into general or serious situations requiring correction or improvement, rather than as instruments whereby individuals or groups obtain special favors. Further refinement of the type of petitions on which the Council will make recommendations and of the information sent to petitioners is indicated. The principal function of the United Nations is not to administer the trust territories but to supervise their administration to ensure that the administering authorities conscientiously discharge their obligations. To the extent that the petition and other functions of the

United Nations violate this principle, the authority of the governments of the trust territory will be undermined, and the trusteeship system as originally conceived will be weakened. The United Nations should make it as easy, not as difficult, as possible for administering authorities to fulfill their trusteeship obligations. Case studies are needed to provide insight into the effect of petitions on decision-making in the trust territories.

The powers of the United Nations under the trusteeship system are adequate to ensure fulfillment of the objectives of trusteeship, but the machinery for exercising them is defective. The trusteeship role of the General Assembly and its relations with the Trusteeship Council have proved unsound. The Assembly is too unwieldy a body and its members too politically motivated on trusteeship issues to enable it to exercise effectively the trusteeship functions assigned it under the Charter. On the other hand, the Trusteeship Council, being to a large extent dominated by the administering authorities and demonstrably less exacting in the exercise of its supervisory functions than it should be, has lost the confidence of the Assembly. This has led the Assembly to assume increasing initiative on trusteeship matters. Actions by the Assembly on these matters, although in some respects beneficial, have also been harmful to the people as well as to governments of certain trust territories and to the United Nations itself. Unless this trend is arrested, serious complications could develop in this field.

The experience of the League of Nations with the mandates system, as well as of the United Nations with the trusteeship system, suggests the possibility that the Assembly might develop confidence in the Council if the recommendations by the Council on problems of interest to the Assembly were founded on studies by outstanding nongovernmental experts. Ideally, the Charter should be modified to differentiate between the trusteeship functions of the Assembly and of the Trusteeship Council, primarily to circumscribe the operating role of the Assembly with respect to trusteeship matters. Such a modification, however, is not essential because the Assembly could delimit, by resolution, its trusteeship functions.

The question now is how can the majority in the Assembly be persuaded not to exercise the operating functions of trusteeship? Many Members might be so persuaded if they were convinced that the Council was acting in the interests of the inhabitants and not primarily in the interests of the administering authorities. One way of bringing about that condition might be for the Council to make greater use of nongovernmental experts in the formulation of its decisions—experts whom the majority in the Assembly hold in high regard. It might be desirable for the Council to appoint, with the approval of the Assembly, a panel of nongovernmental experts who might assist it from time to time in carrying out the functions of trusteeship. Use of such experts would, of course, only contribute in part to producing the fundamental change in attitude and outlook that is prerequisite to the creation of a proper relationship between the Assembly and the Council.

A proper relationship between these organs would, it is believed, call for the Council, under the supervision of the Assembly, to be the only organ that normally exercises the trusteeship functions of the United Nations that are set forth in Article 87 of the Charter. All recommendations to administering authorities would emanate from the Council, except in special cases when the Council might call on the Assembly for support. The Assembly would intervene directly in a question involving a trust territory only in extraordinary cases such as would arise if an administering authority were to violate the terms of trusteeship. Even in such cases, the intervention of the Assembly should preferably be on request of the Council. The role of the Assembly would consist mainly of reviewing the work of the Council, of making recommendations to the Council regarding the conduct of its work, and of considering important problems that the Council might refer to it, or which, on its own initiative, it might call to the attention of the Council. Although the Assembly, through discussion, would keep the spotlight of world opinion on the trusteeship system generally and focus it sharply on individual territories as needed, its primary task would be to see that the Council properly discharges its functions. Such a differentiation in the functions of these organs and the use of nongovernmental experts will be particularly important now that the attention of the Member states has turned to scheduling the steps to be taken by each trust territory toward full self-government or independence.

The trusteeship system has produced impressive results despite its weaknesses, the conflicts it has caused among Member nations, and the confusion it has provoked among the people of some trust territories. It has fostered greater political participation by the indigenous inhabitants at territorial and local levels of government, not only in trust territories but also in some cases in neighboring territories. The advances in Western Samoa from a colonial to a virtually representative government in less than ten years is attributable in part to the excellent work of the Special Visiting Mission of the Council in 1947 and the exemplary teamwork of the mission, the administering authority, and territorial leaders. The achievements in Western Samoa have probably accelerated efforts to develop self-government in American (Eastern) Samoa.

The trusteeship system served as a spur to the transfer of the Trust Territory of the Pacific Islands (and indirectly of Guam and American Samoa) from naval to civilian administration and has provided a petitioning mechanism to speed the long-delayed settlement of land and other claims of the inhabitants of the trust territory. It has strengthened the hand of administering authorities in Tanganyika and Ruanda Urundi against the efforts of settlers to retain or enhance their privileged position at the expense of the Africans. It has informed the Member states of the different political aspirations of the Ewe and other inhabitants in British and French Togoland and thereby perhaps contributed to world understanding of the complexities of fulfilling the principle of self-determination. In addition to facilitating world acceptance of the integration of British Togoland with an independent Gold Coast, the Ewe case appears to have induced the Gold Coast to make special developmental grants for British Togoland, persuaded France to increase the powers of the territorial assembly in French Togoland, and ameliorated border difficulties for the Ewe in both territories. The trusteeship system has also accelerated development programs for the Wa-Meru in Tanganyika. It has reduced the crimes subject to corporal punishment. It has safeguarded the interests of inhabitants of territories associated in an administrative union to a greater extent than they otherwise would have been. It has encouraged the administering authorities to draw upon the technical assistance facilities of international and other agencies, and otherwise to improve educational, health, agricultural, and other programs. It has kept the world community informed of problems and progress in trust territories and thereby allayed, to some extent, suspicion of events in these territories.

Flaws in the trusteeship system are to be expected. It is a pioneer venture in which experience should be carefully recorded and experimentation encouraged. Perfection of this system not only will serve the interests of the inhabitants of the trust territories but also will strengthen relations between the free nations. It might even contribute toward more effective use of international organization in dealing with more critical problems in the world.

CHAPTER V

The Colonial Problem
in Perspective

THE END of colonialism is one of the most significant phenomena of our times. No one can predict when the last territory will achieve full self-government, but there can be no doubt that the movement toward that end is unrelenting. The early achievement by six trust territories of the objectives of trusteeship necessitates immediate consideration of the manner in which the final liquidation of the international trusteeship system will take place. Colonialism is no longer a real issue in those non-self-governing territories in which the people are allowed to move as rapidly as they can toward political objectives of their own choosing. Nevertheless, vestiges of the old colonialism remain that may not submit willingly to the inevitable forces of change. But it can no longer be assumed when political riots and guerrilla warfare occur in colonies that they are indigenous in origin and directed toward fulfilling the aspirations of the territorial inhabitants or that the colonial power is always at fault. The problem has become more complex.

The colonial problem in the United Nations must be viewed against the broader background of Soviet imperialism and of the resurgence through national states of Islamic, Indian, and Far Eastern civilizations that are vying with the West for pre-eminence in world affairs. In addition to the ideological, cultural, and religious roots of anti-colonialism are the economic roots—which extend to underdeveloped countries everywhere. Walter Lippmann, referring to Indonesia, stated:

. . . Colonialism does not end with the grant of political independence. As long as the economic life of the newly independent state is dependent upon the export of a few primary commodities, it will feel itself in a colonial relationship with the industrialized nations to which it exports its primary products. This is the main reason why countries which are no longer political colonies of the western empires, and which have no reason to fear and do not as a matter of fact fear any scheme of reconquest, do nevertheless agitate the issue of colonialism.[1]

[1] *New York Herald Tribune* (June 15, 1954).

The United States Ambassador to India stated it another way. He said: "In India they think of their economic progress as a part of their continuing revolution which has achieved political independence."[2]

There is opposition, among peoples who have recently gained their independence, to Western military bases in their territory and also to military pacts with the West, which one head of state referred to as "colonialism in disguise." Many non-Western peoples have been led to believe that Western domination presents as immediate and dangerous a threat to their national integrity and aspirations as does Soviet imperialism. The nationalization of the Suez Canal by Egypt and the claims advanced by the leading political party in Morocco for rental from the United States for the use of land on which air bases were established pursuant to rent-free agreements between France and the United States are indicative of the sentiment in most of the non-Western world.[3]

The political awakening of dependent peoples thus coincides with the unleashing of powerful forces suspicious of and antagonistic to the West. The typical attitude of non-Communist intellectuals toward the West is one of ambivalence—of admiration and hate, of eager emulation and indignant rejection.[4] Colonial problems provide an outlet for feelings of antipathy and often are the means for advancing national interests. The Conference at Bandung in 1955 dramatized the common preoccupation of the peoples of Asia and Africa with colonialism "in all its manifestations"—Soviet imperialism, traditional colonialism, racism, and other forms of domination by one people over another.[5] Anti-colonialism is a symbol of the revolt against the West, a symbol having application, survival capacity, and influence far beyond what remains of the colonial problem today.

[2] *Mutual Security Appropriations for 1957,* Hearings before the House Subcommittee on Appropriations, 84 Cong. 2 sess. (1956), p. 169.

[3] Unfortunately, the terms "East" and "West" are commonly used interchangeably to refer on the one hand to the Communist bloc and the free world, respectively, and on the other hand to the Asian-African nations and the nations of Western Europe and North America, respectively. It is in the latter sense that the term is used here.

[4] Dankwart A. Rustow, "The Comparison of Western and Non-Western Political Systems," a paper read at the 52nd Annual Meeting of the American Political Science Association, September 1956.

[5] Final communiqué of the Conference at Bandung, *New York Times* (Apr. 25, 1955), p. 6.

There is something unreal about much that has happened in the United Nations on matters relating to dependent territories. There is little resemblance, for example, between the enlightened colonial policy being carried out by the United Kingdom in most of its territories and the rigid, defensive position of that government on questions in the United Nations relating to dependent territories. Nor does there appear to be much relationship between many of the measures proposed by the anti-colonial nations in the United Nations and the conditions and needs of the territorial populations.

This is not to say that genuine regard for the welfare of dependent peoples is not a motivating factor in the approach of most Members to colonial issues. But it is not the only factor, and in some cases, it is not the dominant one. It is also not possible to say that the colonial powers would have accelerated reforms in dependent territories as rapidly as they have without pressure from the United Nations. In discussions of colonial questions in the United Nations, however, the national interests of nonadministering as well as administering Members often obscure whatever recognition might be given, or should be given, to the principle enshrined in the Charter that "the interests of the inhabitants of these territories are paramount." Frequently, speeches are for home consumption. This explains in part the harsh language used in debates on these issues. Moreover, the fact that the United Nations strengthens the hand of the nonadministering Members accounts for their effort to bring colonial issues within the purview of the Organization and, once there, to keep them there.

In short, colonial issues in the United Nations have become enmeshed with larger issues of world politics. The resolution of differences between administering and nonadministering Members and the development of a rational approach within the United Nations on colonial matters are dependent in large measure on the amelioration of other fundamental world issues. The fact that the non-Western world is divided on the issue of communism, as revealed at Bandung and by the Southeast Asia Treaty Organization, provides some hope that a common devotion to freedom may yet provide common ground for understanding among the nations of the free world on colonial issues. The roots of anti-colonial sentiment, however, are doubtless deep enough to keep alive the conflict between administering and nonadministering Members even if the cold war were to end. Perhaps the best that can be hoped for in the immediate future is that organizational adjustments such as suggested earlier in this study will be made to enable the United Nations to function as effectively as possible in the interests of the people of dependent territories and without aggravating other difficulties that beset the world.[6] Unless the present trend is checked, the machinery set up by the General Assembly for implementing Article 73(e) may collapse, the trusteeship system may be weakened, and the influence of the United Nations, which is needed to ensure the speedy advancement of dependent peoples, may be undermined.

Existing internal checks within the United Nations have proved inadequate to halt this trend and to create stability in United Nations activities in these fields. The overwhelming votes in the Assembly against the administering Members, irrespective of the merits of a case or legal factors involved, constitute an ever-present threat to these activities.

The recent increase in the membership of the United Nations is not likely to have a significant effect on the voting strength of administering and nonadministering Members. Three of the new Members, Italy, Portugal, and Spain, will probably vote generally with the administering Members; four, Albania, Hungary, Romania, and Bulgaria, are for some time likely to form part of the Soviet bloc and increase the strength of the doctrinaire anti-colonial Members; and most of the remaining nine will probably vote with the remaining nonadministering Members.

Some problems can be foreseen that may raise new questions or aggravate old ones relating to the role of the United Nations with respect to Chapter XI of the Charter, to the international trusteeship system, and to the political and economic integration into the world community of dependent areas generally. These problems may call for measures that go beyond those set forth earlier in this study.

Future Role of United Nations in Relation to Declaration on Non-Self-Governing Territories

The admission of Portugal and Spain to the United Nations will probably reopen the question of the territories to which Article 73(e) applies and raise more sharply than ever before the question

---

[6] See above Chap. III and Chap. IV.

of the role of the Assembly in deciding whether a Member should begin transmitting information on a territory. Heretofore, similar questions have been dealt with in the Assembly mainly from the standpoint of cessation of information because the majority of the Member states were satisfied with the initial listing by Member states of the territories on which they would transmit information pursuant to Article 73(e). Only Belgium has consistently argued that some Member states administer territories that are non-self-governing within the meaning of Article 73 but have failed to transmit information on them.

In view of the fact that Portugal and to a lesser extent Spain regard their overseas possessions as integral parts of their respective metropolitan areas, it is doubtful that either of them will volunteer to transmit information.[7] Their failure to do so will probably raise a storm of protest not only because these territories fit the popular conception of colonies but also because some of them, such as Goa under Portuguese jurisdiction and Ceuta and Melilla under the jurisdiction of Spain, are located within or near another state that covets the territory,[8] or are inhabited by a people having strong cultural affinities with the people of other Member states.[9]

There might be merit in reopening the question of the territories to which Article 73(e) should apply and the role of the United Nations with respect thereto. There is no doubt that if all Members interpreted their obligations as broadly as did the United States

[7] Portugal makes a special point of referring to them as provinces.

[8] India and Morocco, respectively.

[9] The following overseas areas administered by Portugal and by Spain seem to fit the definition of non-self-governing territories as set forth in Article 73 of the Charter:

Portugal administers eight territories: In the Atlantic Ocean, the Cape Verde Islands, Sao Tomé and Principe; in Africa, Angola and Portuguese Guinea in West Africa and Portuguese East Africa (Mozambique); in Asia and the Pacific, Goa and the Portuguese Settlements in India, Macau, and Portuguese Timor. The populations of these areas range from 60,000 to over 6 millions. The total population is over 12 millions and the total area 803,832 square miles.

Spain administers four territories, all in Africa: Spanish possessions in Morocco, Ifni, Spanish Sahara, and Spanish Guinea. The populations of these areas range from 13,000 to 214,000. The total population is 406,000 and the total area 117,084 square miles.

Excluded from the list are the Azores and Funchal, having 566,000 inhabitants and the Canary Islands, having 842,000 inhabitants, which might properly be regarded as forming part of the metropolitan area of Portugal and Spain, respectively.

Sources of population data: U.N. Department of Economic and Social Affairs, Statistical Office, *Demographic Yearbook 1955* and *Statesmans Yearbook, 1956.*

in agreeing to transmit information on Alaska and Hawaii, both of which are incorporated territories in the Union destined for state-hood, there would be many more administering Members.[10] Some of the most doctrinaire anti-colonial nations, such as India, would be included, and there would be nations from different regional blocs. This would have a salutary effect on United Nations ac-tivities in this field. Portugal and Spain could argue quite effec-tively that if other nations have the sole right to determine their obligations under Article 73(e), they should have the same right. The fact that a territory is separated from its metropole by a vast desert or precipitous mountains rather than by water should not necessarily exempt it from consideration as a territory "whose people have not yet attained a full measure of self-government," but it is unlikely that the Members will agree to re-examine in a generous way their obligations under Article 73(e).

In view of the rapid political advances being made, a steady stream of cases of cessation of information can be expected. These should not provide much controversy, assuming that the certainty of criticism in the United Nations will discourage premature cessa-tion of information. Although administering Members will hesitate to cease transmitting information on their territories before they have been granted independence or a form of full self-government that has overwhelming popular support, local leaders in politically advanced territories may insist on cessation. For example, elected representatives in Barbados or Jamaica could argue effectively that the continued transmissions by the United Kingdom of information on economic, educational, and social matters and discussions, and recommendations by the United Nations relating thereto, constitute an intrusion on the self-governing powers the United Kingdom has already granted them. The question would then arise whether the United Nations should insist on continued transmission in such circumstances.

[10] Senator William F. Knowland stated in June 1956: "I most strenuously do object to this Government having filed such reports [to the United Nations] for the territories of Alaska and Hawaii, both of which are destined to become states of the American Union." When asked why the United States reported on these territories in the first place, Senator Knowland stated: "The preliminary information I had when the matter came up in 1946 was that it had been determined that it might encourage some of the other nations to file reports if we included Hawaii and Alaska." *Congressional Record* (daily ed., June 20, 1956), p. 9596. There is no record that the United States has otherwise tried to persuade India and other countries to report on territories that they administer.

As the larger territories achieve full-self-government, interest will focus on the special problems of the smaller territories. Of the fifty-five territories on which information is still being transmitted under Article 73(e), twenty-one have fewer inhabitants than the least populated Member state,[11] and thirty-three have a population of less than 500,000. Three of the "trust territories" have a population of less than 100,000. Although population is only one of several factors to be considered in determining whether independence is a practicable goal for a territory, it is apparent that none of these territories will either be willing or able to exercise the rights and obligations of sovereignty. If a considerable number were to become separate nations, their requests for admission to the United Nations would probably necessitate review of the membership provisions of the Charter. The United Nations should, therefore, be prepared to recognize a status short of full independence as a proper goal for many territories. There may even be special services that the United Nations or regional agencies can perform in relation to small territories—for example, supplying technical personnel—that may enable them to attain a larger measure of self-government than would otherwise be within their reach. The least that the United Nations and other international organizations can do is to help make a dignified place in the world community for areas such as Puerto Rico, Surinam, and the Netherlands Antilles, which attain a self-governing status involving neither full independence nor complete incorporation in the metropolitan area of a Member nation. The encouragement of voluntary forms of association among territories and between territories and Member states will not only facilitate achievement by many territories of full self-government but will also contribute to integration of the world generally for economic, political, and other purposes.

Conflict among Member states over the political future of the multi-racial territories, the strategic areas, and the disputed territories—*i.e.,* those that are claimed by more than one Member state—will keep alive the question of the application of the domestic jurisdiction clause of the Charter in such cases, inasmuch as the administering Members will probably continue to invoke the clause at the first sign of United Nations intervention. Wholly apart from the legal question of what constitutes domestic jurisdiction, it is apparent that a double standard is at times applied in actions and

[11] Iceland, with a population of 154,000.

recommendations of United Nations organs, which provides legitimate cause for grievance on the part of administering Members. For example, the General Assembly singles out dependent territories in its desire to seek fulfillment of the principle of self-determination, and ignores the equally pressing or even greater need for applying this principle in Eastern Europe and in certain other areas under the control of Member nations. Similarly, it is not clear why the Security Council intervened to restrain the Netherlands in Indonesia but not the Indians in Hyderabad where Indian forces marched while the Hyderabadi were appealing for protection to the Security Council.[12]

If the administering Members have a legitimate grievance that the United Nations sometimes oversteps the bounds of domestic jurisdiction in taking actions on colonial issues, the nonadministering Members have an equally persuasive argument that the colonial powers abuse the domestic jurisdiction clause by invoking it without justification. Given the world-wide interest in colonial issues, the General Assembly would lose its quality as the "town meeting of the world" if Members could not discuss in the appropriate committee or in plenary meetings such matters as the Mau Mau in Kenya, the political rights of Cypriots, or the future status of Western New Guinea.

The only special limitation on discussion in the Assembly that is required in this field is that political information voluntarily transmitted under Article 73(e) will not be separately discussed or made the subject of recommendations in the Fourth (Trusteeship) Committee of the Assembly or in its Committee on Information. Unless this limitation is observed, administering Members would probably refuse to transmit such information, and their ground for doing so would be persuasive. The ruling of the chairman of the Fourth Committee allowing discussion of political aspects of economic, social, and educational conditions in non-self-governing territories is about as far as the Assembly can go in the political field in its consideration of information transmitted under Article 73(e) without raising serious legal and political questions.

It is believed that the Assembly should clarify the jurisdiction of its committees on matters relating to non-self-governing territories. It might be desirable if the terms of reference of the Fourth Com-

[12] Clyde Eagleton, "Excesses of Self-Determination," *Foreign Affairs*, Vol. 31 (July 1953), p. 603.

mittee were formally limited, insofar as non-self-governing (other than trust) territories are concerned, to those of the Committee on Information at the present time, and if no other committee of the Assembly initiated recommendations that are intended solely for application to non-self-governing territories as a group. The general recommendations of the other committees of the Assembly should be normally applicable with equal force in dependent territories and independent nations. Their criteria for discussing and for making recommendations on specific situations should also be the same for both types of areas. The administering Members should derive no immunity from the application of the general powers and functions of the United Nations to their territories simply because of the specific activities of the Assembly in relation to Article 73(e). Nor, however, should the general powers of the Assembly be used to expand its activities in connection with Article 73(e), *e.g.*, to include discussion and recommendations on political information. More frequent reference to the International Court of Justice of questions regarding alleged violation by United Nations organs of the domestic jurisdiction clause might have a salutary effect in this field.

It might be more tidy, from an organizational standpoint, to give the Fourth Committee jurisdiction over all matters in the Assembly relating to non-self-governing territories. Such an arrangement is not recommended, however, because it would sharpen the differences in approach within the United Nations on problems that are common to independent nations and dependent areas. It would also increase the special treatment accorded dependent territories and thereby aggravate the problem of keeping the United Nations from intruding on the domestic jurisdiction of administering Members.

It would be neither possible nor desirable to eliminate review by the Assembly of the information transmitted under Article 73(e). The nonadministering Members will insist on such a review, and it is clear that Articles 10 and 22 of the Charter provide the necessary authority for it. The review is worthwhile because it puts pressure on administering Members to do their best in the territories, provides information on achievements and needs, and encourages greater application of the technical assistance resources of international and national agencies to dependent territories. Furthermore, this review helps create the atmosphere and the basic conditions conducive to political progress but without direct involvement in debate on political matters, which is so strongly opposed by the administering Members, and which, in any event, does not always serve the best interests of the territorial inhabitants.

Apart from the value of this review, the interest of the non-administering Members in continuing it is so great that the means will be sought for providing for it even if the other principal administering Members follow the lead of Belgium and withdraw from the Committee on Information. In that unfortunate event, consideration ought to be given to having the initial review carried out by a group of experts appointed without regard to nationality by the Fourth Committee. The Secretariat of the United Nations could provide the necessary technical and other staff assistance for such a group, but it could not serve in its place and take as detached a view of conditions and needs in the territories without jeopardy to the Organization.

In some respects, the examination of technical information in economic, social, and educational fields by an independent body of specialists would be more useful to the Fourth Committee than that of the politically constituted Committee on Information. However, great care would have to be taken in defining the terms of reference for such a group to avoid giving the administering Members cause for ceasing to transmit information under Article 73(e). Although such an extreme departure from present practice might merit consideration in any circumstances, it is mentioned here only to illustrate the fact that alternative means are available for effective review by the Assembly of this information in the event administering Members withdraw from the committee—assuming of course that they continue to transmit information.

The threat to the continuation of the Committee on Information might be lessened by making its review of information more meaningful and constructive. It is said that the administering Members like to keep old organizational or jurisdictional issues alive in order to divert the attention of nonadministering Members from new and more serious issues. Whether that is true or not, it may be possible to absorb the interest of many Members in a constructive way by enriching the work of the committee. For example, instead of continuing *ad infinitum* the cycle of emphasis on functional topics, a regional emphasis—Africa, the Pacific, and the Caribbean—would seem desirable. Through a regional approach, the information to be examined would become more comprehensible, the comparisons between territories would be more meaningful, and the opportunity would be afforded for considering the manner in which regional commissions and other international agencies are contributing to the advancement of the territories. Development of more systematic standards for measuring both advancement in economic, social, and educational fields and the effort to promote such advancement is vitally needed and would be a proper task for the committee to undertake.

Special international problems of genuine concern to the territories might also be considered by the committee, such as the identification of specific needs for technical assistance beyond that which the metropole can provide and which might be met through multilateral or bilateral technical assistance; the development of conditions that will encourage the use of such technical assistance in public administration—of which there has been very little in dependent territories—such as by encouraging the use of technicians who are nationals of the administering nation or grounded in its concepts and systems of government; and the removal of the present limitation on United Nations and United Nations Educational, Scientific, and Cultural Organization scholarships that normally prevents students in dependencies from using them to study in their metropoles. Efforts of administering Members to convey to nonadministering Members an understanding of the complexity of territorial problems can also be rewarding. For example, a candid and expert analysis of the educational problem in Africa by a British expert proved to be of great interest and value to members of the Committee on Information. In order that representatives on the committee might become familiar with problems and programs in dependent territories, it is believed they should be encouraged to visit those territories as officials of their respective governments.[13] The committee and the Assembly can play a constructive role in this field, and they are more likely to do so if they are shown the way.

The Future of the International Trusteeship System

Among the foreseeable events in the trusteeship field that are likely to have organizational significance, the likelihood of attain-

[13] Any suggestion that they visit dependent territories as representatives of the United Nations would be regarded as an opening wedge for visiting missions and would be strongly opposed by the administering states.

ment by five or six trust territories of full self-government within five years is the most important.[14] The circumstances in which termination of trusteeship is accomplished in each case and the reduction in the number of trust territories and administering authorities will have far-reaching importance.

It seems reasonable to assume that the United Nations will accept the results of the plebiscite that it designed and supervised in British Togoland and will insist on plebiscites in the other territories, with the possible exception of Somaliland, which, pursuant to its terms of trusteeship, is scheduled to become an independent state in 1960. The only foreseeable complication in connection with the termination of trusteeship over the British Cameroons is the possibility of delay in the attainment of independence by Nigeria as it is expected that the inhabitants of the territory will wish to form part of an independent Nigeria—a goal acceptable to the United Kingdom and probably to almost all other nations. Although a unification movement has developed in the Cameroons, it lacks strength, and the United Nations is not likely to encourage it, in view of its experience with unification movements in Togoland.

In contrast, a storm is brewing over the plans of France to conduct a plebiscite in French Togoland without United Nations approval or supervision. France plans to ask the people to choose between continuing the trusteeship status of the territory and incorporating it into the French Union. The Trusteeship Council rejected by a tie vote an invitation by France to observe the balloting. All nonadministering members of the Council objected to the proposed referendum, mainly on the ground that, contrary to the recommendation of the 1955 visiting mission to West Africa, the alternative of independence will not be on the ballot.

The existence of well-organized and articulate nationalist sentiment in the territory underlies the reluctance of France to risk a plebiscite on the independence question at this time. As part of its effort to ensure a heavy vote in favor of incorporation, France has enacted a "self-government" statute for the territory, providing for a local premier and a cabinet responsible to the local assembly and for universal suffrage, but still reserving to France many vital powers in domestic as well as foreign affairs. In the circumstances,

[14] British Togoland, British Cameroons, Somaliland, French Togoland, French Cameroons, and Western Samoa are the trust territories concerned.

it is expected that the majority vote will favor incorporation and that France will ask the eleventh session of the Assembly to terminate the trusteeship status on the ground that such action would accord with the "freely expressed wishes of the peoples concerned." It is likely that most nations will oppose this view, and as the trusteeship agreement cannot legally be terminated without the approval of the Assembly, an impasse could develop that would test the strength of the entire international trusteeship system. If, as seems likely, the people vote heavily in favor of autonomy within the French Union, however, France might acquiesce in another referendum that poses the alternative of independence. The measures taken in French Togoland are likely to accelerate the pace of political advancement in the French Cameroons and to cause the early termination of trusteeship in both territories.

Western Samoa appears to be moving toward some form of self-governing status involving voluntary association with New Zealand. A serious question could arise in connection with the process of terminating the trusteeship status of the territory if the Assembly insists that a plebiscite be held on the basis of universal suffrage to ascertain whether the Samoans accept the arrangements for termination. Samoan chiefs would probably oppose such a plebiscite, consistent with their opposition in the past to popular elections.

The experience of the administering Members and the United Nations in terminating trusteeship in these territories could influence the process by which other dependent territories attain full self-government and also the means for giving effect to the principle of self-determination generally.

Of more practical significance, termination of trusteeship over these six territories may reduce the membership of the Trusteeship Council to eight: four members administering trust territories (Australia, Belgium, the United Kingdom, and the United States), one elected member, and France joining the Soviet Union and China as the permanent members of the Security Council that are not administering trust territories. Conceivably, New Zealand could continue to serve as a member of the Council on the ground that the trusteeship agreement for Nauru designates it jointly with the United Kingdom and Australia as the administering authority for Nauru. The Charter, however, grants seats on the Council to "Members administering trust territories," not to "administering authorities." Thus as Australia alone "administers" Nauru on behalf of the "administering authority" and reports on its administration directly to the United Nations, the legal basis is weak. The practical reasons, however, for New Zealand to retain its seat are strong. It would permit another elected member to serve on the Council. Moreover, after the trusteeship status of Tanganyika is terminated, New Zealand and the United Kingdom as well as Australia would have to continue their membership on the Council as the joint administering authority of Nauru if the Council is to continue to have a balanced membership, assuming that Ruanda Urundi, Nauru, New Guinea, and the Trust Territory of the Pacific Islands will be the last territories to achieve full self-government. Otherwise, the United Kingdom would become a nonadministering member of the Council by virtue of its being a permanent member of the Security Council, with the result that the Council would, contrary to the Charter, have three administering states and four nonadministering states. In that event, the Charter would presumably have to be amended to provide for a different method of constituting the Council.

With fewer territories to supervise and a smaller Council politically weighted in favor of the administering Members, the danger of open conflict between the Assembly and the Council and of interference by the Assembly with the proper exercise of governmental authority in the territories will be heightened.[15] Differentiation in the functions of the Assembly and the Council and use by the Council of nongovernmental specialists who have the confidence of the Assembly may lessen the danger, but a more fundamental change in the composition or functioning of the Council could become necessary.

The proposal for setting intermediate target dates for self-government or independence could provide a stimulus and a basis for measuring progress in the trust territories. If, on the other hand, the proposal leads to the premature establishment of target dates for the final achievement of these goals, it could be positively harmful. It is quite possible, for example, that Africans in Tanganyika who now have far less representation assigned to them in the territorial legislatures than their numbers deserve, will more likely gain full political equality with European and East Indian settlers if the

---

[15] The role of the Soviet Union on the Council would be enhanced as it would be in a better position to demand membership on visiting missions and other agencies of the Council and to pose as a spokesman for the anti-colonial Members of the United Nations.

evolutionary process is allowed to continue than if it becomes necessary to make decisions now on final political objectives. Somewhat the same situation exists in Ruanda Urundi, which is bound to be affected by political developments in the Congo where recent stirrings herald the beginning of an African-led movement for self-government.

Time is on the side of the indigenous inhabitants of the plural societies in Africa, and particularly those under trusteeship and in other dependent territories in which the administering nations have agreed to grant self-government or independence and are actively preparing the people for political participation without discrimination on grounds of race. No one is more keenly aware of this than indigenous political leaders themselves. Once they are certain that political freedom, founded on racial equality, is clearly in sight, they turn to the many tasks that must be performed to ensure that the freedom they win will endure. The role of the United Nations should be to make the accomplishment of these tasks easier, not more difficult. Perhaps the agreement reached by administering and nonadministering members of the Trusteeship Council in 1956 on the practicability of setting intermediate target dates and the hardships experienced by Libya and anticipated for Somalia after 1960 will restrain the Assembly from continuing to press administering authorities for estimates of the dates on which trust territories will achieve full self-government or independence.

Although final target dates cannot be set for every territory, the attainment of the objectives of trusteeship is clearly practicable and foreseeable in all except three territories—Nauru, New Guinea, and the Trust Territory of the Pacific Islands.

Nauru has only 2,000 people. The economy of the island is based almost entirely on the extraction and export of phosphate deposits. These deposits will be exhausted within fifty years, leaving inadequate resources to support the community. Fifty years is therefore the maximum period that trusteeship for Nauru can now be envisaged, as the trusteeship status applies to the island and would not automatically accompany the Nauruans when they relocate elsewhere. The 1956 visiting mission reported "a growing tendency among the people to favour resettlement in Australia . . . when the occasion for leaving this island arises."[16] Nauruans also want to

---

[16] U.N. Trusteeship Council, *United Nations Visiting Mission to Trust Territories in the Pacific, 1956: Report on Nauru*, Doc. T/1256 (June 12, 1956), p. 25.

retain their identity. Australian officials oppose, however, the establishment of a segregated community in Australia. A concerted effort is therefore being made to find another island on which the Nauruans can be settled.

The political future of New Guinea is complicated by various factors. Of all the trust territories, none is as fragmented socially or as isolated from cultural contact with other peoples. Australian authorities have yet to establish peaceful relations with some tribes in unexplored parts of the territory. The rapidity with which change has occurred in the parts exposed to cultural contact indicates that continued acceleration of development programs will in due course bring the people of New Guinea to the point at which they will be able to govern themselves. The problem is further complicated, however, by the fact that the island of New Guinea is divided into three political jurisdictions, one part under Australian trusteeship, another under Australian sovereignty, and the third, constituting about half of the island, under Netherlands administration with Indonesia also claiming sovereignty over it. Ideally, in the interests of the 2,402,000 inhabitants of all three territories,[17] it would be desirable to continue the present status of the territories until the inhabitants are in a position to express their wishes regarding their political future. But the possibility that this will be allowed to take place is remote. Indonesia received assurance at Bandung that Asian and African nations will support its claims to Western New Guinea. Australia would regard the satisfaction of these claims as a threat to its security. It would probably be unwilling to allow the inhabitants of Papua or even New Guinea an opportunity to express themselves freely regarding their political future so long as there exists a threat to the security of Australia. In the circumstances, the termination of the dependency status of each of these territories is likely to provoke a major international dispute.

The Trust Territory of the Pacific Islands presents other distinctive problems. Its population of 65,000 inhabits ninety-seven islands and atolls scattered throughout 3 million square miles of ocean. Self-government is increasing at the island and district level and although representative government at a territorial level should develop in due course, the form in which the territory might achieve full self-government is not apparent. Independence does not seem

[17] 1,207,000 in the Trust Territory, 495,000 in Papua, and 700,000 in Western New Guinea.

to be a practicable goal. Admission as a state of the United States
seems out of the question. Federation with Guam and association
of such a federation with the United States as a commonwealth like
Puerto Rico, on the basis of mutual consent, would seem practicable
and beneficial to all concerned. In any event, such an arrangement
would provide one way in which the objectives of trusteeship and
of Chapter XI of the Charter can be fulfilled in this area and should
not be foreclosed by short-sightedness on the part of either the
Trusteeship Council or the United States. It would be desirable
for the Trusteeship Council, for example, to stop criticizing the
United States for maintaining the headquarters of the Trust Territory on Guam. There is urgent need for the United States to re-
consider the decision to govern a few islands in the Northern
Marianas through the Navy Department.[18] Guam and Rota, both
in the Marianas, and the rest of the Trust Territory are under
the jurisdiction of the Department of the Interior. It is regrettable
that the people of the Marianas, who have close cultural and family
ties, must for the time being be split into two separate jurisdictions,
but that they should be divided into three seems almost incredible.
Moreover, present restrictions on travel between these islands merit
re-examination; and, other measures that will lead the islanders
of the Trust Territory to seek permanent association with the United
States deserve prompt attention. Such measures are: the settlement
of long-overdue land claims that the people have against the United
States, allowing the few Japanese who are married to islanders and
were repatriated shortly after the war to join their families in the
Trust Territory, and exploring all possible alternatives to the conduct of future thermonuclear tests in the islands that might cause
the further dislocation of these people.

[18] The 1956 visiting mission of the Trusteeship Council stated that "it
wonders whether, if it could be arranged without prejudice to essential security
requirements, the interests of the people of the Saipan District would not be
better served by the transfer of the administration of the District to the civil
government of the Trust Territory. In this connection, the Mission wishes to
point out that military requirements have in fact been met in the Marshall
Island [where thermonuclear tests have been held] without the need for establishing a District Naval Administration in any part of that District." U.N.
Trusteeship Council, *United Nations Visiting Mission to Trust Territories in
the Pacific, 1956: Report on the Trust Territory of the Pacific Islands*, Doc.
T/1255 (June 7, 1956), p. 108. The mission recorded a request it received from
the people of Rota demanding the union of all the people of the Marianas as
evidence of the problems created by the division of governmental responsibility
in this chain of islands.

A more fundamental task confronts the United States if it is to avoid being the last of the colonial powers: namely, to perfect the commonwealth concept so that if it is applied to the Trust Territory and Guam as well as other unincorporated territories, it will be recognized by the United Nations as providing full self-government to the peoples concerned. This will require *inter alia* granting each commonwealth representation in the enactment of federal laws that are to apply to it. Such representation could be provided without amending the United States Constitution (1) by granting each commonwealth nonvoting representation in the Congress, (2) by requiring each house of Congress to vote separately on the application of a measure to a territory if objection thereto is raised by its territorial representative, and (3) by requiring in the event of such objection a vote larger than a simple majority for any such measure to apply. Such congressional representation would also contribute greatly to perfecting the commonwealth status of Puerto Rico. The United States, like other administering Members, will find it necessary to make adaptations in its governmental processes in order to fulfill its obligations under the United Nations Charter with respect to the Trust Territory of the Pacific Islands and other dependent territories under its administration.

The United States does not at present feel the pressure of world opinion to the same degree as other administering authorities, partly because the Fourth Committee of the Assembly debates the report of the Trusteeship Council on other trust territories but does not debate the report on the Trust Territory of the Pacific Islands. The latter goes to the Security Council, which takes no more than perfunctory action on it. Until the last year or two, the Trusteeship Council has tended to treat lightly some of the shortcomings in United States administration of the Trust Territory. The prominent role of the United States in world affairs and the fact that its territorial policies are in general less a matter of international concern than those of the traditional colonial powers also tends to lessen the intensity of United Nations supervision of United States administration of its trust territory. As the number of trust territories diminishes, however, closer international supervision over the government of this trust territory can be expected. Termination of the trusteeship status of the territory may pose a special problem because the amendment of the trusteeship agreement will be subject to a veto by the Soviet Union in the Security Council.

It is unlikely that any other territories will be placed under trusteeship. Even with a fundamental change in the government of the Union of South Africa it is unlikely that the latter will agree to place South-West Africa under trusteeship, and there appears to be no way in which it can be legally compelled to do so short of an amendment to the Charter, which would in effect make the continued membership of the Union of South Africa in the United Nations contingent on such action. Although the Assembly committee on South-West Africa, made up of Member governments, has been discharging its task to the apparent satisfaction of the Assembly, there would be merit in replacing it with a body of specialists appointed without regard to nationality by the Assembly. This not only would be more in accord with the arrangement under the League of Nations but also would serve as a pilot project in the use of nongovernmental specialists in supervising trust and other dependent territories.

The United Nations and the Colonial Problem: A Long-Range View

Despite almost daily evidence of the receding tide of Western colonialism, the continuation of a colonial-type relationship in some trust territories and other non-self-governing territories can be expected for many years to come and, with some exceptions, it will be in the interests of the inhabitants concerned that it continue. Although armed revolt and manifestations of stubborn colonialism are given top publicity in the United Nations, the administering Members are moving with the tide, some more than others; it is too strong to resist.

There is evidence of great achievement in colonial administration in recent years, and there can be little doubt of the advantages of enlightened colonialism to peoples who are "not yet able to stand by themselves under the strenuous conditions of the modern world."[19] The task ahead in the remaining territories calls for more from the United Nations than pressure to end the colonial relationship—more, too, than organizational changes to deal with information transmitted under Article 73(e) and with the changing scene in the trusteeship field.

As previously noted, the United Nations can do much to facilitate the integration of the remaining dependent territories into the

[19] League of Nations Covenant, Art. 22(1).

world community. Moreover, it has a distinct obligation to do all that it can to see that the inhabitants of territories that gain their independence do not lose their opportunity for freedom and growth as a consequence. For example, some observers predict that confusion, dictatorship, or domination from the outside may well be the lot of the new state of Somalia unless the United Nations makes some special arrangements to provide assistance after trusteeship ends in 1960.[20]

Even the Gold Coast, which is generally regarded as ready for independence, is confronted by precarious years ahead. Its problems are somewhat typical: concentration of power in the central government with one-party domination and no opposition in sight to contest its leadership; weak local government; rising population and rapid urbanization; deficiency of technical personnel to fulfill the ever-increasing demands on the government at national and local levels; excessive dependence on a single crop for public revenues; and complications resulting from different languages and cultures, conflicts with tribal chiefs, and the disintegration of tribal life. There is dedicated leadership in the Gold Coast, the prospect for economic growth is good, and the people are eager for knowledge and for a better life. Membership in the British Commonwealth also will enhance the security of the community. The outlook now is highly promising. Nevertheless, a catastrophe, man-made or natural, could present a formidable obstacle to continued orderly development.

Will international concern for the welfare and freedom of the people of Somaliland, the Gold Coast, and other dependent territories end with the termination of trusteeship or other dependency status? Will international assistance be only symbolic or will it be adequate to ensure continued growth? Can the United Nations, representing as it does the hope for a peaceful world, afford to let a nation that emerges from international trusteeship become another disease-ridden, poverty-stricken police-state? Facing up to these questions now suggests that the United Nations should apply more discriminately its pressure to end colonial relationships, should help colonial powers to the utmost in seeing that the foundations for democratic government are firmly laid before independence is

[20] Amry Vandenbosch and Willard N. Hogan, *The United Nations: Background, Organizations, Functions, Activities* (1952), p. 295.

achieved, and should be prepared to provide extraordinary assistance to the newly independent nations.

The only legitimate excuse for dependency status is in the advantages it affords for creating the conditions necessary for a community to govern itself democratically, and to meet the rising expectations of its members. If the colonial power does not have sufficient resources for that purpose, the United Nations should find ways to supplement them. If the colonial power fails to use the resources available, then pressure from the United Nations to end prematurely the colonial relationship would seem justified—assuming, of course, that the United Nations is prepared to provide the extraordinary assistance that the community will thereafter require. Extraordinary assistance will probably be needed in any case by most nations emerging from dependency status, but the need will be less if full advantage is taken of the period of dependency, and if pressure is not applied without clear cause to end it prematurely.

This will require international assistance on a far greater level than exists today and involvement of the international community in a constructive way in the development of dependent territories. Techniques for measuring need and growth in economic, social, and educational fields will be required for purposes both of international supervision and of allocating international aid. It is fortunate, indeed miraculous, that the political awakening of dependent peoples and their accompanying demands for a better life come at a time when advances in technology may permit their fulfillment. Meeting these demands provides one of the great challenges of the times. Considering the extent to which colonial issues have become involved in disputes between nations and in the political ambitions of individual nations or groups of nations, perhaps the greatest need today is for all Member states to recognize that the interests of the peoples of dependent territories are paramount and that the promotion to the utmost of the well-being and development of these peoples forms a sacred trust of civilization.